from Somewhere in England

D.A. Lande

Airlife
England

*To all those who served in
the United States Eighth Army Air Force during World War II,
and especially to those who did not return from somewhere in England.*

Copyright © 1991 David Lande

First published in the United States of America by Motorbooks International.

First published in the United Kingdom in 1991 by Airlife Publishing Ltd.

British Library Cataloguing in Publication Data available.

ISBN 1 85310 243 1

On the front cover: A 55th Fighter Group P–38 is silhouetted by the sunset at Nuthampstead. *Robert T. Sand*
On the back cover: No letters from home today for these 357th Fighter Group pilots. *Andrew Morland*
Left inset: A 94th Bomb Group "Lucky Bastard Club" certificate. These certificates were issued to the lucky few who survived a tour as a bomber crewman. *94th BGMA*
Right inset: A decaying Nissen hut at Framlingham. *Andrew Morland*

Printed and bound in the United States of America

Contents

Introduction

This book is an account of Eighth Air Force life told largely in the words of those who experienced it. It's not intended to be a definitive Eighth Air Force history, documenting precise statistics and the chronology of events during World War II.

It is an "everyman's story"—the story of young Americans sent to airfields in the United Kingdom to carry out the daylight strategic air offensive. It is told from the viewpoint of a cross-section of diverse participants—including fliers, ground personnel, Red Cross workers, English observers, families on the home front, and others. It is also told in letters and diary excerpts of those silenced forever during the war.

Quotations are included here not because they sensationalize the time, but because they typify it. The intent is to paint an overall picture of life in the Eighth Air Force—on the ground and in the air—using representative incidents from a variety of participants. Focus is not deliberately on any particular fighter or bomber groups. Nor is focus on the leaders or strategists.

The "big picture" of strategic bombing, easily viewed in hindsight, was not common knowledge among those tasked with flying missions or those supporting the missions. As is universal in military life, enlisted men and junior-grade officers were not privy to the whys and wherefores of their duties, however dangerous they might be. Sweeping theories of the strategists were far removed from the acute realities of combat and logistics challenges of preparing men and machines for air battle.

Pondering the air war in Europe from the safe vantage point of nearly five decades later, it may seem like all glory, glamor, and excitement. But to the people who were there, flying missions or supporting those who did, it was different than that. Diaries, letters sent home, and reminiscences spoken from the perspective of today communicate a different message—about an endurance run of fear and boredom and heartache. For many, the flickering pilot light of hope nearly went out in the darkest days.

After the war, those who returned from England to welcoming hometowns enjoyed the distinction associated with wings and winged-eight shoulder patches on their uniforms. But it wasn't long before their World War II experience faded into the homogeneous mass of memories. In later years, however, the time has re-emerged as distinctive—something truly worth remembering and preserving. And this emergence prompts many of them to return to airfields, once on the cutting edge of the European air war, now sitting derelict in the East Anglian countryside.

They revisit a time in their lives that, for many years, lay dormant or obscure in their minds. And perhaps they seek to verify for themselves that the incredible time happened at all. The sight of an old airfield brings sounds, and the sounds bring smells, and the smells bring images in vivid detail. *From Somewhere in England* offers the memories and emotions evoked as they gaze today upon the fields they left behind, like their youth, in the English fog.

Acknowledgments

I am privileged to know many of those who were there and, through extensive interviews with them, have sought to put a human face on the United States Eighth Air Force in World War II.

I extend thanks to them and many others who contributed, including Karen Laws, Barbara Graves, Sharon Vance Kiernan, Irma Permoser, John Campbell, Dave Osborne, George Lawson, Robert Brismaster, Harry Crosby, and staff of the Experimental Aircraft Association. For their help in finding interviewees and information, I thank also the editors of the following publications: *VFW, Air Force, 8th AF News,* and *The Retired Officer.* Special thanks to Dave Kaphingst for his photo reproduction expertise and Tamarac Travel, Tamarac, Florida, for its commitment to organizing nostalgic England tours.

Prologue

Abandoned airfields can be very moody places. Especially when an airfield once was the wartime home for a US Eighth Army Air Force bombardment or fighter group, and the ubiquitous early-morning haze renders England's vividly green surroundings in soft focus.

It's a time when ghosts come out to toil and play. Devoid of movement, save the swirling mist, an empty runway makes it easy to dwell on the history sealed within its sketchy tarmac and pitted concrete.

The very weather seems to possess a quality of the past—like faded old photographs.

Walking the runway against the capricious Midlands wind, you can still

Farmers still plow up remnants from World War II. Andrew Morland

Rear of the PX (Post Exchange) at Horham, England. Andrew Morland

7

Airfield buildings at Bungay.

hear the deep-throated engines of heavy bombers and escorting fighters—aircraft christened with names like *Piccadilly Lilly, Purty Baby, Petie* and *Stage Door Canteen*—flying right into history. Tall grasses are bent back almost as if in the gale of a slipstream.

Nearly half a century later, the stations seem full of voices, the clump of boots, laughter from an Aeroclub and shouted orders over the thunder of 1200 horsepower engines. A dilapidated hangar still echoes the metallic *clank* of ground crews working desperately in the small hours of the night to repair the ravages of the mission before. Resonant and resolute utterances of intelligence officers and weathermen seem to reverberate mission details to every crevice of a cavernous, long-unused briefing room.

Obscure outlines emerge at intervals: parallel silhouettes resembling the twin tails of a Liberator bomber on a weed-choked hardstand and sleek martial lines like those of Mustang fighters, queuing up for takeoff.

Empty window sockets stare from the half-circle, crumbling masonry front wall of a solitary Nissen hut that once served as headquarters. Presiding over the scene, a soon-to-be-razed, box-like control tower looms—having sat for decades among acres of raspberry brambles, like an abandoned radio, broadcasting creaks and whispers to the English rain.

A cluster of empty huts crouches unobtrusively in a tree-sheltered meadow. Inside them, brooding stillness is permeated by a musty odor much like that of old periodicals buried in back shelves of library archives—1940s *Stars and Stripes* tabloids, and *Life* and *Time* magazines, which once dispatched late-breaking stories about the activities on these very fields. But the smell of dampness and decay was *not* the smell of those vibrant, desperate years so full of life (and death) for men based here. Like the sky, the airfields were never still, but bustled with round-the-clock activities of men preparing for air battle.

Chapter 1

East Anglia revisited

I remember vividly the way it was the last day I saw it. . . .
—Jack Spratt, 92nd Bomb Group

On the eastern shores of England, just opposite Continental Europe, East Anglia thrusts out like a boxing glove into the blue-gray waters of the North Sea.

Along narrow country lanes in the tranquil East Anglian countryside, motionless cows stand knee-deep in buttercups against a backdrop of silver willows. Sheep graze in pastures bordered by ancient stone walls and split-rail fences. Primrose, violets and bluebells ripple through wet meadows, divided by thick hedgerows at regular intervals. It's a static vision captured in an early 1800s painting by John Constable.

Superimposed on this idyllic landscape, however, are traces from a far-from-peaceful time—a time when the English countryside became a battle front for a raging air war. By mid 1942, the sleepy backwaters of East Anglia and English Midlands had been stung alive with the ardor of Americans sent to wage an air war. And as a resident of a typical Midlands hamlet said, "A village of 150 suddenly went to several thousand. The activity became like that on an anthill."

There were more than 120 US Army Air Forces airfields fit like puzzle pieces into the gentle undulations of East Anglia. Smaller in square miles than the island of Hawaii, East Anglia is an imprecisely defined region north of the Thames River and south of The Wash, a major inlet of the North Sea. For its strategic location—flatlands well suited for runways and closeness to Continental Europe—the area became the hyperactive origination place for Eighth Air Force strikes against the Third Reich.

Almost as quickly as the airfields had been animated, they fell silent in 1945, as once more did the East Anglian landscape. Eventually the airfields were abandoned, their once colossal significance lost forever. And like the contrails in the wake of long-vanished aircraft that flew from them, the onetime bustling fields dissipate. The fields that still stand have been preserved more by chance than by design and are being quietly reclaimed by the land.

Some remain mildly active as fields for glider clubs, crop-dusting planes and flight training facilities. Some are now Royal Air Force (RAF) bases. A few became small commercial airports.

Hethel's perimeter track and runway became a test track for Lotus sports cars. Podington airfield became one of England's two commercially sanctioned dragstrips.

Many air stations were annexed to form vast farmyard complexes—one (Halesworth) boasting the world's largest turkey farm. Some, once in rural settings,

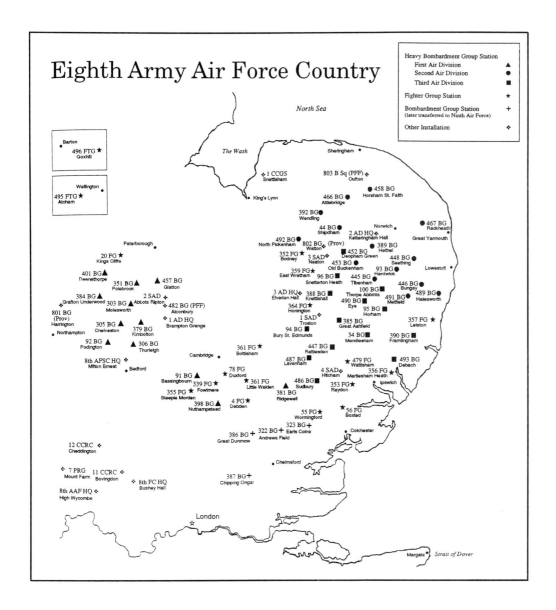

Eighth Army Air Force Country

Heavy Bombardment Group Station
First Air Division ▲
Second Air Division ●
Third Air Division ■

Fighter Group Station ★

Bombardment Group Station +
(later transferred to Ninth Air Force)

Other Installation ❖

were enveloped by cities and industrial parks and are gone practically without a physical trace.

Most stand mute and spectral, engulfed by the overgrowth of peaceful decades. Still overlooking runways, control towers stand poised for the approach of squadrons that will never return. Indeterminate buildings are forlorn and empty.

In a cursory meander through them, one might think, "Ah, if these walls could talk. . . ." But in their own way, derelict walls do talk. In cryptic chronicling of monumental events, the walls tell the story of men who lived out the final days of short, intense lives based in England, of their women, of deadly confrontations in the sky and of targets attacked.

In a shadowy corner of billeting quarters, at a height just above where an

upper bunk had been, hash marks appear in groups of five, each mark representing a mission. They total only twenty, five short of the quota laid down at one point in the war. Nearly indiscernible lettering above a door spells the dictum of the day: "Abandon hope all ye who enter here." These fields were the last place many young Americans ever set foot on earth.

For many survivors of the US Eighth Army Air Force, haunting memories of impossible missions cling with astonishing tenacity. It is the aircrews' vision of nightmarish flights through fierce enemy defenses and of the joy of making that final hash mark in a log book or on a billet wall after the last mission. It is the ground crews' vision of endless hours preparing equipment and of relief after "sweating out" the return of their kindred from embattled skies. They are drawn to this

part of the United Kingdom—back to the scene that witnessed both the best and worst episodes of their lives.

To explain why he has traveled across the Atlantic to the remote regions of eastern England, political science professor John Houk, who also served on a 92nd Bomb Group crew, plucked a quote from the late artist Andy Warhol's augury at a Stockholm photo exposition. He wants to recapture, he said, the elation of being "world-famous for fifteen minutes."

For Dr. Houk and thousands of others who return, this is the ultimate sentimental journey—a trip back to a time when A–2 flight jackets were not a fashion statement, when "bail out" did not refer to government help for failing corporations and when German cities unheard of now, like Schweinfurt and Regensburg, aroused the fervor of the American public. It was a time when an airplane was personified—referred to by name, not merely by tail number.

During each individual's story of "East Anglia Revisited," time runs backward. They drink bitter and milds at the village pub closest to their airfield—the same pub they frequented during wartime. When they get together, GI wisecracks fly as in wartime. They talk about

Chipped and fading artwork still adorns the walls at Shipdham, once home of the 44th Bomb Group. Trevor Austin

comrades and places unseen for decades, as if frozen in time. They refer to "kids" not seen since 1945. On a typical itinerary are visits to English people befriended during the war and, of course, to their old airfields.

For many, these former Eighth air stations are the worn footlockers that contain life's fondest memories and greatest tragedies. Although now ghost towns, the stations live in the minds of those who survived—composite scenes re-created from diaries now disintegrating at their folds, brittle yellow newspaper articles, threadbare uniforms with winged-eight shoulder insignias, and old songs—like the standard "In the Mood," played there by Maj. Glenn Miller's Army Air Forces band.

It also forms anew in the imagination from photographs whose images spring into three dimensions, permanent and ineffaceable from the entropy of rapidly passed decades. Yesterday comes back in innumerable detail—detail that overlays the scenes of airfields as they are today with memories of when they were new and intact.

For some, the contrast between recollection and reality evokes inexpressible emotion. There is a mixture of reverence and pathos for the memorials at places like Mendlesham and Grafton-Underwood, and the remnants of ancient runways clogged with weeds. Many of the returning visitors pick up a small chunk of concrete runway to take home.

"Seeing it again brings back sentiment and emotion," said L. G. Spillman, who returned to Podington in the summer of 1989. "I can't say a lot of fond memories, but there was some fondness, too. I thought of things I hadn't thought of for many years—like mission mornings when it was so foggy that we couldn't even see to get to the mess hall. On those mornings we relied on goodie packages sent from home and ate nothing else. And I remembered people, some killed in the war, who I'd not thought about for years—faces came to me, not necessarily names."

Visiting Thorpe Abbotts, home to the 100th Bomb Group, Roger Lyons commented: "I walked around with a map of the base and tried to identify the buildings. I found the hospital. Couldn't find the barracks site for sure, but when I got near it I remembered how we played ball there in the evenings."

About his pleasant perusal of Alconbury, still in use as a military installation,

A 303rd Bomb Group crewman chalks up yet another mission on the door to his hut at Molesworth. Sharing the hut were crews from three aircraft: Hunga-Dunga, Sky Wolf *and* Spook. John Campbell

Ralph Ballinger of the 904th Signal Company said:"They gave me a cook's tour of the place. It looks different with new buildings added and some old ones taken away. The hangars are still here. Base headquarters is new, but located where our old headquarters site was. The dispersal area is now lighted tennis courts and baseball diamonds. And our old mess hall has been moved, possibly up the street and converted to a club."

Al Giesting found the 352nd Fighter Group's station at Bodney "sown in barley. Only the permanent buildings were still there. The hangars of the service squadron are used for grain storage. The fields were back in crop, but the airfield is still held by the Air Ministry."

Carroll Lewis, pilot in the 379th Bomb Group, likened his return to Kimbolton to "the feeling portrayed by Dean Jagger in the movie *Twelve O'Clock High*—the waving wheat fields and cows grazing over a peaceful English countryside where such intense activity took place." He recalled Kimbolton as "a place you would leave early in the morning possibly not to ever return. . . .Friends were made and lost there—memories would remain forever of that most important place."

Not only those stationed at the fields return to recapture something from bygone days. Barbara Pathe, a Red Cross worker who motored in "clubmobiles" to bases in the vicinity of Bury St. Edmunds, went back shortly after the war in the early summer of 1950: "It was a happy time of normalcy, except for the rationing that still prevailed. I did miss the excitement of living in the midst of all those vital young Americans, and surprisingly I missed being awakened by the roar of bombers rendezvousing over Bury for their flights to Germany."

And even some who had never been to England before come to see where a family member was based. The flying club at Hethel has taken a number of grandchildren on flights over what remained of a grandfather's airfield.

Spouses are also absorbed by the fields which, perhaps, had been previously only represented by an APO address for wartime letters. "When our group went back to King's Cliffe to dedicate the monument in 1983," said Jack Ilfrey, 20th Fighter Group pilot, "our wives got a kick out of our anxiousness to point out places we knew around the airfield."

Others wizen in disappointment at the demise of what still stood sturdy in their minds. Hiram Drache viewed in astonishment the remains of Glatton, home to the 457th Bomb Group:

"My heart began to throb as we neared the base from the south, and it hit a high when I saw the water tower and the thatched-roof, white house, then the chapel spire [at Connington] in the distance. At first it seemed like nothing had changed, but within a few minutes I realized that . . . except for the main runway, it was all gone.

"I [stood] at the end of the runway while recalling the many anxious minutes I had spent lying on my stomach in the nose of the B–17 watching the ground

pass underneath me. . . .We then walked to the former site of our 748th Squadron area. I stood stunned as I observed a plowed field with not one memento of those days that were once a highlight in the lives of so many. We kicked the grass and looked among the trees in search of one small token of those days. There was nothing.

"I visualized where the squadron office had been, and then the huts I had lived in, first as a young crew member and later as squadron navigator. I was speechless and hurt to realize that except for those of us who actually lived there, few will know . . . about what was once there."

"It was just an old sod field—long abandoned," commented pilot Charles Cummins about the 361st Fighter Group's station at Bottisham. "The village is still there, but most everything at the field is torn down. They're putting a highway through the middle of it."

Howard Moebius, 357th Fighter Group pilot, went back to Leiston in 1975: "I saw it again just as they began grinding up the runway. A workman said, 'If you had waited until next year to come, this would be all farmers' fields.'"

"It's almost like I read about it somewhere," one returning veteran said. "Like the place existed only in fiction. But I was really here."

Vaguely familiar, often overpowering emotions are evoked as they study the remains of the fields, searching for the dim outline of their youth in overgrown Nissens made surreal by the sun-and-shadow of now thick woods, and macadam runways blurred by Mother Nature's mist—and sometimes the mist of sentiment that envelopes the eyes from within.

"I must admit that when I look down what is left of our main runway [at Nuthampstead], my eyes become misty as I recall the many takeoffs for combat missions," said Mark Magnon, a 398th Bomb Group pilot. "The pub that was part of the base is still in business. And the adjacent farms are now operated by the children who used to watch us take off."

Returning to England for the first time since March 1945, Jack Spratt paused where he believed a hardstand had been—the hardstand he knelt upon and kissed after completing his thirty-fifth and final mission as a ball turret gunner for the 92nd Bomb Group:

"I remember vividly the way it was the last day I saw it—with hardstands and

Section of wall extricated from a razed air-field building at Bottisham. The wall is now intact at Thorpe Abbotts, thanks to the efforts of EWACS. Trevor Austin

buildings. When the plane was back here in its position on the hardstand after my last mission, I was the first one out of the waist door. I knelt on the ground and kissed the concrete and picked up a handful of dirt.

"The crew I had flown with—not my own—didn't know it was my last mission. They were a green crew with only three missions. I didn't know them or how well the pilot could fly, so it made the emotion of getting back even more dramatic.

"There's great joy in making witness to this place I lived for nine months, not knowing from the first mission on that I would ever come back to this English soil. It's an incredible feeling to come back after forty-four years and think, *That's where I once took off and didn't know if I would ever return.*"

Recapturing the elation of long ago is one reason they come back. But Spratt also came to meet with old friends. Two others quoted previously, John Houk and L. G. Spillman, served on the same bomber crew and experienced the rare emotions of returning together to see their air station at Podington.

Houk commented: "It's surprising how we have resumed friendship, even though there's been really no ties in the interim. I'm amused by the fact that we argue over little details. Walking around the base, one says, 'I know it was here.' Another says, 'No, it was there.' But the experience has brought us close together once again."

Spillman added: "We wanted to find the 327th Bomb Squadron area, even though someone I'd spoken with in San Antonio said that area of the base is now a pig farm. With that hint, the driver immediately knew where to find it. Our bath house was still standing—seeing that reminded me of how far we had to walk from our barracks."

Some describe it as "a time when a lot of living was crammed into a short time" and "an intense period that was burned into your memory." It brings back some joyous thoughts—of pride for partaking in our nation's victories and satisfaction for lifelong friends made.

John Wood, 381st Bomb Group ball turret gunner, said: "It's an experience that's embedded in my mind. When I close my eyes, I still sometimes see enemy fighters coming head on through the formation."

Wood went back alone to England in 1954 to see Ridgewell: "I stood there on the old runway, all cracked up with grass

"There was some rowdiness. Not like we know it today in the terms of vandalism and excessive noise—but rowdiness such as one gets when a group of good-natured young men get together. There was good humor and a certain amount of bravado as they paraded up and down the road in the blackout trying to impress the local girls."
—John Mills, Bedfordshire youth

Diss Railway Station has changed little since 1944. John W. Archer

growing through it. And I could hear the wind. That was something you didn't hear there during the war, because there was always an aircraft engine running up or some other noise. But when I returned, it was just so deathly quiet as the wind whistled through. I stared at the runway and thought about how, after missions, I went with my crew to the White Heart Pub at Great Yeldham."

"That which is bitter to endure may be sweet to remember," wrote Thomas Fuller, in *Gnomologia* (1732). But not all is sweet to recall.

A return to East Anglia can bring arrestingly sad thoughts. Some come here to have it out with painful memories, but not necessarily communicate them. "I know several individuals who were sole survivors out of a crew of ten," a 448th Bomb Group veteran offered. "They don't want to talk about it."

Ravaged by emotion experienced not quite so acutely for decades, another responded, "Losing friends was the hardest part. A crew was close—maybe even closer than brothers. And I just can't bring myself to think about it—ok?"

Therein lies perhaps the predominant reason they return: to pay homage to beloved men who also might be in the

prime of maturity, had they survived the war. To remember with pain and unutterable gratitude those who didn't return—like they did—to anxiously awaiting families and comfortable lifestyles in postwar America. They come in tribute to those who "found their graves in the sky" or met death on cold, windswept airfields in this foreign land.

"The loss of friends was the most painful experience," almost any of them will tell you. But friendship forged in wartime was the best experience. Special bonds were created, not only on an individual basis, but between two cultures of people. Those bonds still exist today. Returning Eighth veterans are met by an adoring British public who, as C. L. Anderson of the 390th Bomb Group said, "treat us royally." Many return to see, for the first time, the people of Great Britain free of blackout and rationing. Even the most detached observer can't help noticing that the relationship is extraordinary.

Click-clacking into key railway stations like Diss (home of a favorite phrase: "Dis is Diss") and Norwich, just as many had during the war, reunion-attending veterans are greeted by "mobs of fans"— townspeople in the heart of what the English themselves have dubbed "Eighth Air

Force Country." Bands play Glenn Miller favorites and signs read, "Welcome home, Yank," "Gum, chum?" and "Hi, Dad."

The memory is alive and well in the hearts and minds of those who counted aircraft flying out in the early morning and counted them as they came back in the late afternoon. Even though many decades have passed since the last raid was flown against Nazi Germany and the last truck exited an airfield gate, the Eighth Air Force is still part of life in the English countryside.

In village pubs, locals still talk about the young Americans who frequented the establishments, playing darts with them and "becoming like one of the townfolk"—although they were prone to discontinue their visits abruptly. Inquiries at the local airfield invariably yielded responses like, "He didn't return from a mission" or "There was an accident on the field."

"The pubs were small and friendly," said B–24 pilot Robert Bieck of the 453rd Bomb Group. "We always griped about the beer. However, I have been back to the U.K. over a hundred times since the war—and I now like the beer."

And today, it's sometimes difficult for an Eighth veteran to pay for his own beer in a local pub. Townspeople jump at the chance to reminisce with their American guests about their own individual involvements with the Eighth Air Force. An unmistakable message one gets is that a unique love affair exists between the British in small East Anglian villages and GIs once stationed there—despite initial suspicions and "differences" in culture.

"They became 'my family' for the eight months I was in England," Saul Kupferman of the 306th Bomb Group commented about a Bedford family. "A true love affair formed. Looking back, I strongly feel that the love and friendship they offered me during those trying times, as well as the home atmosphere, played an important part in my survival."

During his visits since the war, Kupferman stayed with surviving family members, at their insistence. They welcome him with open arms, as did he when the family visited the United States.

From the Thames Valley to The Wash, they still recall vividly when bombers and fighters thundered overhead. Once quiet air and earth vibrated with the ferocious intensity of supercharged engines of war. Many say it's the most excitement ever to come to their sleepy hamlets.

"It was a time when excitement reigned," commented Englishman John Mills, a young boy during the American "invasion." "Even now I feel those years were the most intense and most exciting and most formative years I've experienced."

English children became enamored with the young foreigners, who seemed to possess the swaggering self-confidence that no harm could befall them. The GIs moved onto government-commandeered land with not only armadas of aircraft, but seemingly bottomless pockets of goodies that the children had never known in their short, war-usurped lives. Their memories are of Christmas parties thrown for them, of chewing gum and candy bars and fruit in a world of strict rationing.

Many of these children, as adults, have become the keepers of the sites. Some prevent deliberate destruction and work to preserve them, in a sense, as shrines to these larger than life figures known in their youth. A guardian of remembrance is John Gray, who was sixteen years old when the Eighth left in 1945.

Gray played tennis with the Americans and attended the 200th and 300th mission parties for the 390th Bomb Group, whose airfield occupied approximately forty acres of the Gray family farm. The lavish Gray home is still neighbored by a small city of Nissen huts, once billets for the group's 371st Squadron. One of those Nissens has been carefully dismantled and sent to Davis-Monthan Air Force Base in Tucson, Arizona, where it was reconstructed for the 390th Bomb Group museum there. "Along with it went all the 'amenities'—electric light fittings and pot-bellied stove," noted Gray.

Americans hailed as heroes by the local populace are remembered regularly. Like Kimbolton-based pilot, Lt. John Aherne, who stayed in his disabled aircraft to guide it over the village of Bozeat. Below him in mist-shrouded houses, lived families like his own—mothers, fathers, children. He fought the controls of his fatally stricken bomber until past the populated area and then shuddered downward like hell on a wing. Englishman Gerry Darnell witnessed the ordeal:

"One very foggy morning I was walking up the driveway of a farmhouse at Bozeat and heard the drone of an aircraft obviously in trouble. The noise grew louder and out of the fog appeared the shape of a B–17. I watched in horror as it

"The closest town was a typical English market-town, where the people accepted us with kindness, courtesy and friendship. . . ."
—James Goodson, 4th Fighter Group

"The times bred togetherness and camaraderie like I have never experienced since."
—Mark Magnon, 398th Bomb Group (H)

crashed into the paddock of the farmhouse that I was about to visit.

"Fire tenders and ambulances rushed to the scene, but bombs aboard had exploded and little could be done. Lt. Aherne had ordered the members of his crew to bail out and all were safe."

A service attended by all villagers was held for Lieutenant Aherne in the Bozeat church. A plaque commemorates him, and people continue to pay him tribute at the Remembrance Day Service held on November 11 each year.

In a number of village churches, saints and prophets in stained-glass windows are oddly partnered with the American eagle or Flying Fortress.

No matter where you travel in the region, even after decades since the airfields were active, you're never more than a few miles from traces of the Eighth's passing—whether it's physical vestige or an ineradicable memory attached to a particular place. Subtle and not-so-subtle reminders are everywhere.

Even at airfields like Bottisham and Fowlmere, declared "redundant" by the Air Ministry after the war and promptly bulldozed into extinction, there seems to be something still looming above dead foundations and shallow, manmade contours. One can still sense proportions and dimension amidst the wildflowers, and beech and oak trees trying to reclaim the sites. A forest of mature trees stands on the site of more than one derelict airfield, where it is said that during the war a tree was planted for each airman lost from a group.

At Ancient House in Horham, English resident Alan Johnson pointed to the patched ceiling and told matter-of-factly about a hole blown there at daybreak one morning in 1943. A bomb- and fuel-laden bomber failed to lift off before reaching the end of the runway: "The concussion blew out windows in the village and knocked a hole in my roof."

Exploring the dazzling green countryside near Wincanton, Somerset, a flash reflection of midday sun might catch your eye as you cross stone wall-bounded fields. There, set in a stone wall, is a bronze plaque that reads: "This tablet was erected by the people of Wincanton in Honour of United States Airmen who lost their lives when their Flying Fortress 'Old Faithful' crashed in flames at Snag Farm near this spot, when returning disabled from an operational sortie over Toulous, France, on 25th June, 1944."

The plaque is one of hundreds of tiny gems set in the vast green brocade of East Anglia. It memorializes succinctly the loss of the Peter Mikonis crew from the 91st Bomb Group. Lieutenant Mikonis had coerced an olive drab B–17G, *Old Faithful*, for more than six hours after a German flak battery found its mark on number three engine. Details of the crew's last six agonizing hours will never be known for certain. According to the official Description of Accident report, dated June 29, 1944, "The aircraft was seen to leave the formation at approximately 0900 hours." Known facts are that they finally reached the sanctity of England, sighted by an armored division private at 1545 hours, or 3:45 P.M. The private is quoted as saying, "I was walking to my girl's house when I happened to look overhead and saw the wing of the plane snap in two. . . . " The still-smoking right wing collapsed, causing the bomber, limping along at tree-top level, to instantly roll to its back and slam into a farmyard bounded by the stone fence noted earlier. Its crew was killed instantly.

If you're seeking lodging on Lavenham's High Street, you'll likely go to the Swan Hotel (known previously as the Swan Inn), where a portrait of Brig. Gen. Frederick Castle is prominently displayed. Ask any of the hotel's staff about it and you'll hear a story of heroism that occurred on Christmas Eve 1944. Departing from Lavenham airfield, General Castle led the largest Eighth Air Force mission of the war.

Lost in the raid were fifty-six US aircraft, including General Castle's B–17. The staff might show you a copy of the citation for General Castle's posthumous Medal of Honor—the last of fourteen Medals of Honor awarded to members of the Eighth Air Force—which reads:

"He was air commander and leader of more than 2,000 heavy bombers in a strike against German airfields on 24 December 1944. En route to the target, the failure of one engine forced him to relinquish his place at the head of the formation. In order not to endanger friendly troops on the ground below, he refused to jettison his bombs to gain speed and maneuverability. His lagging, unescorted aircraft became the target of numerous enemy fighters which ripped the left wing with cannon shells, set the oxygen system afire, and wounded two members of the crew. Repeated attacks started fires in two engines, leaving the

Flying Fortress in imminent danger of exploding. Realizing the hopelessness of the situation, the bail-out order was given. Without regard for his personal safety he gallantly remained alone at the controls to afford all other crew members an opportunity to escape. Still another attack exploded gasoline tanks in the right wing, and the bomber plunged earthward, carrying General Castle to his death. His intrepidity and willing sacrifice of his life to save members of the crew were in keeping with the highest traditions of the military service."

Unobvious stories—stories that one might never know unless one happens to ask—lie behind names of localities, like Maude Gray Court on St. Benedict Street in Norwich. When builders sought a name for a redevelopment on St. Benedict Street in the late 1980s, the "golden boys" from nearby Rackheath were remembered. The place was named Maude Gray Court after a B–24J named *Maude Gray* that often was crewed "by a group of boys who frequented the Ten Bells pub on St. Benedict Street," according to a local newspaper. Obviously, the memory of men and missions is strong.

One returning veteran revisited Coombe House, a combat rest home for fliers, which has been occupied by St. Mary's School for girls since 1945. He was graciously given a tour by Roman Catholic nuns, who showed traces of long-ago American visitors—in the form of signatures and graffiti scrawled on walls behind school lockers.

East Anglian farmers still plow up fragments of shattered aircraft and ordnance. They still drive their tractors on airfield perimeter tracks that provide smooth and convenient passage from one field to another. Maycrete and Nissen huts, once serving as Aeroclubs, post exchanges, mess halls and chapels, are now used for hay storage, stables and equipment sheds.

In the Tilbury-juxta-Clare area, a farmer, Eric Meekings, still cultivates the field where *Egg Haid* and *Schnoozle*, two B–17s, plummeted to earth in a single, flaming mass after a post-mission collision on Jan. 21, 1945. Pointing across hedgerow-divided fields where he's toiled since boyhood, Meekings said, "I can still see the difference in color of the soil while cultivating."

A group commander's house, located in communal site number three of Ridgewell, is owned by Carole and Bob Martin. "They built these to stay," Carole Martin remarked. "Six-inch-thick drive. Four-inch watermain pipes instead of the usual half-inch. And as you can see, nothing is sagging or falling off." Just outside is an

"My most vivid memory is the 2,000-plane raid on Christmas Eve 1944. Our group was second over the target. The group ahead of us was the lead group—with General Castle leading. Even though they were quite far ahead of us, we could see them going down, one after another, like Roman candles. Enemy fighters and flak were turning them into blazing fireballs."
—George Swanson, 94th Bomb Group (H)

A Ridgewell Nissen, now a shed for implement storage. Andrew Morland

air raid bunker used now to shelter firewood from the rain instead of protecting life and limb from Luftwaffe attack.

Ridgewell's station morgue also still stands, modified into a one-stall garage located just behind a postwar home. But the station's control tower "was razed for no particular reason," according to Dave Osborne, the local Ridgewell contact for the Friends of the Eighth (an organization of the finest ambassadors found anywhere).

Framlingham's control tower, restored as a museum, was reopened in August 1980. Control towers at Seething and Thorpe Abbotts and other airfield buildings across East Anglia also now serve as museums filled with airfield artifacts.

Artifacts come from many sources, among them veterans once stationed at the fields, but much comes from enthusiastic efforts of local people. Britons like Ron Buxton make a hobby of researching World War II crash sites. Relying on records still in village police files, which document crew, mission and witnesses, they are able to pinpoint crash locations. As a result, many of these unearthed items have been put in the airfield museums.

A group of young Britons, each with a unique talent, has joined together to form an organization they call EWACS (standing for Eighth War Art Conservation Society). Their specialty is rescuing from destruction wartime murals or "frescos," artwork painted on walls of airfield buildings. When a building is about to be razed, they go into action with chisels, concrete saws, forklifts and any other equipment necessary to extricate a whole section of a brick wall in one piece.

Many towers have found a number of uses other than museums and farm buildings. Podington's control tower and others are occupied as private residences. The former control tower for the 361st Fighter Group at Little Walden is now an immaculate architecture office, its renovation preserving the integrity of the original design. But now, observation windows—once the vantage point for controlling P-51s at takeoff and landing—overlook highway B1052 (south out of Hadstock) that employs the northeast-southwest runway for the straightest section of the route.

Throughout the region, English residents remark that a hangar still standing at the nearby airfield or the local corn exchange was the setting for a performance by Glenn Miller and his band within weeks or days of Miller's disappearance on a flight over the Channel.

"Nothing has changed here—even the wits [width] of the roads," remarked

Inside an air raid shelter. Andrew Morland

Englishman Mike Orlebar, about the area surrounding Podington.

The English and their countryside coax memories from the Americans who lived history there. The human mind loses much more than it retains, yet it is a computerlike storehouse of information, available at any moment to be tapped. Instantly, sometimes involuntarily, a memory is triggered by a song, a locality, a jingle, a word fallen out of vogue, an odor, a distinctive sound, a particular person after years of separation. Thoughts nestled deep in the mind's recesses thrust into the forefront of consciousness and long-lost emotions are revived, fresh as the day they were experienced.

Eighth Air Force veterans—whether transported to England by air, by sea or solely by their minds' power of conveyance—look upon airfields that, to them, are still possessed by intense life. And flashbacks from a most unusual war stand front and center.

Many of the fields were operational not even three years. Yet they exude a profound presence of the past, of events crucial to the outcome of war on an unparalleled scale that would determine the destiny of the world. It was an era when young Americans were sent to the British Isles, without any particular wonderment, as part of the greatest air striking force the world has ever known.

"Radio equipment had a distinctive, acrid smell. It permeated aircraft radio compartments. Now, when I'm in a radio shop and I get a whiff of that, I think of a B-17."
—Harry Crosby, 100th Bomb Group (H)

Chapter 2

The Yanks arrive

We had sealed orders that weren't to be opened until we left the ground. Our pilot opened them immediately after we lifted off and read over the interphone that we were assigned to the Eighth in England.

—Lloyd Nelson, B-24 gunner

A postwar return greatly contrasts the first time the Americans came to airfields in England.

In a flurry of excitement over new surroundings and the promise of adventure, the youth of America breezed into the war-weary British Isles where rationing and shortages had prevailed since 1939. Some had not been out of their home states before, let alone off the North American continent.

The generation had grown up with spectacular air heroes like Charles Lindbergh and other transoceanic flyers, hailed globally for early aviation exploits. While other kids read homework assignments, they sometimes feigned interest in textbooks, their attention riveted to a concealed copy of *Flying Aces* magazine tucked into the binding. And from these they became enthralled with Capt. Eddie Rickenbacker, William Avery Bishop and other World War I flyers, who were the personification of all the glory and glamor in the world.

But these same boys, equipped with children's dreams and men's courage, didn't view themselves on this grandiose scale. Most were civilians-turned-temporary-soldiers in their late teens or early twenties who, prior to induction, had de-livered groceries or helped with milking chores or played baseball in the local sandlot. Some had plans to attend State U the next fall—but all put their plans on hold.

They joined the United States Army Air Forces (USAAF) and were assigned to the Eighth Air Force. They were further assigned to a *group*, the basic operational unit to which their primary affinity formed. Fliers and ground personnel, based on training and experience, were assigned to fighter groups, bombardment groups (popularly termed "bomb groups") and so on.

C. L. Anderson offered a description of his 390th Bomb Group crew which was, like most bomber crews, a microcosm of America:

"I was a farm boy, born and raised near the little town of Patterson, California. Our radio operator was also a farm boy, as was our waist gunner who came from a Texas farm. The navigator was a percussion musician from New York. [Tendons in his right arm severed by flak, this navigator's musical career ended over Hamburg.] The tail gunner—a Golden Gloves boxer—was a nineteen-year-old kid from Pennsylvania. The engineer, also nineteen, was the son of a banker in

The youth of America answered the call.
USAF via John Ziebell

Iowa. The bombardier was from the outskirts of Chicago. Our pilot grew up on an Oklahoma farm and had moved west with his parents to Stockton, California. I guess we were just a bunch of kids."

"A bunch of kids" like these, along with spartan air stations and the aircraft based at them, were the reality that represented America's ideals—the ideals of purging the world of tyranny and defending the intangibles of democracy and freedom.

The Atlantic crossing

The journey from the United States to Great Britain was sometimes a memorable, even hazardous experience. Jack Ilfrey, 1st Fighter Group pilot (later 20th Fighter Group pilot), made the trip in a P–38 Lightning. Along with him flew three other P–38s and a 97th Bomb Group B–17. In July 1942, they flew from Maine to England with stops in Labrador, Greenland, Iceland and Scotland. "In that part of the world, the weather is very unpredictable and always bad," Ilfrey said. "Our flight made the trip without difficulty. But others who left at the same time weren't so lucky. Six P–38s from our squadron and two B–17s made emergency landings on the Greenland ice cap. Fortunately, all the boys were rescued. We learned later that the flight had been given false weather information from a

German submarine." (Those eight aircraft remain buried in ice and attempts are under way to recover them.)

Matthew Robb, 388th Bomb Group navigator, recalled his crew's trek to Knettishall by a similar North Atlantic route:

"We were sent to Kearney, Nebraska, for overseas assignment. There we were given all new equipment—from safety razor to sheepskin clothing. For me a new sextant and watches. A brand-new B–17 from Topeka included a new, extra engine in the waist. We spent a week learning about the southern route to England—via Florida, Cuba, Guiana, Belem, Trinidad, Khartoum, Cairo, Casablanca and then to either Ireland or England.

"Then, we were awakened early one January morning and told we were the first such group to fly the *North Atlantic* route in winter. We were to get all our gear into our new plane for a pre-dawn takeoff to fly to Presque Isle, Maine. The generator on number two engine was causing the magnetic compass to be off, so we had to fly fence-rows to realign the compass. There would be no such geographical lines in Europe to work with.

"[After Presque Isle,] we took off for Nutt's Corner, Ireland at 9:30 at night. We were to fly at 11,000 feet using celestial navigation. A fix gave me a starting point and another gave me ground speed, drift and direction. We encountered a storm

The ETO, as painted on a wall at Hethel, once the home of the 389th Bomb Group. Trevor Austin

and levelled off at 22,000 feet. We were north of course and got farther north each time [I] took another fix. We were headed for Norway instead of Ireland. A big correction had to be made. . . .I gave our pilot a heading of 135 degrees. He made the turn and [I] figured ETA. I turned on the radio compass and was thrilled to see it center on zero. Everything worked out perfect—except that we arrived one hour and fifty-six minutes early. At that altitude, we had gotten into a direct tail wind [jet stream] that doubled our ground speed. The Emerald Isle appeared and we were there."

"We had sealed orders that weren't to be opened until we left the ground in the States," said Lloyd Nelson, B-24 top turret gunner. "Our pilot opened them immediately after we lifted off and read over the interphone that we were assigned to the Eighth in England." The crew responded with tentative whoops and hollers, because the accomplishments of the Eighth was already well known, but their enthusiasm was guarded, "because the heavy losses were known, too," Nelson said.

Jack Spratt's first sight of England was from his ball turret's 360 degree view: "We were used to the wide open spaces in America. England looked like a checkerboard with its borders of hedgerows and fences. I saw thatched roofs and other roofs made of red tile. . . ." Tail gunner L. G. Spillman likened England's farming fields to a giant crossword puzzle.

As the crews studied their new home below, East Anglians searched the sky to identify the source of a din different than the RAF aircraft they were accustomed to. "My father and I heard the sound of an unfamiliar aircraft," recalled John Mills, then fourteen years old. "It was 7:30 in morning in the early months of May 1942. We saw [what I later learned was a] B-17E, flying at about a thousand feet. It still had the words 'U.S. Army' in large letters on the underside of the wings. [That identification was omitted once the Eighth became operational.] The units soon started arriving in force and we saw B-17s and B-24s in increasing numbers."

The majority of the ground echelon was sent to England by ship. Given a one-way ticket on the *Queen Mary* (along with the other members of the 466th Bomb Group's ground echelon, among the 18,000 GIs aboard), John Pendleton departed New York harbor: "It was the only time I've ever seen the Statue of Liberty. That impressive sight remains indelibly implanted in the mind of all servicemen leaving the good old U.S.A. aboard a ship taking them to a war."

In constant danger of German U-boat attack, convoys zig-zagged across the Atlantic. Ralph Ballinger of the 904th Signal Company recalled being positioned at "the 'coffin corner' of the convoy, because it was a faster ship. But an oil line ruptured and we had to drop out. Finally, after repairs, we caught up with the rest of the ships just after dark. Fortunately, the convoy was not attacked."

First impressions

After fourteen days on the Atlantic, Fred Bartz's troop ship landed at Liverpool. Bartz, 306th Bomb Group cook, commented: "I wondered what the hell I got into. England was cold, and it rained constantly for days."

"It was a damp cold," added Dean Morehouse, 361st Fighter Group pilot. "It penetrated more than the dry cold of North Dakota. And it was foggy. We couldn't see the buildings across the street."

Some fliers also came by sea. A pilot for the 94th Bomb Group, Frank Halm's first reaction when he landed in July 1944 at Drennock was "absolute amazement at how green it was—the most impressive green I had ever seen. I lived in an Oregon valley where it's also very green, but there seemed to be an even deeper texture to it here."

Sent to Horham with the 95th Bomb Group, Glen Lunde was struck with the multitude of "beautiful small farms" and the sight of "English farmers working in white shirt and tie."

Gilbert Falck was assigned in late December 1943 to the 91st Bomb Group, located at Bassingbourn. He commented: "The 91st was given England's 'West Point' of the air. Barracks were two-story brick buildings with steam heat. The officer's mess, club house, ready room, etc. were all first class."

This was in contrast to what Robert Bieck of the 453rd Bomb Group found when he "entered a different world" at Old Buckenham:

"The base was not really finished. There was some obvious poor planning—like the roads. They were concrete, but for itty bitty British cars. Our six-by-six trucks, with their double tires, hung over either side of the road. It took an agonizingly long time to reconstruct the roads.

"Trucks hauled us to our new abodes, pneumonia tubes called Nissen huts. Like others, we had a tough time trying to get [heat] from the little stoves in the hut."

Andrew Low, later a major general, described his first reaction to Old Buckenham as "grim" in response to "much mud and rudimentary facilities."

James Goodson, a pilot in the famed Eagle Squadron and later ace in the 4th Fighter Group, dismissed his base at Debden as "primitive" and commented on the broader picture: "An American's first impression of England is always that of an older, less modern country. The standard of living was much lower in England, as was the standard of comfort. There was almost no central heating and even most hotels had electric or gas fires in the rooms. In the winter, one was *always* cold."

"Our showers were outside," said John Pendleton of the 466th Bomb Group about Attlebridge. "Four walls and no roof. During cold weather there was always ice on the floor, wall, and pipes. But we were lucky—we *could* shower, shave, and clean up regularly."

About the 361st Fighter Group's new home at Bottisham, Charles Cummins commented: "It was a small sod field that wasn't too impressive to us. We had been training in the States on long, hard-surface runways. But we adapted to it. And it was a pleasant place, located by a small village just outside Cambridge. We had it all to ourselves—no one else wanted it."

"We were out in the country," said Francis Cunningham of the 466th Bomb Group's intelligence section. "There were no gates—practically no security measures. It's no wonder German intelligence was good."

Soon after arriving in early 1943, the 94th Bomb Group was stationed temporarily at Earl's Colne until its aircraft arrived. Carl Lose recalled the first night when "Axis Sally welcomed us to England and the Germans dropped a few bombs to let us know they were aware of our presence."

Weatherman Aaron Kaplan recounted the 18th Weather Squadron's introduction to Lord Haw Haw soon after the squadron's arrival to High Wycombe:

"Lord Haw Haw gets on the air and said, 'Hi ya, Yanks.' We laughed and thought, 'What's going on?' And he continued, 'We missed you yesterday, Yanks, but we're coming tomorrow night to get you.' And we laughed again.

"The question was: How much of the thing is walls or is the whole thing ceiling?"
—Preston Clark, Jr., 94th Bomb Group (H)

Axis Sally, tantalizing voice of the Axis airwaves. EAA Aviation Foundation Photo Archives

The Axis airwaves

"Calais One, Calais Two, Bremen, Luxembourg and Friesland . . ." chanted a Nazi announcer. It was the signal that Axis Sally was coming on the air with a radio program of popular music laced with propaganda, broadcast to England and other Allied countries.

"Hello, gang," came the cheerful, seductive female voice. "Throw down those little old guns and toddle off home. There's no getting the Germans down."

Her melodious voice was the kind that coaxed one's ear to follow up and down, as it caressed a harangue designed to undermine morale: "I'm afraid you're yearning plenty for someone. I just wonder if she isn't running around with some 4-Fs back home." This was her preface to a pop song like "Somebody Else Is Taking My Place" or "I Wonder Who's Kissing Her Now."

Axis Sally, actually Mildred Gillars, was American-born, but turned traitor out of love for a German officer. She and Lord Haw Haw, actually William Joyce, another propaganda radio announcer, were tried after the war. She served twelve years in federal prison and Lord Haw Haw was hanged.

Lord Haw Haw, "welcoming" radio host, at the outbreak of war. EAA Aviation Foundation Photo Archives

"The next night, we're playing cards, and I have jacks back-to-back. I thought, 'Here's where I knock 'em dead.' All of a sudden the air raid siren goes off and we scatter . . . to the air raid trenches. High Wycombe is on a hill . . . made of limestone. They dug these trenches out of the limestone and didn't allow for any kind of water drainage. Some of the guys jumped in and almost drowned.

"We waited and waited. Finally, we saw the sky light up . . . [the Germans] dropped flares and it was like daylight. The Germans had control of the air in these days and could come and go as they pleased.

"High Wycombe was on a hill and there were two other hills and two other towns. They were bombing and bombing [but mistakenly on] another hill instead of ours. Otherwise, I wouldn't be here to tell the story.

"Ruby Kranz was a schoolgirl living in Naphill, a town on a neighboring hill. She and her family also heard Lord Haw Haw's broadcast. He said: 'We know where you are Pinetree. And we know where you are little Naphill, nestled in the Chiltern Hills in Buckinghamshire. We'll be visiting you tonight.' There was no doubt that he was talking about us. We laughed about it, but we were really scared."

Three bombs, all duds, landed within a hundred yards from the Kranz house. The attack had been one of many experienced by Naphill's residents and others across the region since early in the war. The English naturally were frightened by such attacks, but defiant and good-humored about it all. And the newly arrived Americans gradually became accustomed to the constant possibility of attack by random buzz bombs or more precise manned aircraft.

Jumping in with both feet

No time to hesitate for German propagandists' scare tactics, the embryonic Eighth Air Force, commanded by Brig. Gen. Ira Eaker, immediately began preparations for an aerial offensive.

"We flew Spitfires to learn the countryside, formation flying, and to become accustomed to clouds," said Robert Powell, Jr., stationed temporarily at Atcham until the 352nd Fighter Group arrived from the States. "Training commands were too cautious and careful to keep clean safety records that they didn't teach all new pilots all they needed to

High Wycombe (code-named "Pinetree"), headquarters for Eighth Air Force Command, was located in what had been an exclusive girls' school—Wycombe Abbey. Former oc- *cupants left behind a bell by each bed labeled, "If you need a mistress in the night, ring twice." 8th Photo Tech Squadron*

know in combat. We had to learn more after we were there."

"From somewhere in England"

Once settled, the natural instinct was to write home and tell your family where you were stationed. However, in an effort to thwart the enemy's excellent intelligence network, no one was allowed to specify assigned location beyond writing "from somewhere in England."

Censors screened letters to prevent such disclosures, but there were ways around that. Some preplanned with their families that, in each piece of V-Mail, the first word's beginning letter would be a letter of their location, and the family would put the succession of letters together by order of date to spell the name.

Ralph Ballinger said: "I mentioned in my first letter home about a certain hotel I had stayed at on West Jackson Boulevard in Chicago during radio school. It happened to be the *Bedford*, and even though I didn't mention Bedford explicitly in the letter, they picked up on it right away."

They wrote about their new homes and wartime conditions, albeit cryptically in view of necessary censorship, to their families in America, where life was relatively far removed from war.

And they themselves—not long ago also far removed from war—plunged into the incredible experience of an air war, waged radically in the full light of day....

V-Mail sheet—V for victory.

Pilots of the 357th Fighter Group find no letters from home today. John Ziebell

You would have laughed yourself silly the other day - if you could have seen me. We hit it rough up there & one time I flew around the waist like a bullet — somehow I shorted my electric flying suit & caught on fire. The whole crew swore up & down they never saw me move so fast & judging by their laughter I must have carried a prize expression of anxiety. I moved so fast that in doing so I ripped my flying suit & stopped my oxygen — how one guy can get in such a mess in two seconds is beyond me. As soon as I could breathe again, I took some rugged kidding & well deserved it.

—Jack Kirschbraun,
March 15, 1944
letter to family

Chapter 3

There are no milk runs

There are no milk runs. Old-timers among the combat men know and the new ones learned it today.

—381st Bombardment Group (H) operations report of mission 101-179 to aerodrome at St. Avord, France

In the darkest hour before dawn, aircrews walked to briefing and murmured among themselves about where the target might be. Clues sometimes leaked out ahead of time: "For instance, the gas load," recalled Don Morse, 92nd Bomb Group flight engineer/top turret gunner. "That gave away the range. We could figure roughly that the target had to be within a certain radius of the base."

In the early days of the daylight strategic bombing effort, range was a critical issue. A target deep inside enemy territory meant more layers of enemy defenses and the absence of fighter escort when bombers needed it most.

Until briefing, the target was anybody's guess. Possibly a close one, not heavily defended on Continental Europe's coast. In nomenclature of the day, a milk run. Or the *other* kind—a deep penetration through a gauntlet of flak batteries and eager squadrons of enemy fighters, all whose singular objective was to shoot them down.

"At briefing, I considered any mission to be perilous," said G. W. Pederson, 306th Bomb Group gunner. "There's always a chance of something bad happening, even if the mission *looked* like a milk run."

Battling the weather

Difficult missions were not solely the accomplishment of enemy efforts. Weather in England is notorious for rapid, severe changes. Like enemy defenses, weather was a hazard to reckon with. But between the two, weather was often more difficult to predict.

Weatherman Art Gulliver of the 18th Weather Squadron explained: "Predicting weather in England was difficult and entirely different than predicting weather in the United States. England's maritime climate results from the Gulf Stream coming up south of Iceland and back down north of England and Scandinavia. The moisture was the problem—there was so much of it. And weather changed rapidly. In the North Atlantic, particularly in winter, the storms came in every eighteen hours on average."

Weather incessantly caused delays. It heightened to fever pitch the already high tension. It idled minds primed for action, giving fear a chance to seep in. "There was a lot of chatter on the interphone," said 100th Bomb Group navigator Harry Crosby. "You'd hear boyish voices cracking dumb jokes in the nervousness. There was lots of nervous talk and razzing of one another, like 'Do you

Predicting weather in the United Kingdom was a challenge. During the Eighth Air Force's campaign, 25 percent of all days were nonoperational because of weather. 100th BG

The hallmark of England: fog. 100th BG

have guns or did you leave them on the hardstand?' Meanwhile, I sat there sweating and hoping the clouds would clear off so that I could navigate visually instead of by dead reckoning and radio during assembly."

G. W. Pederson added: "England's weather was usually bad. Fog, rain, snow, drizzle, gloom. I was briefed for at least forty missions more than I flew. If there was any chance that the weather would be good enough to fly, we'd be briefed for a mission and we'd be ready for takeoff. I'd get all that adrenaline flowing and tension built up, and go through the work of getting the guns ready. Then we'd be told the mission was delayed an hour. This compounded the tension. We'd wait the hour and they'd come around again to say it's delayed another hour. This sometimes went on for several hours. Then, finally, the mission would be scrubbed. It was always a great let-down when we didn't go on the mission. You'd burn up all that energy just getting ready."

"The frustrations of weather probably caused as much suspense as enemy action," observed Hiram Drache, 457th Bomb Group navigator.

Despite adverse conditions, the 94th Bomb Group was ordered to prepare for takeoff. Heavy snow reduced visibility to near zero at Bury St. Edmunds. Frank Halm's crew was assigned as group lead. "We generally knew our way around the perimeter track," recalled Halm. "We turned on alternate landing lights as we taxied, to verify that we were still on the taxi strip. But soon the landing lights were covered with snow and we didn't know where we were."

Eventually, Halm's Fort groped its way to the runway, but as the four propellers sliced the cold air, churning up a blizzard of accumulated snow, "it went to black daylight," said Halm. "Our commander came out and looked over our aircraft. There was a pile of snow on the wings and across the top of the aircraft. None of us 'green airkids' knew much about the hazards of icing and drag."

The group commander instructed ropes to be thrown over the outer wing panels and see-sawed to get the ice and snow off. Jeeps ran up and down the runway to provide tracks to follow.

Halm ran his four engines up to full power before releasing the brakes. "That was scary," he said, "but we were young and had a job to do. We took off, but were

only three feet off the ground a hundred and fifty yards off the end of the runway."

A second bomber got off. The third lifted off, but stalled, did a half roll and blew up. The risk of taking off over the wreckage was too great. Other bombs strewn about and hidden in snow might go off. Halm concluded dismally, "The mission was cancelled for weather—and no credit as a mission for it."

Living on borrowed time

The weather gave fliers time to consider the bleak odds of survival—a one-in-three chance for bomber crews initially deployed to England. With these odds, it was generally understood that the initial quota for a combat tour was twenty-five missions, "because you didn't have much chance of living after eight missions," asserted William Blackmon, Jr., 381st Bomb Group waist gunner, "so there wasn't any point in asking you to stay around more than twenty-five."

"Veteran flyers were a rarity," commented Ken Stone, original 381st Bomb Group crewman. "We all felt we were living on 'borrowed time.'"

G. W. Pederson was one of the original "clay pigeons" of the 306th Bombardment Group—the name derived from an April 24, 1943 *Saturday Evening Post* article titled "The Clay Pigeon

"I thought I'd either finish my missions or get killed. Becoming a prisoner of war was never on my mind. I felt that way because I saw so many go down and I saw so few get out. And if they did bail out, we didn't see what happened to them on the ground. We figured that angry civilians killed them."
—William Blackmon, Jr., 381st Bomb Group (H)

Bomber crewmen who completed a tour became part of the elite "Lucky Bastard Club." Each bomb group had its own certificate design. The example shown is from the 94th Bomb Group. 94th BGMA

Squadron," which described the 367th Squadron, 306th Bomb Group, as being shot down like clay pigeons during the bracing days between October 1942 and August 1943. During that time, their loss rate was highest in the Eighth Air Force. The first man of the 367th Squadron to become a prisoner of war, Albert W. LaChasse, still refers to himself as "first pigeon."

"On a mission to Antwerp on April 5, 1943, three crews from our 367th Squadron were lost," Pederson said. "Until that time, I thought I had a chance of surviving my twenty-five missions and going home, but after that I was sure I was going to be killed on my next mission."

Saul Kupferman arrived at Thurleigh, home to the 306th Bomb Group, on Oct. 15, 1943, the day after the second costly mission to the ball-bearing factories at Schweinfurt. "Only three planes returned, which accounted for all the empty bunks in my barracks," said Kupferman.

"Walking into the empty bay after the second Schweinfurt raid, I felt desolate," said pilot Lester Rentmeester of the 91st Bomb Group. "Based on statistics, I was positive I would not complete my tour."

But still, to many, death was something that "happened only to the other guy." Andrew Low, command pilot in the 453rd Bomb Group, was "unwilling to accept it could happen to me. Others yes, but not me."

"At briefings early in the war, they gave an idea of expected losses—often two or five percent," said John Wood, 381st Bomb Group gunner. "If they had said, 'We expect only two people to come back from this raid,' I would have wondered, *Who will the other guy be?*"

"We had the feeling that we were immortal," said C. L. Anderson of the 390th Bomb Group.

Lloyd Nelson of the 453rd Bomb Group spoke for many when he said, "You always figured it'd be the other guy who'd go down—not you."

Nelson's pilot, Robert Bieck, affirmed, "No one, absolutely no one in my crew ever expressed doubt that we might not make it back." The Bieck crew completed a tour of missions in B–24s with no deaths or injuries. Some fliers saw a correlation between their firm belief that they

A ball turret gunner climbs into his turret. John Campbell

Little Mac
"George McLaughlin was one of four ball-turret gunners in the 535th Squadron small enough to wear his parachute in the turret," said Tom O'Brien of the 381st Bomb Group. "'Little Mac,' as we called him, used to stay up all night reading the Bible. One night he said calmly to me, 'Obie, I have to tell you something. I'll never go home again.'

"I laughed and reassured him. He had only a few missions to go. But he made me promise to do things for him after he was gone. He had many items already packaged in pre-addressed envelopes to send to the States. I watched his plane go down on the very next mission. I thought if anyone would get out of that aircraft, it'd be him—all he had to do was unlatch the turret's hatch and roll out into the slipstream. But Little Mac didn't make it.

"For years after that, I had dreams where I saw just his face and he'd speak to me softly: 'Obie, I have to tell you something.' I'd wake up in a cold sweat shouting, 'For God's sake, tell me!'"

would survive and the fact that they *did* survive in the face of menacing odds.

Mark Magnon, once a nineteen-year-old captain and 398th Bomb Group pilot, commented: ". . . the word was out that only about one out of three would complete a combat tour—meaning that two of three would either lose their lives . . . or wind up as POWs. Despite this, I was always confident that my crew would complete the tour. This confidence permeated my crew. . . ."

Reciprocally, doubt of survival sometimes coincided with death. Magnon continued: "A friend . . . felt from the very beginning, even in primary flight school, that ultimate combat would be his undoing. And, unfortunately he was right . . . a direct hit on his second mission killed the entire crew."

"I always had the feeling that it wouldn't happen to me," said Ken Stone. "After all, I was flying with two Lords . . . my pilot, Marvin D. Lord and the real Lord."

Talismans and rituals

Although few admit to being superstitious, fliers practiced a litany of superstitious *dos* and *don'ts*. Many clung to what they believed would bring them through. These sometimes took the form of a certain sequence in dressing or a ritualistic schedule, or a talisman—an object that seemed to bring luck.

Harry Crosby's first experience with a B–17 crash happened before he left the States to begin his thirty-seven death-defying missions as an original member of the Bloody Hundredth Bomb Group. The B–17's pilot, John Brady, brought his ship down on a dry riverbed in Idaho, destroying the aircraft but injuring no one. A woman on the scene gave Crosby a talisman: "She gave me a sprig of Scotch heather and said, 'Carry this with you.' To this day I carry it in my billfold. And I must say I have been lucky. Out of the eleven on board, I was the only one who completed a tour. The rest were killed or became POWs."

On nights before missions, it was not unusual for fliers to lay out flying clothes carefully in precise order over chair backs. And when not scheduled to fly, the same men dropped clothes in disarray. One pilot wore the same sweatshirt on all of his missions. One crew always paused outside their B–24 to stand in a circle with their hands stacked in the center and bowed their heads in a moment of silence.

Many people were driven by talismans and rituals," explained Lester Rentmeester. "They tried to do the same things that they did before successful missions. Many people carried rabbits' feet or wore the same scarf." And there were unconscious rituals: "Our pilot always said over the interphone, 'Tallyho, boys,'" Lloyd Nelson recalled. "And we were on our way."

Takeoff

On bomber and fighter stations across East Anglia, crews sat anxiously in vibrating war machines. Everyone watched for takeoff flares that would send them on their way into the dingy sky.

"We taxied out of the hardstand and got into line on the perimeter track that went around the runway," said C. L. Anderson. "Then we'd run up the engines to make sure everything was working properly. For long missions, we'd shut down the engines and tanker trucks would come to top off the tanks to replace fuel used in taxiing and running up."

"Takeoffs were always a little unnerving," said Ray Patulski, 490th Bomb Group navigator. "Since I had an airspeed indicator and a first-class view of the runway through the nose, I relayed airspeed and distance to the end of the runway."

"On one particular takeoff, when we finally did lift off," Joe Curley recalled, "the pilot said, 'Whew! The pitot tube was frozen and I didn't know how fast I was going.'"

G. W. Pederson, initially positioned as a gunner in the nose of a B–17E, where plexiglass made his seat the "best view in the house," watched "the end of the runway coming up and it seemed always that we became airborne at the very last possible moment."

As the aircraft thundered to an ear-splitting crescendo halfway down Rattlesden runway, Bernarr Cresap of the 447th Bomb Group thought to himself, *Lord, you know we've got to get off this runway pretty quick now. I don't expect you to repeal the law of gravity just for us, but if you could just fudge it a little bit, I sure would appreciate it.* Just at that instant the runway was gone and there was a sudden smoothness.

"Every takeoff was a maximum performance takeoff, because the planes were loaded to the limit," commented Lester Rentmeester. "If it was a shorter mission, there was less gas, but there would be more bombs. . . ."

Forming up

Another risk involved the close proximity of fields and the fact that groups were taking off and forming up simultaneously, all over East Anglia. Departures were carefully orchestrated to lessen the chance of collision. However, in the typical dense cloud cover of early morning England, collision was a constant danger when there was no notion about where other planes might be.

Hundredth Bomb Group lead navigator Harry Crosby explained the intricacies of forming up:

"Standard meteorology for England was clear evenings and cloudy mornings. We'd often go into clouds at 200 feet. We tuned in the frequency of our 'splasher six' or buncher beacon (a low-power radio compass beacon) on our radio compass and set a course for it. The beacons were set up in such a way to not overlap each other, even though bases were close together.

"We'd fly a corkscrew up—climbing like a spiral staircase over the beacon. Finally, we'd pop out into the clear,

sometimes at 12,000 feet, sometimes at 20,000.

"Behind us, other planes popped out of the clouds and got on our wing to form the squadron. Then the two other squadrons of our group came through. One went higher than us and the other went lower, to form the group.

"In our case, we then had to rendezvous with the 95th and 390th Bomb Groups, who were to be over a given point at a given time. Then these three groups flew on to form up an air division, often with absolutely no view of the ground.

"None of the missions were milk runs. Just forming up was frequently catastrophic. Planes collided trying to rendezvous—and down they'd go.

"Not only did we rendezvous the bombers together, we rendezvoused with the fighters. We were to be at a checkpoint at a certain time. Early on, we had British Spitfire escorts that could fly with us only eight or nine minutes (because of limited range). So if we came eight or nine minutes late, we'd have no fighter support."

There were visions of giant, ghostly silhouettes slipping just past them in the soup, as they went higher and higher to

A 10/10 cloud cover under formation of B-24s. 8th Photo Tech Squadron via Bob Brismaster

break through the clouds. Assembly was always done above cloud tops—at whatever altitude that might be. Ray Patulski said: "Because of the effect of the North Sea's cold water, there would be a lot of cumulus clouds—puffy, fair-weather clouds—so you'd have to circle around them. On days of heavy stratus clouds, you wouldn't break out for several thousand feet.... With a lot of airplanes taking off in a limited area, there were occasions when you were groping your way through the clouds and you'd see another airplane just missing you...."

Observing from a B-24 turret, Lloyd Nelson saw "ships everywhere at different altitudes, going in every direction, searching for their groups to tie in with. We searched the sky for 'colors of the day'—flares being shot out of a group's assembly ship."

"We joined the formation flying in a race course pattern," Robert Bieck added. "Each group had a rally ship painted in a distinctive, if not bizarre fashion. Once the three groups in our wing were assembled, then we vectored toward the rest of the division—no easy thing. One of our greatest fears was that one formation would be dragged through one another. It happened on occasion and the result was exploding, spiraling wreckage, parachutes and many deaths."

A typical formation consisted of three twenty-one-plane bombardment groups joined together to make a combat wing. Four wings joined together to make an air division, which flew in procession to the target. There were three air divisions in the Eighth Air Force.

The B-24 Briney Marlin *looking for other members of the Second Air Division to form up.* 8th Photo Tech Squadron via Bob Brismaster

High-altitude combat

Flying at high altitude, vast contrails (the condensation of exhaust) would form. Anything but beautiful to bomber crews, contrails were terrifying, because they formed gigantic pointers, betraying the formations that had nowhere to hide. Flak batteries could sight in on them and prepare well in advance to send up barrages. German fighters sometimes hid themselves in the bombers' contrails, and then attacked from the rear unannounced.

Turbulence made it difficult to maintain position within the tight confines in the combat box designed to protect them. Danger of collision was constant. At 25,000 feet, the physical adversities tor-

"Our pilot told the top turret gunner to watch a B-17 out of position, sliding back and forth overhead because of the turbulence caused by the thousand-plane air stream. The top turret gunner screamed, 'Look out!' and the pilot thrust the stick forward. I was at the right waist gun position and flew up and hit the ceiling, then the floor. Pinned by gravity, I could move only my eyeballs...." —Glen Lunde, 95th Bomb Group (H)

The combat box

Because strategic bombing was new, leaders made up the rules as they went along. One new tactic (devised by 305th Bomb Group commander Curtis LeMay) was called the "combat box," intended to frustrate enemy fighter attacks. Designed especially to help protect vulnerable bomber formations on deep-penetration, unescorted raids, the combat box organized bombers into a wedge-shaped labyrinth to get maximum defensive firepower from their many guns.

A combat box stacked and staggered the aircraft of a bomb group's three squadrons, each squadron consisting of six or seven aircraft. A bomb group actually consisted of four squadrons, but typically the four squadrons rotated position in the combat box: high squadron, low squadron, lead squadron, and the fourth was allowed to "stand down" for the mission. At the point of the lead squadron was a bomber manned by a highly qualified crew called the lead crew.

Tight combat box formations not only helped in defense against fighter attack, it concentrated bombs in tighter patterns on a target. But the tactic also greatly increased the chances of collision, as turbulence buffeted the airplanes.

mented the body like fear tormented the mind.

Clyde Coenen, 487th Bomb Group bombardier, kept watch on a thermometer in his aircraft's nose: "Since you determine trail for the bombsight according to air pressure, temperature and other factors, I had a thermometer right there. The coldest I saw was 78 degrees below zero."

"We wore our oxygen masks from ten thousand feet on up," Lloyd Nelson said. "Condensation inside the mask caused problems." The moisture from breathing would condense and freeze, plugging free passage of oxygen. At intervals it was necessary to squeeze the oxygen mask tube to prevent anoxia.

Another problem of condensation was its effect on visibility. Phil Garey of the 94th Bomb Group commented: "The plexiglass was so close to the head of the tail gunner that condensation sometimes built up there and froze, effectively blinding lateral vision. A rag did a poor job of wiping it off. I tried a razor blade once and ruined the plexiglass."

There was no good alternative to the umbilical cord of oxygen. Garey recalls once having to leave his tail gun position to move a starboard fifty-caliber machine gun to the port side. "The gun had mal-

functioned and that's where they need the firepower most. I put on a 'walk around' oxygen bottle that was supposed to last five minutes. I lifted the bad gun and set it down. Then I lifted the other and moved it into position. The next thing I knew, 'Pappy' [a thirty-one-year-old waist gunner] was holding pure oxygen to my face and shaking me. With the extra exertion at high altitude, the bottle lasted about a minute and I had lost consciousness. Fortunately, there were no after-effects and I was back in my position minutes later."

Perhaps the worst of the natural adversities was frostbite. "It was somewhat endemic," Robert Bieck commented. "Waist gunners had the biggest problem, because of their exposed positions in the rear fuselage. But the electric suits helped them immeasureably."

Heated flying suits, especially early versions, still left something to be desired, however. "If any part shorted out, then everything shorted out," lamented waist gunner William Blackmon. "I remember on one occasion I called my pilot over the intercom and told him, 'I can't stand it any longer. My heated boots are out and my feet are killing me. How about dropping down a little bit so I can warm up?' Of course, he couldn't risk everybody's life on account of me. So I ran all the way

Contrails, beautiful designs in the sky, were the horrifying, stark fingers that pointed to *approaching formations.* 8th Photo Tech Squadron via Bob Brismaster

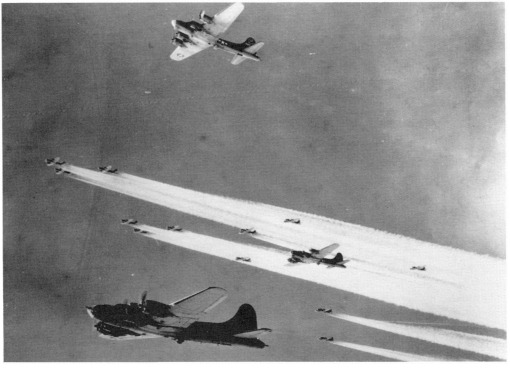

from the Ruhr Valley back to England."

"The whole aircraft was cold, damned cold," Bieck continued. "And that included the cockpit, which was supposed to be the best seat in the house. It was always somewhat of an anomaly to me to find my feet and hands so cold and at the same time my back would be perspiring. I became disenchanted with wearing an electrically heated suit after I burned my right leg from a short circuit in the suit's wiring. I continued to wear the heavy leather sheepskin flight clothing—nothing in that outfit is going to fail."

The natural tendency in the "heat" of battle, when guns jammed, was to pull off heavy flight gloves, which resulted in frost-bitten hands. A solution to this problem was for gunners to wear skin-tight gloves beneath the heavier gloves to allow the gunner some dexterity that bulky gloves would not allow.

"Most of us wore two or three layers of clothing and we moved our fingers and toes as much as possible to help prevent frostbite," said Wilton Fremaux of the 379th Bomb Group. "Even today my fingers hurt when placed in cold water."

Fighter escort

The Eighth on occasion turned back because of weather, but never because of enemy resistance. Bombers continued on course when the shorter-range fighters were forced to turn back because of lack of fuel.

P–47 Thunderbolts fought well against Luftwaffe fighters, but could not escort bombers all the way to deep-penetration targets. P–38 Lightnings had longer range, but were insufficient in number for large-scale operations from England and were plagued by mechanical difficulties in Europe's cold and damp climate. It wasn't until July 1943 that P–47s, equipped with auxiliary fuel tanks, accompanied bombers across the German border. "The P–47 was a big, heavy airplane—a durable airplane," said Charles Cummins, 361st Fighter Group pilot. "But the problem was the gas it used. Even with belly tanks, you couldn't go too far." And the long-range fighter, the P–51 Mustang, didn't begin substantial escort until February 1944.

"I was always grateful to see our fighter escorts," Ken Stone said. "They were my heroes. Unfortunately, when they left us at the German border, we entered Germany protected only by our own guns." Low on gas, the fighters reluctantly banked away from their "big friends" and swooped westward. The bombers beat on alone to face the fury of German fighters defending their homeland.

The Royal Air Force also shared in protection of American bombers on daylight raids. G. W. Pederson recalled the heroism of RAF pilots in April 1943: "We were just about over the coast on the way back out from Belgium and were under heavy [usually frontal] attack by enemy fighters. A lone RAF Spitfire positioned itself two or three hundred yards ahead of our formation in an effort to break up the head on attacks. He lasted at most a minute and a half. A German fighter shot him down—didn't come out of the dive at all before going into the Channel. Despite nearly fifty years, that bravery is as vivid in my mind as if it happened today."

Bandits

Low on fuel, fighter escorts scarcely veered away when the battle-hardened Luftwaffe, the German Air Force, appeared as ominous specks ahead. "They were outstanding professionals who pressed their attacks," noted Andrew Low, 453rd Bomb Group operations officer.

"German fighter pilots were almost fearless in attacks from all angles and levels," said Wilton Fremaux. "Only tight formations gave us the concentrated firepower necessary to protect ourselves."

But even tight formations were far from invulnerable. Enemy fighters looked for chinks in the armor—gaps in the bomber gunners' fields of fire. Massive head-on assaults became a favorite and most effective Luftwaffe tactic. "I think fighter attacks inspired the most concern among crews," said Robert Bieck. "They seemed to fly so fast if the attack was head on. And they created so much damage in such a short time. . . ."

Ball turret gunner Ralph Price of the 381st Bomb Group experienced the greatest fear of his life when he first witnessed "planes exploding into balls of fire, knowing that ten men burned to death and knowing that it could happen to us." Five miles above the earth, there was no place to hide.

Gilbert Falck recounted heavy fighter attack for twenty minutes prior to a raid on Magdeburg, Germany: "I can still see the guns blinking on the leading edge

"On one mission we went around Berlin deliberately to draw up fighters. It was a beautiful day. The city was in full view below and the sky contained a mass of airplanes from both sides. I had the right nose gun in hand and was watching an Fw 190 barrel-roll in on us. I was so fascinated watching him and how beautifully he flew that I did not pull the trigger."
—Hiram Drache, 457th Bomb Group (H)

"At 29,000 feet, I looked to my left. Only 40 or 50 yards away was a Ju 88, just emerging from the clouds, sent to get our altitude to radio to their gunners on the ground. I called, 'Bank her left chief,' because I couldn't position my guns in the top turret to fire at it. I gave it a long burst and it went back down although I'm not sure if I hit him. But he was surprised as hell to find himself in the middle of our formation."
—Harold Loch, 91st Bomb Group (H), *Memphis Belle* gunner

"Over Wilhemshaven, William Wyler (film-maker of the *Memphis Belle* documentary) wanted to fly in my position in the top turret with a motion picture camera. So I took the right waist gun. A Messerschmitt came down in an 80 degree dive and I couldn't raise the barrel high enough to get it in my sites. He narrowly missed colliding with us. A minute later, another Messerschmitt was coming at us, firing all the way and tracers streaked past on both sides of me. The fighter pilot came close enough that I could see his face. Wyler was not paying attention to the near misses that nearly got us. He wasn't shooting the guns, but interested in getting the best film footage. He flew three raids with us in the *Memphis Belle* and two in two other airplanes in our squadron."
—Harold Loch, 91st Bomb Group (H), *Memphis Belle* gunner

Seated bombardier charging the twin fifties of B-17G nose turret. 94th BGMA

of the attacking fighter's wings. It was an awesome feeling, knowing they were trying to shoot us down. Clyde [Mason] and I wrestled the plane into crazy evasive positions, which must have put a strain on the [rest of the] crew. . . . [and a strain on the aircraft]. We noticed that all engine gauges were operating in the red.

"The noise was deafening. The top turret twin fifties were blazing away, as were the nose guns. Fighter after fighter kept coming through our formation. It was a veritable hell."

"The twenty-millimeter fire from FW–190s and Me–109s looked like flash-bulbs popping all around," said William Blackmon, who had two confirmed kills as a waist gunner. "At a time like that, it's either him or me."

Firing cannons and machine guns and launching air-to-air rockets, enemy fighters slashed through the formations almost at will. Ken Stone recalled his closest brush with death: "The [enemy fighter] shells were timed to explode a certain number of seconds after leaving the gun barrels. I'll never forget seeing five shells explode, one after another, directly in line with my turret. If we had been going faster, I wouldn't be [alive today].

Ball turret gunner Robert Strehlow of the 452nd Bomb Group said: "We saw what looked like a thin layer of clouds at

eleven o'clock ahead, level with us. It was a mass of fighters. They came right through the formation. My left gun was hit by something and it jammed the whole works inside the receiver. The turret was rotating jerkily after that. I looked back and as far as I could see were parachutes and burning wreckage of airplanes."

On John Wood's fifth raid, in a 381st Bomb Group B-17 named *Tinker Toy*, pilot William Minerich was beheaded by enemy fighter fire. Wood recalled: "Enemy fighters attacked head on. A twenty-millimeter shell came right through his window and hit [Minerich]. I came forward when the copilot called for help on the intercom. It was unbelievable—I got up there and had to take a second look. The pilot was just sitting there with his hands in his lap. And it wasn't like his head was cut off. I didn't see it laying on the floor—it just wasn't there. The copilot was hurt, but maintaining control. I wiped the blood off the instruments so that the copilot could see."

A notation in a flight surgeon's diary read: "There was hardly a square inch of the entire cockpit that was not covered with blood and brain tissue."

Interrogation reports about the Oct. 8, 1943 incident recorded: "His engineer was unable to stand on his turret platform because of the slick layer of blood cover-

Tinker Toy, *the "jinx ship" of the 381st Bomb Group. Crewmen examine the hole of a 20 millimeter shell that pierced the ship. The* shell exploded in the pilot's face, killing him instantly. *USAF via Karen Laws*

ing it. Lt. Sellers (copilot) flew the ship home, holding perfect formation and successfully performing evasive action. Sgt. Miller, the engineer, handled throttles at landing."

"One was petrified with fear," Lloyd Nelson said. Even with the sub-zero temperature, "the water ran down my face. They were in a large mass at ten o'clock level—looked like a swarm of bees. They came at us, a dozen at a time. I was terribly frightened, but continued firing. German pilots were very good—and I don't think they wanted to go down any more than we did."

Ralph Price added: "There were times when attacking fighters passed so close I was sure I could recognize the pilot if I saw him again. The German pilots were good and apparently fearless, especially when they were defending Germany itself."

"I came face-to-face with a German pilot," Ed Pickering said. "I had about seven seconds of firing time. I cannot describe the fear." Pickering shot down the enemy and others from his group observed it—a confirmed kill.

Don Morse experienced both elation and remorse in his first confirmed kill. He said: "I was doing what I was trained to do—tracking the target in my gunsights and firing. My reactions were routine, like a robot. All of a sudden, the fighter that had been bearing down on us blew up into a fireball. I thought, 'Wow, I got him!' Some of the wreckage hit our ship. My natural inclination was to turn around and take a look—that's when the remorse came. I didn't see a chute. I suddenly felt different about the whole thing."

Gilbert Falck commented: "During head-on fighter attacks we would scrunch down in our seats with our helmets low on our heads, while we tried to hide behind our flak suits—all this while flying formation, doing evasive action and directing gunfire on attacking fighters. When the fighters attacked, we wished for flak. When the flak got heavy, we wished for fighters."

Flak

There was little relief in seeing enemy fighter formations veer away and head home. "As soon as the enemy fighters left us, then came the flak. . . ." said Gilbert Falck.

Massed around major industrial centers, German flak batteries filled the sky with wing-tearing, fuselage-ripping piec-

"On our third mission over Cologne, flak ripped a hole in the tail section big enough to fall through. It tore the parachute off my back and dented my flak suit between the shoulder blades, injuring a disk in my spine. I was scared to death—when I reached around and touched my back, the torn parachute silk felt just as if my insides had been torn out."
—Ed Pickering, 401st Bomb Group (H)

"There was no sound except for the engines and air rushing through cracks. The intercom was quiet except for the necessary checks and orders. If we fired our guns, that was intrusive. But flak was silent unless very close. Then unless it actually hit the aircraft, there was just a dull 'whoosh!' I'd watch flak tracking us or see a barrage of it, and it was as though I was detached from everything."
—Phil Garey, 94th Bomb Group (H)

Severed by flak, a B-24 tail free-falls. 8th Photo Tech Squadron via Bob Brismaster

es of jagged metal. Fond of long words made of two or more words grafted together, Germans coined *fliegerabwehrkanone* from words that meant aircraft defense gun. Four letters were drawn from the word to make a shorter form: F-L-A-K—short and sharp, like the burst itself. In the parlance of American fliers, "the word flak by itself would be used to refer to the shells, the black smoke residue following the explosion of shells, or a steel fragment of a shell," explained Bernarr Cresap.

Resembling ink splatters against the blue blotter of the sky, flak was a mesmerizing agent of death. "Flak . . . seemed like a harmless puff of smoke until you saw holes opening up in your wings or oil streaming from an engine," said Ralph Price. "When airplanes fell from the formation in flames you knew it was more than just smoke."

"My greatest fear in combat was flak," C. L. Anderson said. "With fighters, you had a chance to fight back. With flak, you were like a duck flying over a blind—you couldn't counteract. When you started on the bomb run, you didn't alter course or altitude, so they could zero in on you."

"I didn't envy the fellows assigned to bombers when they approached the tar-

get," commented fighter pilot Dean Morehouse. "In fighters, if the first few blasts of flak didn't hit you, you could vector out of it—glide to the side or change altitude. The bombers had to fly right through it."

Bomb run

The critical sweep over the target was called the bomb run. As puffs of black, slow-dissipating smoke filled the sky, bombers faced a pinnacle of peril. At the Initial Point (IP), the bombardier took over control of the bomber. Straight and level flight for twenty to fifty miles was necessary for accurate bomb delivery. Without accuracy, it was all an absurd sacrifice.

"The longest moments of my life were when the bombardier took control of the plane after the IP and we were frozen in on a track going to the target while flak was exploding all around," said Hiram Drache.

Ken Stone explained: "The anti-aircraft gunners would send up a box barrage of exploding 88 millimeter shells directly over the target, and we had to fly straight through the flak barrage. We couldn't take any evasive action until we

Piston from a B-17 exploded by flak. Clyde Coenen said: "It's a hard piece of evidence of what happened up there."

Saved by a flak suit

Lead bombardier Clyde Coenen was stunned when an object suddenly shattered through the plexiglass nose before him as he prepared to sight in on a target of industrial complexes below. The object whistled past his ear. "It was a piston from a nearby B-17 that had exploded from a flak hit," he said. "It went over my shoulder. Immediately after that, a piece of flak struck me in the chest. The worst part was that I reeled back off the stool and landed on the piston—square in the middle of my back. 'I'm hit! I'm hit!' I yelled. I was mortally wounded for all I knew."

But when the flight engineer came forward a few moments later, he found Coenen back on the stool. "My arm was black and blue, but the flak suit absorbed most of the impact. Normally, we'd take off the heavy suit after danger of flak had passed. But that day, I wore it all the way back across the English Channel."

had dropped our bombs. As long as you could see the flak bursting, it was OK. If you heard exploding and ripping through the metal of your plane, you were in trouble."

After bombs away, the next logical step was to ensure that all bombs had fallen from the racks before closing the bomb bay doors. "Following procedure, our pilot called the radio operator to check if the bomb bay was clear," said Glen Lunde, 95th Bomb Group waist gunner. "It was not clear. The radio operator called back that a whole rack of bombs were hung up and propellers were spinning—meaning they were *armed to explode.*" Working over the bomb bay at 25,000 feet, the crew tried to dislodge the bombs using the crank intended for manually lowering malfunctioning landing gear. Finally, after several frantic attempts, the bombs fell.

"After bombs away," Gilbert Falck said: "the formation usually nosed down about two thousand feet to pick up speed to clear the area. The return flights usually brought more enemy fighters, as our route back was different from our route to target. Gas gauges were checked, the fuel/air mixture was made leaner and we began wondering what the weather would

be like at the home base—and if we'd have enough fuel."

Return to base

The flight home was a mirror image of the flight to target. All the same hazards, just in reverse order. Some fliers resorted to instinct—just a gut feeling about what to do. On a mission to Leipzig, Germany, ball turret gunner Robert Strehlow's crew found their oxygen supply depleted before reaching the target. They were forced to drop out of formation and below 10,000 feet to make the long trip home alone. Strehlow recalled, "The navigator suddenly said to make a 45 degree turn right. The pilot said, 'Roger.' Then all hell broke loose. Flak bursts were all around on the left—and they would have had us if we'd stayed on course. It was pure luck they didn't hit us. After that incident, we zig-zagged all the way across enemy territory." Strehlow asked the navigator later if he had seen muzzle flashes on the ground, prompting a call for a turn. The navigator replied, "No, it just felt like it was time to turn."

Clyde Mason's crew was just crossing the coast of France when copilot Gilbert Falck saw a gun flash on the ground.

On the bomb tags (as labeled in calligraphy):

1 Chemnitz – (MARSHALLING YARDS) FEBRUARY 6, 1945
4 Frankfort – (JET COMPONENT PLANT) FEBRUARY 17, 1945
6 Nurnburg – "MARSHALLING YARDS" FEBRUARY 20, 1945
7 Bremen – (BRIDGE) FEBRUARY 24, 1945
8 Munich – (TEXTILE ROAD) FEBRUARY 25, 1945
10 Leipzig – (MARSHALLING YARDS) FEBRUARY 27, 1945

11 Ulm – (MARSHALLING YARDS) MARCH 4, 1945
12 Essen – (BENZOL PLANT) MARCH 8, 1945
14 Swinemunde – (OIL STORAGE PLANT) MARCH 12, 1945
16 Hamburg – (SUBMARINE PENS) MARCH 20, 1945
17 Ramsdorf – (MUNSTER AREA) (JET AIR FIELD & OIL REFINING) MARCH 21, 1945
18 Alchorn – (Holland) (JET FIGHTER FIELD) MARCH 22, 1945

20 Steenwijk Meppel (Holland) (JET AIRFIELD) MARCH 24, 1945
201 Ziegenhain Meppel – (Holland) MARCH 24, 1945 (JET AIRFIELD)
22 Kiel – (SUBMARINE DOCKS &) APRIL 3, 1945
24 Nuremberg – (MARSHALLING YARDS) APRIL 4, 1945
26 Munich – (AREA – MANNHEIM) APRIL 9, 1945
27 Landshut – (MARSHALLING YARDS – MUNICH AREA) APRIL 11, 1945

Some fliers saved a bomb tag from each of their missions. Glen Lunde's calligraphy on these denote the target and number of missions he completed as a gunner with the 95th Bomb Group.

"One, two, three," he began to count. "... fourteen, fifteen." At that blinding instant, flak scored a direct hit. The cockpit filled with fire and smoke. Rather than leave the protection of the formation, they elected to limp along with it as best they could. Only the copilot's controls were operating. "Upon returning to base [at Bassingbourn], I made a good landing but soon found I had no brakes," said Falck. "I rolled nearly to the end of the runway, then put the plane in a gentle ground loop to the right. I came to rest on the grass." Only then did they realize that they had taken a direct hit where the left wing and fuselage join. "It was major damage. Our lead plane told us that they thought the wing would come off in

On March 6th, I went on my first mission. It was one HELL of a rough sortie for my first. Our target was a Ball-bearing factory 16½ miles East of Berlin – our secondary target was the center of B. The primary target was visible – BUT for some reason we hit the center of Berlin. Our primary target had 16 flak guns our secondary had 450. I hope & pray I never see such flak barrages again. Fighter opposition was intense – our escort was good. Coming to the target we had flak at the Dutch Coast & in spots along the route. As we dropped our bombs we had terrific flak – the ship directly ahead of us blew up – we had hits in our tail assembly & one between the tail & waist. Fighters attacked the formations all the way back. Only one ME109 came into our range. It was 45° below zero. We had a mid-air collision with the plane next to us – smashed our right wing & aileron – however we were not in too tough shape & made it back over our last flak barrage on the coast. One crew to the rear hit the silk. We had open waists & a fast ship – No. 649

Mar. 6, 1944, entry from Jack Kirschbraun's diary.

Badger Beauty, *100th Bomb Group B-17, was shot down and salvaged by the Luftwaffe. Among other Luftwaffe uses, it flew inconspicuously alongside Eighth Air Force forma-* tions *and pummeled its unwary, former kin with 20 millimeter shells.* 100th BG via Harry Crosby

flight. We were glad we didn't know that until we were back safely on the ground."

"At least twice we came back by ourselves," Phil Garey said. There generally was reluctance ". . . to let a strange plane into a formation. Group leaders were wary of captured bombers spying or attacking."

"We were on a 'milk run,'" Don Morse said, "an 'easy' mission, not too deep, to the marshalling yards on the outskirts of Paris. After we hit the target, we turned around to head back. I had my guns pointing to the rear and suddenly, a flak burst in front of us sent shrapnel rocketing through the plexiglass back of my turret. It parted my skull open and knocked me clean out of the turret and tore off my oxygen mask. The copilot came down out of the cockpit to help, disconnecting his own oxygen without giving it a second thought and putting his mask on me." Blood seeped in a constant stream from the deep head wound, soaking his flight suit. Administering a compress from the first-aid kit, the copilot started to pass out. Morse grabbed an emergency oxygen bottle hanging on the wall and put it on him. They found themselves helping each other.

Despite being seriously wounded by flak, Morse experienced what he described as the happiest moment of his life: "After we were hit by flak, we lost

altitude—and the protection of the squadron. We fired flares out so that fighters in the area would come down and protect us. Immediately, two P-47s appeared—one on each side. They had to put their flaps down full to match our speed. They took us over the Channel and once in sight of the coast, they left us."

Ken Stone added: "It was a great relief to see our 'little friends' meet us on our return over France, Holland, or Belgium. But the only time I relaxed was when we were back over England. The White Cliffs of Dover were the most beautiful sight to behold."

Just as weather often caused difficulties with departure, landings (already precarious from battle damage) were sometimes disrupted. "When fog reduced forward visibility to zero," explained Lester Rentmeester, "barrels of gasoline were sometimes set on fire to dispel the fog. They were partially successful. My favorite aid was a slow-moving aircraft flying directly over the runway, since you could see things directly below you but very little horizontally."

"Ground cover [clouds] usually meant breaking formation," Gilbert Falck said. "The group would break up into squadrons, then flights, then singles. We'd break through the cloud layer and be lined up with our runway with planes in single file. It was an exciting time."

Chapter 4

Little friends

There was an occasional flash and a ring of smoke where a bomber had been. Then the massed Me-109s dived down in another head-on attack. I rolled into a dive and led the group down to cut them off. One [appeared] in my sights, still out of range, but closing fast. . . . As I pressed the [trigger] button . . . [I saw] yellow flashes along the grey and black fuselage, then . . . a wing and debris floating past.

—James Goodson, 4th Fighter Group

Framed against the grayness of early morning England, dark forms of men walked alone to sleek silhouettes of aircraft. Wisps of fog curled around wings, as they climbed aboard.

Sliding into a cockpit no bigger than half a phone booth, a fighter pilot entered his solitary world of exhilaration and deadly one-on-one aerial confrontations. Before he clapped his canopy shut making his isolation complete, his crew chief offered a few final words of wisdom and only half-kiddingly sought reassurance that the bird would be returned in its present condition.

The engines, already warm thanks to the ground crews' preflight, caught easily and settled quickly into a smooth, powerful resonance. Already this morning, the pummeling sound of bombers had shattered the silence of rural England. Their thunder persisted invisibly as, high above the shroud of gray gloom, bomber crews endured the fatiguing tedium of forming up. Like the bombers, fighters flew from airfields in East Anglia. (To help compensate for fighters' shorter range early in the war, most fighter sta-

tions were located closer to England's eastern shore.)

Pilots in the first flight released their toe-pedal brakes and crept smoothly from their dispersal points. As they lined up abreast on the runway, other flights followed on the perimeter track.

Without delay, flight after flight, squadron after squadron hurtled down the runway and arced gracefully toward the gray scud that congealed into solid overcast at higher altitude.

Wheels were raised into their wells. Radios were checked at low altitude, so the enemy wouldn't pick up transmissions. Trim adjustments were made to compensate for the drag and weight of belly tanks.

"Forming up took hardly any time at all for fighters," said Karl Dittmer, who completed a tour as a 385th Bomb Group pilot and went on to fly twenty-one combat missions with the 352nd Fighter Group. "We often took off four abreast and joined up on course."

Based in East Anglia, fighter pilots faced the same weather notorious for delaying and complicating bomber oper-

"I never came close to hitting anyone in the soup—at least not that I know of."
—John Ziebell, 357th Fighter Group

"During the group's first combat missions, the P–38s flew without adequate heating systems. Instruments froze over. And ground crews practically had to pry the pilots' hands off the stick."
—Robert Sand, 55th Fighter Group

P-47 Thunderbolts of the 56th Fighter Group—Zemke's Wolfpack. John Campbell

Standing before Lady Gwen II, *a 353rd Fighter Group pilot describes his latest battle.* John Campbell

"We played around a lot more in fighter squadrons—buckets balanced on doors and practical jokes like that. In bomb squadrons, we were just too tired. If we flew three bombing mission in three days, we were exhausted. Flying a bomber in tight formation was hard work, even though we could take turns at the controls with our copilots. Formations in fighters was much easier. We didn't expend nearly as much effort concentrating on keeping position. Plus, most of my missions in fighters were less than five hours long. In bombers, I had one mission ten hours long and several that were nine—a lot of that time and energy spent in forming up before we even began across the Channel."
—Karl Dittmer, 385th Bomb Group (H) and 352nd Fighter Group

ations. "The weather was probably responsible for more fatalities than the enemy," said James Goodson, 4th Fighter Group pilot. "This was particularly true of new pilots, who did not have sufficient instrument-flying practice."

Squadrons broke out of the cloud tops into the glare of the sun. Without weather interference, the rendezvous course quickly merged the little friends with the big friends in bomber formations. Although they flew at the same high altitudes as bombers, fighter pilots experienced less environmental punishment in the close quarters of heated cockpits than bomber crewmen. However, frostbite was a problem in the earlier models of the P–38 Lightning.

"During the winter of 1943–44, there were some difficulties flying P–38s at the high altitudes the bombers flew," explained Jack Ilfrey, commander of the 79th Squadron, 20th Fighter Group. "Some of the pilots got frost-bitten hands and feet, because there was almost no heating system in those models of P–38. And at high altitude, the oil froze up and pistons blew out. Thank God that in a P–38, if one engine goes, you still have one to get home. With the introduction of the P–38L, a lot of those heating problems were rectified."

In P–47s and P–51s, "frostbite was not a problem, unless the canopy was damaged," commented Goodson. "In that case you could always hit the deck."

Knights in the sky

Air-to-air combat was a deadly test of skill that relied on pilot skills, gunnery, and stamina. Sometimes likened to medieval jousts, fighter combat cast pilots as the knights in armor, meeting the enemy in the arena of the sky. Riding their "mounts," they charged toward opponents trying to impale them—not with a lance but with a stream of lead. Like the bomber crews' impersonal battle, it was a detached method of mortal combat, accomplished by pressing a button on the stick. There was no ghastly moment when the lance pierced an opponent's chest. The result of accurate aim was a cloud of momentarily-lingering molecules that an instant before had comprised a plane and pilot.

Although the nature of combat was different, Eighth Air Force fighters shared with bombers the same hazardous skies of Nazi-held Europe, where every cubic

foot of sky harbored potential danger. "By the time I left England, almost all the pilots were new—about eighty percent of the group were replacements," said Dean Morehouse, original member of the 361st Fighter Group. "We didn't talk much about odds of survival. Those who came back were the lucky ones."

The fighter pilot's war was a far different experience than that of bomber crewmen. "There was a world of difference between crewing a bomber and a fighter, particularly in the attitude you took," said Karl Dittmer. "In a bomber, you were a flying target. You took a defensive stance—always wanting to avoid or ward off enemy attack. In a fighter, even though you were escorting and technically 'defending,' you actually had the attitude of being on the offensive—aggressively on the lookout and ready to go after the enemy."

Youth was an especially important qualification for flying fighters. Along with it came quicker reflexes in a vicious environment where fractions of an inch were the difference between hit and miss, and split-second decisions meant life or death.

"I once read a report about myself written by a commanding officer I respected very much," said Robert Powell. "He described me as an officer who doesn't always determine all the facts before making a decision, but who had an uncanny ability to make the *right* decision. I wondered, *Is he saying I'm not thorough—just lucky?* After I thought about it, I came to the conclusion that he was describing a fighter pilot. You don't always have time to get all the facts before you make a decision, but you make the right decision or you're a dead man."

While bombers avoided confrontations with enemy defenses in their journey to and from targets, fighters actively sought adversity. "They *looked* for trouble," commented B–24 pilot Robert Bieck. "They were every bit as aggressive as German fighter pilots."

By nature, fighter pilots were competitive—with the enemy and even among themselves. Pilots who destroyed five enemy planes became an ace. They aggressively sought to increase their score of victories.

"We all hoped we'd run into German fighters," said Robert Wright, 361st Fighter Group pilot. "I enjoyed air-to-air combat."

A first mission

From the log of Dayton Castor, Jr., a description of a first combat mission flying a P-47 with the 353rd Fighter Group:

"January 4, 1944. They show up very plain—those huge black crosses against the silver grey of the wings. All of a sudden you realize that the man sitting in the cockpit of that little silver job has cannon and machine guns which will blot out your life if he can maneuver into position. Your mouth becomes dry, the hair on the back of your neck stands stiff, and the sound of your breathing that echoes back through your radio system is short and raspy. You realize also that you have several tons of airplane mounted around several large guns which will cut his airplane to bits if you can but outwit him. . . .

"You aren't afraid—at least you don't think of running away, even though you have the necessary power and speed to do it if you desired. I remembered a theory of psychology which said that one's emotions result from bodily reaction. Perhaps if one allowed the situation to overcome him and he knew that he could not escape he might become afraid. Your flying is instinctive. Everything the Army has drilled into you during the years of practice and training comes into play. Your eyes are concentrated on that silver streak. Each action of that plane brings a reaction in your plane without conscious thought on your part. You can feel the increased rpm of your engine and then you realize that your left hand has automatically increased the prop pitch. Each time your head turns to look for the ring and dot in the gun sight. There is no feeling of speed even though somehow your eyes have registered that you are doing over 350 airspeed. You could never be certain enough to swear before a jury that your engine instruments were operating correctly, yet you know they are for each one says OK in your brain. Speed, distance, angle off, deflection are all computed by your brain and the stick comes back a little more to give him the proper lead. Your finger has been touching the trigger on the stick all the time. Yet your excitement has not caused an ounce of pressure which would fire the guns before you are ready.

"Long ago your mind realized you were fighting a Me-109 not an FW-190. All the things about turning radius, roll, speed, horsepower, climb and dive that you have read or heard come to the front. You can see that square cut cockpit, that very small rudder and slim fuselage, as he turns to the left. More stick, more rudder comes into play. Two ring lead ought to be enough. Throttle comes back— you're going to overrun him at this speed. He sees you plainly now. He turns tighter. More stick, more rudder! No time for a high speed stall now. Just a little more lead. NOW! Your plane shakes all over. The instruments vibrate. Tons of energy are being expended in each wing. Is that smoke from him? No, just more vapor trails as he turns tighter and has opened all the power he has. Trigger still down. It happens fast. Either you hit him or he couldn't stand looking into those flaming .50 caliber guns. From the tight left turn to tight right in the flick of an eye. The whole top of his plane is in front of you for a second, then he is gone. Roll with him. Again training comes in to get you out of the spin that your over-enthusiastic turn caused. You're way downstairs now after you recover from the spin. All by yourself. If you got him, OK. If not, well another day. Back on the stick. Trade in some of that 400 mph for altitude—and friends. Sure is lonesome down here."

"Fighter pilots had to have a little of the killer instinct in them. Like a boxer, you have to want to put the other guy away. You have to want to win."
—Robert Powell, Jr., 352nd Fighter Group

"We hoped for the opportunity to shoot down enemy planes," affirmed Robert Powell, Jr. "We wanted the chance to test our skill against the German pilots one-on-one."

But this aggressiveness could also be fatal. "I watched another Mustang dive down to intercept enemy fighters rising up through the clouds to attack a bomber formation," said John Ziebell, 357th Fighter Group pilot. "He began his descent from very high altitude and got going too fast. He tried to pull out of the dive, but compressibility did him in. I saw the wing fold, but didn't see the crash. He never came back."

As the European air war intensified, it became increasingly clear that the costs of unescorted daylight bombing raids were prohibitive. The fighters of the Eighth assumed a vital role in daylight strategic bombing: to protect the bombers found highly vulnerable to the Luftwaffe's single- and twin-engined fighters' slashing attacks. But in this escort role, Eighth fighters performed a service crucial to the bigger picture. They were clearing the skies for invasion of the European continent.

Schweinfurt: a convincing lesson

Raids on the ball-bearing factories at Schweinfurt, Germany, helped make painfully evident the flaws of early theories about bombers alone penetrating enemy airspace, striking targets and returning with acceptable losses. Schweinfurt, along with Regensburg, was attacked on Aug. 17, 1943 with a loss of thirty-six and twenty-four bombers respectively.

The Eighth Air Force returned to bomb the same objective in Schweinfurt on Oct. 14, 1943, a day that came to be known as Black Thursday. This time, sixty B–17s were shot down out of the 315 that reached the target. In cold statistics, this represented a nineteen-percent loss—far beyond the loss rate generally deemed acceptable. In flesh and blood, sixty bombers lost meant 600 young men.

Escorts flew as far as they could, and had to turn back at the Belgian-German border. As bomber crews watched the tails of their escorts become tiny specks behind them, specks in front of them grew rapidly into the angry form of bandits stacked for massive head-on assaults. The last sight the little friends had of the bombers were flaming masses plunging earthward. The Luftwaffe was waiting in silent proximity at Germany's threshold—just outside the escorts' range.

"When the thirty-six original crews [of the 381st Bomb Group] entered combat on June 22, 1943, we were a well-trained unit, our morale high," said Ken Stone of the 381st Bomb Group. "However, this changed after the first Schweinfurt mission on August 17, 1943. We had dispatched twenty-six planes and only fifteen returned. Our morale was at an all-time low. By October 9, 1943, a little over three months [later], the 381st lost twenty-six of the original crews, a seventy-two percent loss. Of the nine original crews in our squadron, only two crews completed twenty-five missions."

After these devastating losses, bombing operations were curtailed for some

time. Finally, in January 1944, a sleek new shape appeared in England's skies. The Mustangs had arrived—long-range escort was a reality.

The advent of long-range fighter escorts brought about a dramatic change in the complexion of the air war over Europe. Touting a bomber's range and fighter's performance, P–51s could escort bombers all the way to target. Along with this came modifications of tactics that encouraged strafing and deliberate confrontations with the enemy.

"The P–51D with drop tanks was a godsend," noted Lester Rentmeester. "They didn't prevent fighter attacks altogether, but reduced them by 50 percent immediately and more later on."

Bombing of aviation-related industry was not the only crippling blow dealt to German air power. Even more devastating was fierce air-to-air combat that irreparably diminished German front-line fighter strength. The enemy lost 692 precious fighters and along with them a share of their best pilots—225 dead or missing and 141 wounded.

Two 357th Fighter Group Mustangs, one in camouflage paint scheme and the other unpainted. Later in the war, most Mustangs were left unpainted. USAF via John Ziebell

Three Mustangs bring a lone Fortress home. USAF via John Ziebell

Now the Eighth Air Force deliberately attacked targets, like Berlin, to lure the Luftwaffe into battle to defend. Experienced German pilots were being lost far more rapidly than skilled replacements could be trained.

By June 1944, when the invasion took place, the fighters had overwhelmed their opposition to such a degree that Gen. Dwight D. Eisenhower, Supreme Allied Commander in Europe, shared one bit of comforting news with troops about to land on the Normandy beaches on D-Day morning. He said crisply: "You needn't worry about the air. If you see a plane it will be ours."

Big Week

Of the long-awaited long-range fighter, an immediate culmination was the Big Week. During a week beginning on Feb. 20, 1944, the Eighth along with the Fifteenth Air Force (based in Italy) dropped

A gunner's view of an Me 410. 100th BG

William J. Sullivan's notes on an Apr. 24, 1944, mission to Landsberg, Germany.

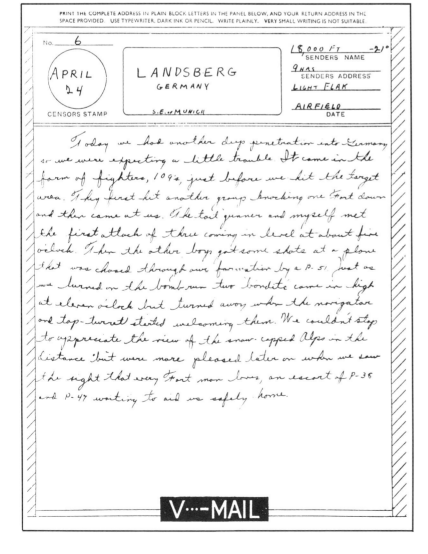

nearly 10,000 tons of bombs—approximately equal to that of Eighth Air Force's first year of operations—on aircraft production centers. There were over 3,300 Eighth Air Force bombers dispatched with the loss of 137, over the six days that constituted the Big Week. There were over 2,500 fighter sorties and total losses of only twenty-eight. The four-percent loss rate for the bombers attests to the effectiveness of fighter escort.

Bombers accompanied by long-range escort devastated German aircraft production at a critical point in the war: when Allied invasion of Continental Europe was imminent.

Facing the enemy over the Fatherland

Aerial combat with an enemy over his homeland was an awesome assignment. Especially when adversaries were seasoned veterans of aerial combat. "We knew the enemy's capabilities and we respected them," said Dayton Casto, Jr., 361st Fighter Group pilot.

James Goodson said: "German pilots had, on average, much more experience than ours and were therefore superior. As a result of heavy losses towards the end of the war, they had to use pilots who were less experienced, but their best were still superior to our best."

"German pilots were well-disciplined, aggressive, and very brave," observed Robert Bieck. "Their task was an overwhelming one, indeed. For the German pilot, there was no such thing as a tour of duty. You simply flew until you were wounded or killed. It's no wonder their top aces had over 300 planes to their record."

"The yellow-nosed 'Abbeville Kids' were tremendous pilots," commented Charles Cummins, 361st Fighter Group pilot. "Of course, they weren't kids at all. They were old, experienced pilots," who claimed over 2,700 Allied aircraft shot down by war's end.

Deep penetration escort

By spring 1944, one fighter group was usually assigned to cover each bomber combat wing box. However, it remained a challenge to cover every part of the vast formations over the entire route.

A typical escort formation placed one squadron, divided into two sections, ahead of a bomber formation. A second squadron also divided into two sections and flew on both sides of the formation. The third squadron flew top cover approximately 4,000 feet above the bombers. Fighters constantly weaved or orbited to compensate for the slower speed of the bombers.

"Our job was to make sure our bombers got back," said Powell. "Always on my mind was the fact that inside each one were ten men."

As bomber formations approached, German pilots scrambled at airfields dispersed throughout the route in occupied countries like Belgium, Holland, and Denmark. John Ziebell of the 357th Fighter Group said, "You heard on your radio, 'Bandits at XX,' and you'd take off after them."

Fighter pilots had to be ready at almost any instant to bank sharply in high-speed turns and power dives to meet the challenges of the approaching enemy. As pilots veered to fend off attackers of bomber formations, G forces (gravity forces) withstood easily by fighter aircraft put incredible strain on a pilot's circulation system. Effective pressurized flight suits or "G-suits" were not available until very late in the war.

"If you made a quick turn to lose an enemy behind and felt yourself graying out, it was terrifying," said Powell. "But most of us developed techniques to deal with it—like leaning forward and screaming if necessary to put pressure on the blood vessels in the neck to help prevent from blacking out."

Recalling an escort mission 31,000 feet over Berlin, Goodson offered a fighter pilot's stream of consciousness:

". . . the great fleet of B-17s sailing majestically through the black puffs of flak. Then the massed Me-109s dived down in a head-on attack. I rolled into a dive and led the group down to cut them off. One [appeared] in my sights, still out of range, but closing fast. A quick glance behind, then concentrating on the 109, seeing the black crosses and, as I pressed the button, the yellow flashes along the grey and black fuselage; then an explosion and a wing and pieces of debris floating past. Racking the P-51 'round in a tight turn, blacking out for a moment and, when vision clears, pulling up into the next wave of 109s coming down, closing on one of our P-51s. 'Yellow four, break hard right!' The 109 follows this but I'm inside and hit twice in the cockpit. Suddenly, there's nothing but a few of our own P-51s around."

March 1945 Escort *cover.* USAF via John Ziebell

Flak

High over strategic targets, flak was a threat to both bombers and fighters, but fighters could avoid flak when bombers could not. "When the bombers ran into flak on their bomb run, we got the hell out of there," said John Ziebell. There was nothing to be done, except watch the bombers fly through it.

"We felt sorry for the bomber crews on bomb runs," said Robert Wright. "They couldn't make any maneuvers to dodge the flak. All we could do was watch them go into the target—flak bursting all around them."

"When we were being tracked by flak," said Robert Powell, "we simply did a little chandelle maneuver and the flak would follow with a chandelle behind us but usually without effect."

"Escorting bombers was actually pretty safe," said Charles Cummins. "When the Germans started tossing up flak, bombers had to fly through it over the target and we could fly around and meet them on the other side. The more dangerous encounters with flak were during strafing."

Strafing

As range of their aircraft increased, the fighter groups' role expanded beyond escort duties. Instead of the singular duty of sweeping enemy fighters out of the

"When our fighter group was selected to fly escort on a shuttle mission to Russia . . . some of us on the ground crew flew as waist gunners in B-17s of the 390th Bomb Group. We were to maintain the P-51s. To see that little single-engine fighter over enemy territory, 600 miles from home, had a very profound effect on me. It put a whole new perspective on the word maintenance . . ."
—Bill Weith, 357th Fighter Group

"Five Me 110s came suddenly and we knew we'd had it. Then out of the clear blue sky, three P-51s came and the 110s disappeared."
—Hiram Drache, 457th Bomb Group (H)

"We lost a lot more pilots after we began strafing. Over enemy airfields, I watched tracers coming up at me and I just gritted my teeth and hoped they wouldn't hit me."
—Robert Wright, 361st Fighter Group

"A friend and I had strafed locomotives and accidentally crossed an airfield. Small arms fire hit him in the mid-section of the wing and his P-47 flipped over and smashed into the deck, just off my wing. It shook me up later when I thought about it. But at the time it just made me mad. So I strafed the hell out of the airfield."
—Dean Morehouse, 361st Fighter Group

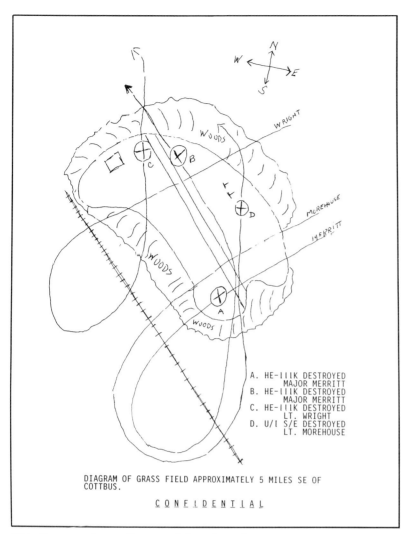

A. HE-111K DESTROYED
    MAJOR MERRITT
B. HE-111K DESTROYED
    MAJOR MERRITT
C. HE-111K DESTROYED
    LT. WRIGHT
D. U/I S/E DESTROYED
    LT. MOREHOUSE

DIAGRAM OF GRASS FIELD APPROXIMATELY 5 MILES SE OF COTTBUS.

C O N F I D E N T I A L

This diagram of a strafing attack by pilots of the 361st Fighter Group was typical of those drawn during post-strike debriefing.

"We knew flak was the greatest danger, but we did not hesitate to strafe airfields, which is how I got shot down. I accepted fear as a healthy and normal reaction."
—James Goodson, 4th Fighter Group

path of the bombers, fighters were put on the offensive—hunting targets of their own in the sky and on the ground.

The dramatically extended range and performance of the Mustang left no place in northwest Europe safe from daylight attack. "We went from strictly escort work to penetration ahead and behind the bombers," said Cummins. "After escorting them a ways, we'd go down on the deck and strafe assigned targets or targets of opportunity."

It was known that the expanded role would increase fighter losses, but the now steady stream of fresh pilots and planes from the United States would fill in vacancies. Strafing was a particularly hazardous activity that claimed the lives of many fighter pilots and downed seemingly invincible aces like Duane Beeson (4th Fighter Group) and Francis Gabreski (56th Fighter Group), who were taken prisoner.

"Strafing" is a German term adopted by the Allies to describe aircraft shooting ground targets. Strafing airfields, usually defended by light flak weapons, resulted in heavier losses to fighters than escort duties, because strafing surrendered most of the advantages of being airborne. Dean Morehouse commented: "Our biggest losses came from strafing targets. You could expect flak and a hail of small arms fire."

Strafing trains was a very effective means of disrupting vital German supply lines. Like a hawk spotting a squirrel, fighters dove on them, raining destruction. But this kind of "squirrel" often concealed formidible defenses. "German trains had flak cars, often pulled immediately behind the engines, sometimes one in the middle and on the end," explained Jack Ilfrey, 20th Fighter Group ace. "The flak cars were somewhat disguised like boxcars, but we knew they were there. In those days of steam locomotives, you could easily see the rising steam of a train from a long distance. One day, I spied one and went down to blow up the boiler, but the flak cars were ready for me—they shot me down." (Although 200 miles behind enemy lines, Ilfrey evaded capture. Dressed like a French farmer, he bicycled to friendly lines and eventually returned to England.)

Low-level strafing meant close-range return fire from any direction. And if an aircraft was hit seriously, the deck rose all too rapidly to meet it. Bailing out was not an option.

The hazards of strafing may have influenced Eighth Fighter Command in its decision to give full victory credits for aircraft destroyed on the ground. The USAAF was bent on continuing the devastation of the Luftwaffe, which had begun to refuse aerial combat in order to conserve its diminishing air strength. Giving full victory credits was an inducement to leave the relative safety of air-to-air combat for strafing. It meant 'acedom" for five victory credits for aircraft destroyed in the air or on the ground. Eighth Fighter Command was the only unit in all of the US forces to adopt this rule.

"That type of combat was the worst," said Ilfrey. "You can't do anything about people shooting at you from the ground, like you can when someone is shooting at you in the air."

Powell said, "Regardless of how good a pilot was, strafing was risky. Like shooting dice, sooner or later you're going to crap out."

But consistent with the character of fighter pilots, many welcomed the dangerous challenge. "Going to P-51s almost doubled the length of our missions," said Morehouse. "Long missions became almost boring. We welcomed going downstairs and strafing."

After attacking targets of their own, fighter groups often were scattered. If there weren't escort duties for the bombers' return, individual flights returned on their own. If a group united for the flight back, planes flew in loose formations until they neared East Anglia. Then they tightened into proud formations as they approached their home airfield—a show appreciated by the anxiously awaiting ground crews.

The Eighth's fighters carried the assault into the heart of Germany and achieved successes in ways easily measured—in contrast to the incalculable force of the bombers. When bombers landed and strike photos were interpreted, the extent of damage to the German war machine was never precisely known. Fighter accomplishments were largely a matter of numbers—victories scored during a mission.

P-38 pilot Jack Ilfrey with the King's Cliffe based 20th Fighter Group. John Campbell

"It was easy to see the results of your work when you strafed a train," said Dean Morehouse of the 361st Fighter Group. USAF

A Mustang lands at Leiston on Dec. 10, 1944. USAF via John Ziebell

Chapter 5

Sweating it out

As we sweated out the group's return, I saw grown men—the crew chiefs—cry when their plane didn't come back. It was like they were at a funeral and they had lost their mother, father, and best friend. . . .

—Evelyn Cohen, Second Air Division Headquarters

Everyone gathered on the flight line. Men from ordnance, armament and engineering. From communications, intelligence, operations and transportation. From the photo lab, mess hall, hospital and Aeroclub. All were drawn together, their affinity rooted in the concern for their flying kindred.

Against a backdrop of panoramic woodlands and farm-dotted hills, some of them slumped over bicycle handlebars or sat in vehicles with motors silent. Others tossed a baseball. The subdued gathering gave the impression of tranquility. But these were tense moments of uncertainty. Everyone here was preoccupied, their attention riveted to the sky.

All eyes flashed at intervals to the east, drawn irresistibly to the sky above a distant church spire that beckoned like a finger. Any moment now, specks would appear in that piece of sky. In this strange world of shuttle-battle, combatants were dispatched at a specified takeoff time, reached their destinations on a schedule something like a commuter train, and returned often within minutes of the ETA—or not at all.

Before the unaided eye could detect them, someone with binoculars on the control tower roof thrust an indicatory arm toward the horizon. All heads turned. Others pointed and nervous murmuring arose. Specks, barely yet distinguishable, appeared against the backdrop of the heavens. Then a glint of sunlight ricocheted off a distant fuselage like a reassuring wink.

Everyone strained to count those precious specks, each bearing (hopefully) an uninjured ten-man bomber crew or a fighter pilot.

"Every crew chief was attached to his plane and pilot," said Al Giesting, 352nd Fighter Group crew chief. "All of us watched intently for our own to come back in."

"Bombers often came back with flares flying to indicate injured aboard," said Norm Schleitwiler of the 351st Bomb Group armament section. "Planes were sometimes severely damaged—parts torn off. Landing gear sometimes didn't come down. Everyone felt bad when flares were flying and ships were missing."

"There was what seemed like a universal holding of breath as the planes approached," recalled Barbara Pathe, who watched the activity from a Red Cross clubmobile. "Then an intense concentration focused on counting them in and on reading and reacting to the flares,

Sky watchers. As the ETA approached, all attention turned to the sky. 94th BGMA

and finally a flurry of ground activity and anxiety over missing planes."

Not only on air stations were eyes fixed on returning formations. "We'd count them back," said Ruby Kranz, Buckinghamshire resident. "We saw the stragglers, smoke pouring from them, flying low and slow—just clearing village houses. The air just vibrated."

Control tower: the nerve center

The control tower, usually a box-shaped, two-story masonry structure with balcony and sometimes a watch room on the roof, was a base's eyes and ears.

"Air controllers were on alert 24 hours a day, mission or no mission," noted Don Hope, Alconbury flying control officer.

Group and squadron commanders, if they weren't flying the mission, wore a path pacing on the roof or second floor balcony. Teletypes chattered inside. Exhibiting the latest information about a group's aircraft, a giant status board presided over the tower's operations room. Flying control personnel were the first to know how many aircraft were missing and had the somber task of erasing the names of pilots and aircraft from the status board.

The alert room on the ground floor front buzzed with nervous energy of men

ready to respond to any emergency on the ground. Rescue vehicles were poised for immediate response in front of the tower.

Stormy returns

The old nemesis of weather had severe impact on the weary aircraft and fliers who had fought through six or eight

Ambulances stand ready on the field as formations appear in the east. EAA Aviation Foundation Photo Archives

458th Bomb Group's mascot Uncle Peter with young nephew, Monk (left), and niece, Glamor Girl (center), patiently sweat out the return of the group's B-24s to Horsham St. Faith in 1944. Robert Neel

hours of flak and enemy fighters to return home. From the weather station, generally located on the ground floor of the tower, forecasters like Art Gulliver kept abreast of weather developments. He explained: "Even after the centralized forecast system was formed, those of us at weather detachments were on our own for the local landing forecast. Because the ceiling often was low or the fog heavy, forecasters advised about where to divert aircraft. We received reports from other bases every hour and sometimes every half hour via teletype so we knew what bases were still open."

"Our planes were returning from a mission only to find the field fogged in," said Bill Weith, 357th Fighter Group mechanic. "Flares were set out to mark the runway, but they didn't help. We could see the planes from the ground. But apparently the sun reflecting off the fog dazzled the pilots' vision. Some landed on the perimeter track, some on the runway, one P-51 lost a wing and crashed nearby, and many diverted to other fields."

When aircraft had to divert from a home base due to weather, many times they found refuge in the runway at Bovingdon, located at higher elevation than surrounding fields and consequently, often clearer. At those times, Bovingdon's controllers sprang into action. "Suddenly, when Mayday calls started coming in,

From a checkered mobile control vehicle, air traffic controllers direct aircraft during landings. USAF

An air controller signals aircraft with an Aldis lamp. USAF

everything broke loose," said Howard Dicken, Bovingdon air controller. "Bombers and fighters from different fields streamed in. You'd direct an aircraft to the active runway and suddenly find another aircraft, wheels up and on fire, coming from the opposite direction."

Dicken, who went on to make a career of air traffic control in civilian life, recalled the challenges of split-second decisions in wartime air control:

"When the Mayday calls started coming, it was the controller's job to determine which aircraft had priority to land. If we saw a red flare from an aircraft, even though there was no radio contact, we knew they had wounded on board. They had priority to land. But if one was on fire and one had wounded, the priority always went to the one on fire.

"We put extensions on our mics and earphones so that we could walk more freely around the second floor walkway. You constantly held a Vary flare pistol in your left hand and the carbon mic in your right. At that time we did more air control using flares—we'd give the aircraft with the lesser trouble a red flare to wait. Just as soon as you fired the pistol, you cocked it and got ready for another.

"[When an aircraft radioed from some distance out and declared Mayday] we asked the pilot to count to ten and back. In the meantime as he's transmitting, we revolved a VHF homer loop antenna on the roof of the tower. When we got a 'null' [total silence], we knew the loop was directly aligned with the aircraft. We rotated the divider on a compass rose and read the reciprocal, which was the direction the aircraft needed to find the field. Immediately we radioed this heading.

"There were so many days when the adrenaline was running. It was always a feeling of elation when a Mayday was on the ground safely."

Crashes

Crashes on East Anglian airfields became commonplace. Returning aircraft had often limped along for hundreds of miles after encounters with German defenses. Aircraft bearing wounded and exhausted men approached home fields— or any field available—on a wing and a prayer, which meant almost anything could happen at any instant.

"I turned around just in time to see a terrific explosion in our bomb dump," recalled Roger Lyons, 100th Bomb Group

Watch office on the flat roof of Alconbury's control tower. Don P. Hope

A rare scene during the war—an empty control room. 94th BGMA

RESTRICTED

FM 24-9

WAR DEPARTMENT

BASIC FIELD MANUAL

◆

COMBINED
UNITED STATES - BRITISH

RADIOTELEPHONE (R/T) PROCEDURE

December 28, 1942

RESTRICTED

BASIC FIELD MANUAL

COMBINED UNITED STATES-BRITISH RADIO-TELEPHONE (R/T) PROCEDURE

1. Purpose.—This radiotelephone procedure (R/T) shall be used in combined operations of the United States and British Forces. The use of matters shown in brackets, as [Hullo], is optional.

2. General Instructions.—*a.* Messages transmitted by radiotelephone are not necessarily written down, but operators should whenever possible make a short note of their purport. They must, therefore, be kept short and to the point. This brevity is best achieved by the use of standard phraseology. Messages which must be given by the receiving operator to another person should preferably be written down.

b. Speech over the radiotelephone will be clear and slow with even emphasis upon each word. Words will not be run together.

c. Messages will be spoken in natural phrases and not word by word.

d. In the interests of security, transmission by radiotelephone will be as short and concise as possible consistent with clearness. (See par. 9*e.*)

3. Phonetic Alphabet.—When necessary to identify any letter of the alphabet the standard phonetic alphabet is to be used. This alphabet is listed below:

Letter	Spoken as	Letter	Spoken as
A	ABLE (AFIRM)*	E	EASY
B	BAKER	F	FOX
C	CHARLIE	G	GEORGE
D	DOG	H	HOW

*Names in parentheses shall be used when the *United States Navy General Signal Book* is used.

Pages from a flying control manual, circa 1943. There was inherent simplicity in the language of the air. All excess verbiage is trimmed away to make every utterance succinct and unmistakable in meaning. Vital information transmitted back and forth from disembodied voices could, and often did, mean the difference between life and death.

BASIC FIELD MANUAL

Letter	Spoken as	Letter	Spoken as
I	ITEM (INTERROGATORY)*	R	ROGER
J	JIG	S	SUGAR
K	KING	T	TARE
L	LOVE	U	UNCLE
M	MIKE	V	VICTOR
N	NAN (NEGAT)*	W	WILLIAM
O	OBOE (OPTION)*	X	XRAY
P	PETER (PREP)*	Y	YOKE
Q	QUEEN	Z	ZEBRA

*Names in parentheses shall be used when the *United States Navy General Signal Book* is used.

Examples

a. Encrypted groups—LUXOW will be spoken as " Love Uncle Xray Oboe William."

b. Difficult words will be both spoken and spelled. Example : " Catenary—I spell—Charlie Able Tare Easy Nan Able Roger Yoke—Catenary."

4. Pronunciation of Numerals.—When figures are transmitted by radiotelephone the following rules for their pronunciation will be observed :

Figure	Spoken	Figure	Spoken
0	Zero	5	Fi-yiv
1	Wun	6	Six
2	Too	7	Seven
3	Thuh-ree	8	Ate
4	Fo-wer	9	Niner

5. Call Signs.—Call signs composed of letters or letters and figures must be transmitted by means of the phonetic alphabet and numeral pronunciation.

Examples

Call sign AB shall be transmitted as " Able Baker."
Call sign P3 shall be transmitted as " Peter Three."

6. Component Parts of a Message.—Every radiotelephone message is composed of three basic parts : the *Call*, including precedence (priority), if any ; the *Text* (subject matter) ; and the *Ending.*

RADIOTELEPHONE (R/T) PROCEDURE

The Call

7. Form.—The call of a radiotelephone message may take one of the following forms :

Case I—full call	*Examples*
[Hullo]	[Hullo]
Call sign receiving station	Able Baker
This is	This is
Call sign station calling	Peter Three

Case II—abbreviated call	*Examples*
This is	This is
Call sign station calling	Peter Three

*Case III—link call**	*Examples*
[Hullo]	[Hullo]
Link call sign	Able Baker
	Charlie

*NOTE.—The link call sign procedure is a special arrangement not at present in general use. When prescribed for specific combined use further instructions will be issued.

b. Precedence (priority).—Precedence designations are seldom used in voice (R/T) procedure, but if used will be spoken in clear as the last part of the call, for example, "PRIORITY"* or "IMPORTANT",* etc.

Table of United States-British Precedence (Priorities).

United States	British
Urgent	Emergency
Operational Priority	Immediate
Priority	Important

The Text (Subject matter)

The text (subject matter) may consist of plain language, code words, or figures. If it is necessary to spell out a word, the phonetic alphabet will be used.

The Ending

Every transmission will end with one of the following procedure words :

Word	Meaning
a. Over	My transmission is ended and I expect a response from you.
b. Out	This conversation is ended and no response is expected.

An RAF Stirling bomber crash at Bury St. Edmunds (Rougham). USAF via Leroy Kuest

radio repairman. "A crew from another group had bailed out of a disabled plane, which fell into a grouping of 500-pound incendiary bombs."

"We witnessed many crash landings," said Leroy Kuest, 94th Bomb Group air mechanic. "A P-38 and a British Stirling bellied-in on the grass. We watched two B-17s trying to land at the same time—one crashed and the other lifted off again, circled and came in for a perfect landing. One B-17 approached the field with an engine out and a wing too low. When he hit the runway, he knocked off the landing gear on one side. The plane lurched off the runway on to the grass and the remaining gear acted like a plow share, throwing mud up in the air. It started for our tent and we all ran to get out of the way, but it stopped about two hundred yards short. We expected it to blow, but it didn't. Propellers on one wing were bent back, but it eventually flew again."

"Hydraulic system shot out, a fighter bellied in our field," said Weith. "The pilot had not turned off the gun switch and inadvertently touched the trigger, spritzing the area with fifty caliber slugs. One of them tore out the back of the instrument panel of a P-51 I was checking out."

British farmer Percy Kindred recalled: "An old man working with me blurted out, 'What's the matter with that airplane?' I looked up and could see a B-17 wobbling. Two engines were out—one feathered and the other windmilling.

A contorted B-17 in a heap on a hedgerow. 100th BG

A P-47, piloted by Glenn Duncan of the 353rd Fighter Groups, came unwillingly to rest in an English field after engine problems on Apr. 27, 1944. John Campbell

Medics aided by ground and aircrew members carry a badly wounded flier from a B–17. 94th BGMA

Crewmen begin to sift through the wreckage of a crash-landed B–24 Liberator, looking for survivors. 94th BGMA

It was in terrible shape. It swung around and got lined up with the field. Just as he dropped his wheels, a tractor went across his path. The poor devil pulled up to miss it and tried to circle for another approach. The plane got halfway around, but suddenly just dropped. All on board were killed."

Medical help

Flight surgeons were on alert to treat man-made wounds and nature's wounds. Dr. Willard Klockow, 453rd Bomb Group flight surgeon, commented that medical work on Eighth Air Force stations tended to be either "flood or drought. The floods occurred when our men were bombing especially dangerous targets, as at Brunswick, Germany and the Ploesti oil fields in Rumania."

Hundredth Bomb Group flight surgeon Clifford Kinder explained: "Each of the four squadrons had its own flight surgeon assigned. Individual bases were not equipped to handle the more serious injuries. In our case, at Thorpe Abbotts, we evacuated seriously injured patients immediately to the 65th General Hospital, located about twenty miles away."

"We met all planes as they came in," said Kinder. Sometimes crews emerged from their aircraft without a scratch. Other times, they came out on stretchers.

Safe on the ground

"We always counted the planes circling to land and were very happy to see the wheels of our aircraft touch down safely on the runway once more," said Carl Lose, 94th Bomb Group crew chief.

On fighter stations, ground crews knew immediately if their returning aircraft had seen action, even if no damage was visible: broken tape seals over the wing gun muzzles were a "sure-fire" indication. Fighter pilots communicated victories to awaiting ground crews by waving the appropriate number of fingers.

On bomber stations, just a glance at a heavy bomber often told the story: huge chunks of vertical stabilizers missing, dirty fingers of smoke trailing one or more engines, and flares flying to indicate wounded on board.

Fliers deplaned and looked, often in astonishment, at the damage to their aircraft. L. G. Spillman said: "First thing we

Medical staff and others gather to help an injured flier. 94th BGMA

Above and beyond the call of duty

In the bedlam of war, the extraordinary and unexpected became the norm. Such an example occurred at Thorpe Abbotts on a morning in May 1944 when, as always 'Doc' Kinder and others from the group's medical staff met a returning straggler, a B–17 described simply as an aircraft that "might be dangerous." Those standing by ready to give aid knew nothing beyond that.

The aircraft rolled to a gentle stop and the crew, with the exception of the tail gunner, quickly deplaned. The station ordnance officer peered in the damaged tail section to find the tail gunner, alive but unconscious, wedged tightly between the tail bulkhead and—a bomb.

Over the day's target at Laon, France, a bomber in a higher squadron had taken evasive action to avoid flak during the bomb run. A result was a misdirected 100 pound bomb falling squarely into the lower bomber's tail section and severely injuring tail gunner Raymond Cohen. The bomb was armed and embedded nose down in the tail compartment.

Movement of Sergeant Cohen or the bomb could have spelled abrupt tragedy. An ordnance man poked an exploratory arm through a jagged hole and was eventually able to thread a length of wire through the bomb lug, thereby relieving pressure from the nose fuse. Then he gently loosened the armed tail fuse and extracted it.

A medic went in through the tail's escape hatch, but was unable to pull the gunner free. Using heavy telephone wire found on a nearby truck, the men wound a coil around the bomb and pulled it away from the wedged gunner.

Kinder crawled through the cramped, battered tail section and tried to pull the gunner gently from his berth of torn metal and shattered plexiglass. Finding that the thong of the gunner's boot was caught, Kinder stretched with knife in hand to cut it and the gunner was carefully pulled free.

Sergeant Cohen was rushed in an awaiting ambulance to the station hospital, where he died from head wounds without regaining consciousness. An RAF bomb disposal squad later removed the bomb.

Such actions were "above and beyond the line of duty," but the fact that the gunner was still alive prompted willing risk of death for Doc Kinder and all involved. When asked to comment about the incident, Kinder simply replied, "We got very attached to our squadron's crews. If one of them was injured or killed, it bothered us a great deal. We did what we could."

---

did after landing was to inspect damage. One of my crewmembers pointed to a hole where flak had gone cleanly through the fuselage, inches behind where my head had been."

Camaraderie

Extraordinary camaraderie characterized the groups. There was a closeness that made them as "close as brothers, closer in some cases," as one airman put it. These relationships sprang from indomitable trust and confidence in one another. The result was more than simply the "cohesive fighting units" the military sought to build.

In bomb groups, many crews had a special trust reserved for the pilot—a trust that prompts men, now retirement age reflecting back, to speak reverently of a pilot, then perhaps just twenty years old, as something more than a boy, maybe more than even a man, and without a doubt the best pilot there was.

In fighter groups, it made for close relationships that superseded rank, as in the affinity between a pilot and crew chief. And between pilots there were unwritten codes of allegiance.

"There was brotherly love," said Robert Powell, Jr., pilot in the 352nd Fighter Group. "We knew our lives depended on each other in combat. We developed some fantastic camaraderie that still exists today. The same was true between pilots and crew chiefs. My crew chief was a great big guy, two or three years older than I. He used to tuck me in that airplane like a mother tucks in a baby—putting the straps on me and patting me on the back."

"Relations between pilots and ground crew were excellent," according to James Goodson, an ace with the 4th Fighter

---

"We waited till it was practically dark. Finally, our plane came—all banged up from flak. I could tell our pilot, Bill Kemp, was hurt. When we directed him into the revetment, we normally had him spin around and come to a stop and cut the engine. But he just kept going around in a circle—one foot on the brake."
—Joe Redden, 361st Fighter Group

"[Our crew] went everywhere together— drank together, took our passes together. If one of us got into a fight, it was for all of us, no exceptions."
—Phil Garey, 94th Bomb Group (H)

"Relations between pilots and ground crew were excellent. Crew chiefs identified themselves with their pilots and vice-versa. The crew chief's name was always on the plane underneath the pilot's. A pilot returning from a successful mission would say to his crew chief, 'We got another one.'"
—James Goodson, 4th Fighter Group

Group. "Crew chiefs identified themselves with their pilots and vice-versa. The crew chief's name was always on the plane underneath the pilot's. A pilot returning from a successful mission would say to his crew chief, 'We got another one.'"

"I've never seen ground crews with devotion like that since," said Frank Halm, of the 94th Bomb Group (retired after thirty years service). "They were unbelievable. Highly knowledgeable and experienced. They really looked after the aircrews. The early losses helped convince them that this wasn't a kid's game, and while the flyboys might have gotten the glory, they were also taking a beating. Ground crews worked so that you would have everything possible in your favor. They were our best friends."

Dealing with loss

The extraordinary camaraderie between airmen, and between airmen and their ground crews, often made inevitable losses even more difficult to accept.

"After a crew had flown five or ten missions on your aircraft, you got to know them well," said Leroy Kuest. "The hardest thing was knowing they had been shot down. We always tried to find out if any chutes came out—and hoped they had landed safely."

"If the pilot lost was from your barracks, you couldn't help thinking a lot about him," said Dean Morehouse, 361st Fighter Group pilot. "His gear was gathered up quickly and taken to headquar-

Lt. Robert Powell, Jr., demonstrates the warmth between pilot and crew chief. John Campbell

ters. We'd have a bull session in the officer's club and talk about it, which usually eased the feelings some."

Francis Cunningham, 466th Bomb Group intelligence, added: "When a friend was killed, you had to bear it and go on. You could go out at night and get drunk—but that's what they said was Hitler's secret weapon: English pubs. Probably more Eighth Air Force members were hurt traveling by bicycle to and from pubs than anywhere else."

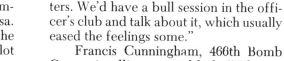

> mello & Campbell finished their 25th mission today. Fry & I are next to finish. mello & Campbell have their orders to leave. They don't want to go until the crew finishes. I sure do hate to see the crew split up after being together for almost a year.
>
> —Ken Stone,
> December 24, 1943
> diary entry

"As we sweated out the group's return, I saw grown men—the crew chiefs—cry when their plane didn't come back," said Evelyn Cohen, who often traveled from her Second Air Division Headquarters office at Knetteringham Hall to the nearby airfield at Hethel. "It was like they were at a funeral—and they had lost their mother, father, and best friend. They worried that they had done something wrong that might have caused the airplane not to come back. They tormented themselves with the question, 'Did I do everything possible for that aircraft last night?'"

It was no wonder that people in the ground echelon became hesitant to form close relationships with their combat-flier counterparts.

Bloody Hundredth crew chief Clarence Schroepfer said, "After a while, we didn't want to get to know the aircrews well. I came to England in 1943 when there were some heavy losses. We had gotten close to the early crews, but so many were lost we didn't want to know the later ones."

"I felt satisfaction as I watched the group return and relief if all came back," Roger Lyons commented. But implying the withdrawal that ground crews often eventually took, he sighed, "Since we had mourned the deaths of the original crews, we didn't come to know the replacement crews. It became more impersonal."

After experiencing heavy losses, many in the ground echelon reluctantly limited themselves to professional relationships as a psychological defense.

But even without close personal relations, reality couldn't be avoided. "It was evident what they had gone through," one ground crewman asserted. "When we cleaned up the aircraft, we sometimes found some poor soul's blood or pieces of clothing. Once in a great while, we found a little piece of body...."

G. W. Pederson had the experience of being first assigned to the ground echelon in the 306th Bomb Group's intelligence section and later to a combat crew. He said: "[After I became a B-17 gunner], my old friends in ground units responded to me almost like people respond to someone with a terminal disease. Neither I nor they thought I was going to be around much longer."

Ironically, withdrawing was also the way many aircrew members dealt with the fear of losing friends. After "being hit hard" by the loss of some of his closest friends, Robert Bieck "decided that one could become too close to friends. I elected to be as distant as possible [short of] being a jerk. Other than my immediate crew members, I did not form any hard, fast relationships. When someone was lost, I did feel badly about it, but it was not like losing a brother."

> At 3 A.M. 51 ships took off, every ship available went. Ours did not go as we had an engine change. More than 4000 ships + over 16,000 aircraft stormed the coast of France in the Normandy area. Gliders went over 9 planes wide + 200 miles long. Paratroopers dropped in great strength 31,000 allied airmen flew the planes, 600 naval guns pounded the coast. Airborne troops landed inland at several points at about 3 A.M. 7,500 sorties were flown between 12 P.M. & 6 A.M. + 10,000 # of H.E. were dropped. At 6:30 first naval assault was started. More than 900 gliders took place in this. Very little opposition was encountered from the Luftwaffe. Since D-Day has started we have had little rest + have been sending 2 missions out a day.
>
> —Leroy Kuest
> June 6, 1944
> diary entry

"Since we counted the planes out and back, we knew how many were missing . . . we always wondered who they were. Then we'd hear about how, on base, this man or that man cried, because mates were gone."
—Ruby Kranz, Buckinghamshire youth

"The thought was always there: How many would not return today? We got to know the aircraft by nicknames. Standing by the perimeter fence, it was easy to see if a certain aircraft had failed to return."
—John Archer, Suffolk youth

"You never knew the fate of a lost crew for certain. We saw guys go down and never knew what had happened to them, then years later saw them at a reunion; they had become prisoners. That's sweating out a mission."
—C. L. Anderson, 390th Bomb Group (H)

A photo specialist operates a Siltzman enlarger, designed for correcting tip and tilt of strike photos. Enlarged photos were pieced together to make large photographic mosaics. 8th Photo Tech Squadron

Bieck noted that the USAAF was quick to recognize the social problems of losing crews and "handled the situation in a clever, subtle manner. They always had replacement crews arriving in time so that there would be no empty breakfast tables."

Pederson acutely suffered the loss of friends:

"I never really learned a good way of dealing with friends who were killed. The one way I found to counteract this was to try as much as possible not to become close to the new crews who came in. It was less painful when they were shot down—and most of them *were* shot down. This meant one had a steadily dwindling circle of friends.

"I became almost a recluse—as close as one can be a recluse in the Army anyhow. I ate by myself, went into town by myself. All my old friends on the aircrews were gone."

"When someone was lost," asserted Ray Patulski, "there was no funeral service. Closer friends would get together and talk about it—and have a drink 'in memory of. . . .'"

James Goodson of the 4th Fighter Group commented, "When there was a funeral service, it was far more distressing."

Charles Cummins, 361st Fighter Group pilot, commented on how fighter groups differed from bomber groups in dealing with and rationalizing death: "You form a block around it and at first, you think, *He was killed because he wasn't as good as I am. I stayed out of the trouble he got into.* But it was just bravado. Later, you think, *His chances ran out on him and mine simply haven't yet.*"

What might have been misinterpreted as stoicism was actually a basic reaction essential to survival: human resilience—the ability to forget and go on. Frank Halm, 94th Bomb Group pilot, said: "I couldn't let it affect my performance. You're in your early twenties—you get emotional for a minute and then it goes away. It was back to business as usual. I don't recall many tears."

On the homefront

On the homefront they "sweated it out," too. Although families in the States could not be among those gathered on flight lines, they were there in spirit.

Nor could they know when missions were under way or what perilous targets

Three 100th Bomb Group wives look for word about their husbands' work from airfields somewhere in England. Left to right: Geraldine (Mrs. Howard) Hamilton, Margaret Ann (Mrs. Ev) Blakely and Jean (Mrs. Harry) Crosby. Harry Crosby

were planned. Perhaps their sweating it out was accentuated by the knowledge that their loved ones faced grave, but undefined perils. And a potential crisis loomed each time Western Union delivered a message or the postman delivered the mail.

Maxine Spillman (wife of tail gunner L. G. Spillman) said: "I was seventeen and pregnant when he went over. He was gone nine months. It was tough on my nerves, and there wasn't much I could do to get it off my mind. I couldn't find out more than anyone read in newspapers. They'd say so many planes went down— and I knew it could have been one with him. But then a month later I'd get 'the letter' and knew he had survived once more."

The necessary censorship of letters in wartime often prevented family members from knowing any more than any person who picked up the local daily. However, word sometimes did get through. Harry Crosby recounted:

"I thought censoring was absurd and the press releases about missions were often inaccurate and frightening. For instance, the press really screwed up word of the Regensburg raid, so I wrote a letter to [my wife] Jean about what really had happened. An army press officer in the Chicago area gave the list of wives in the area who were sweating it out at home, so that newspapers could get stories about them. About this time, a newspaper reporter came to do a story on three [100th Bomb Group wives], because of the recent news about the terrible Regensburg mission. And Jean said, 'That's not the way it was' and proceeded to straighten out the reporter by reading my letter. The letter got into the paper and the censors were on me. From then on, all my letters were carefully censored . . . and she would receive riddled pages."

Of course, not only young wives were sweating out missions on the homefront. It would be a severe understatement to say the Eighth Air Force was a "mother's worry." Hiram Drache said: "I always recorded the precise time when we were in our greatest danger in combat. At those identical times, but seven or eight hours different on the clock, my mother in southern Minnesota would be having nightmares. After the first such event my mother went to the family doctor who, in his wisdom, said that it was ESP and that I was in difficulty. My parents recorded those times [too] and I

hinted in my letters the days when I had a problem. The events in Minnesota and Europe coincided timewise."

Debriefing

The welfare of airmen was an obvious concern to commanders, but bombing accuracy was prevalent on their minds as they met lead crews on hardstands after a mission. As crews exited aircraft, they were asked what had been accomplished. Commanders hoped for the sake of the mission and their crews that the target had been bombed effectively and they wouldn't have to go back again, thereby paying a "double-admission price," as Gen. Ira Eaker described it.

After feeling with relief the hardstand clicking under their boots, fliers were driven immediately to post-mission interrogation, sometimes called debriefing. It was extremely important to question fliers at the first possible moment after a raid while impressions were still fresh in their minds. "The S–2 officer quizzed them on what they'd experienced," explained Francis Cunningham of the 466th Bomb Group intelligence section. "Fliers had a fifth of whisky set before them. The main things on their minds were enemy aircraft and flak— often we heard, 'Flak was so thick, you could have walked on it.'"

Red Cross hostesses served coffee and orange juice and doughnuts. Doctors provided medicinal whisky. The atmosphere was set to be conducive to easy and open communication. Controlled and factual reports of the strike and losses were recorded. "But [there was] a lot of unspoken communication and subdued comments among the crews," said Barbara Pathe of the Red Cross. "It was a drawing together which briefly excluded outsiders and surrounded the stricken crews with momentary space."

"At debriefing, it seemed they questioned the navigator the most," said navigator Ray Patulski, "because he was supposed to be the so-called trained observer. I was responsible for commenting on the success of the bomb run and if I saw any airplanes go down—and how many chutes I saw. I reported on enemy fighter activity and the weather. The debriefing didn't take long—they did it as well and as fast as they could."

Fighter interrogations were generally less formal than that of bomber crews, although squadron S–2 officers asked similar questions about enemy fighter numbers, tactics, markings, friendly aircraft lost or in distress, enemy sea or ground activity, all with time of sighting and location. Claims for victories required proof in the form of a written statement, confirmation by witness, if any, and gun camera film.

Robert Powell, Jr., 352nd Fighter Group pilot, commented: "Our interrogations were more informal. We took our shot of Scotch from a tray that the flight surgeon offered. Then we'd tell the intelligence officers about anything unusual—sightings of unusual aircraft, etc. If you had strafed an airfield, you could make a sketch showing positions of enemy planes and those [that] were destroyed, along with your route of strafing."

A perpetual cycle: the next campaign begins

Each mission was an individual campaign. As propellers clanked to a stop and hoarfrost still clung to the underside of wings, ground crews sweating in the group rushed to examine battle damage. And with that examination, mobilization for the next campaign already had begun. . . .

Chapter 6

In the small hours . . .

Our mission on the ground crew was to make damn sure our airplane was in the best condition possible—as good as if we'd be flying in it ourselves.

—Joe Reddin, 361st Fighter Group assistant crew chief

Just as the English said about the sky, the airfields, too, were never still. During night and day, an unseen army (unseen by the enemy) labored to meet the tremendous challenges of supporting an armada of aircraft and men to fly them. Since the Eighth Air Force flew daylight raids, much of the mission preparation on the ground was done at night.

As darkness descended on the field, loud speakers called for blackout curtains to be drawn shut. These were largely idle hours for fliers, who huddled around tiny tortoise-shaped coke stoves, or went to a station club or nearby village pub to blow off steam. No matter where they were, however, a thought remained prevalent in their minds: *Will there be a mission tomorrow, and where to?*

To the unseen army, the ground echelon, work was just beginning. To them, June 21 did not bear sole distinction as the longest day of the year. They had many "longest days." Twenty-four hours a day, seven days a week, fifty-two weeks a year, relentless activity persisted at every Eighth Air Force field.

"Before maximum effort missions, there was maximum work most of the night," radio repairman Roger Lyons explained simply. Schedules that would appall union bosses of today were routine. Unlike fliers, ground personnel could not "stand down" on account of weather and made no hash marks toward a certain quota of missions or combat hours to complete a tour. They were there for the duration. Many in the ground echelon were members of the original complements of air groups and remained with the same groups throughout the war. Day after day, night after night. . . .

Mission planning

Much of the groups' nighttime activity hinged on the orders from the next higher echelon of command, the combat wing. The wing had fleshed out the order handed down through the air division by Eighth Air Force Command.

Operations staff waited breathlessly for orders to come via teletype at the message center. When they did, the duty officer began calling the long list of numbers. Phones all over the airfield rang and bodies jerked out of bed at communications, armament, ordnance and so on. Ghostly figures emerged from brief slivers of light at doorways of blacked-out buildings, parrying thrusts with dim flashlight beams through the moist darkness.

The S-2 (intelligence) building became a hub of activity as S-2 officers and others gathered in the War Room, the

A P-38 gets the full treatment. Ground crews were the shepherds over the stable of aircraft, putting them in the best possible condition for *the mission to come.* 7th Photo Recon Group via George Lawson

"room of secrets." After the order was decoded, the old man (group commander), Air Exec and Operations Officer conferred on the mission assignment for the coming day.

Activities on bomber and fighter stations largely paralleled one another with, of course, the exception of bomb-related activities. Preparing for briefing presentations, S-2 personnel determined locations of enemy defenses and plotted routes on floor-to-ceiling maps at the front of the briefing room. For bomber crew briefing, tacks connected red wool yarn or ribbon from the IP (Initial Point), where aircraft were to turn toward the target, to the AP (Aiming Point), where the bombardier took control of a bomber, and to the MPI (Median Point of Impact), where the bombs were to strike. For fighter pilot briefing, maps showed zones of escort or rendezvous points and possibly strafing targets.

Group navigators and bombardiers were busy deciphering the field order and ramifications for them. A member of the weather detachment provided them vital weather information, since wind and other weather factors drastically affect bombing accuracy and aircraft speed.

Along with group operations, the commander's staff determined airmen,

planes, routes and target identification, flak evasion and navigation. Vital details, such as bomb specifications, were immediately passed on to the appropriate sections.

Bombing up

A bomb group's armament section and ordnance section were tasked with some of the most dangerous responsibilities on the ground. They performed their work more than carefully, because "you're allowed only one 'oops,'" as one ordnance man said.

Bombing up, or loading and fusing of the bombs, began when the field order was passed along from Operations. "I'd receive the field order and go to the barracks to make sure the boys of the armament section were alerted," said 92nd Bomb Group armament officer Edwin Lundell. "If takeoff was scheduled for six o'clock, we were out at the hardstands at midnight loading bombs."

For bomb groups, the field order specified bomb loads—poundage and type (delayed action, incendiaries, and so on). These details were communicated to the ordnance section, which was responsible for delivery of specified bomb loads to designated aircraft. At a remote part of

A bomb handler rests on a load of 500 pound GP M-43s. Their job was the most dangerous *on the ground—the first mistake was usually fatal.* Norm Schleitwiler

the field (remote for obvious reasons) was the bomb dump, sometimes called "boom town," where bomb handlers and chemical warfare personnel loaded deadly cargo on to trailers for transport to the hardstands.

In the meantime, armament section personnel had already been inside the bombers, ensuring that bomb releases, racks and bomb bay doors functioned properly.

Loaded trailers were parked directly under a bomb bay. Bombs were cleaned (to help prevent wobbling during the fall), fins were screwed on and shackles adjusted. Armament men transferred the bombs from trailers to slings under the aircraft and hoisted them up to the bomb rack.

"You needed at least three men to load bombs," Lundell continued. "One below to put a sling around the bomb and two men to hoist the bombs up into the bomb bay from the trailer that the ordnance people had delivered."

Once loaded, the ordnance crew fused the bombs—a very dangerous procedure. Lundell remembered a tragic day at Alconbury soon after the Eighth Air Force arrived in 1942:

"There weren't enough hardstands for all the aircraft on the field. Bombers were parked wing-tip to wing-tip. A [transient] group was there because their base was not ready for them. They received the orders for a mission, the first

ever for that group. Everyone was excited and standing by their aircraft. Normally during fusing of the bombs, aircrews were not in the vicinity.

"The ordnance men were fusing the bombs after we had loaded them and suddenly a bomb exploded inside an aircraft. It blew up the aircraft, as well as two or three on either side. Many men were killed."

Just as pilots painted nose art on their planes, armament personnel often painted bombs with personal greetings for the Fuhrer. Norm Schleitwiler

Often, the omnipresent drizzle made the handling of a bomb something like attempting to hug a well-soaped baby, and bomb handlers were equally careful not to drop one. "They said if you dropped one from four feet, she'd go up, fuse or no fuse," one bomb handler commented. "We never dropped one, so I couldn't confirm that."

If the drizzle turned worse prompting cancellation of a mission, the ordnance-armament team had to repeat their work, only in reverse. Bombers were not left loaded, because the subsequent field order likely would call for different loads, possibly different aircraft.

Other members of the armament section were trained specifically in power-operated gun turrets, the guns themselves, and still others in the intricacies of the bombsight.

Mechanics

Meanwhile, the engineering section's ground crews persisted at their work. What had begun as an examination of battle damage, immediately after a group's late afternoon return, often turned into an all-night marathon of repair.

"We'd bring 'em back with engines gone and big holes and they'd work all

night . . ." remarked C. L. Anderson, about his thirty missions with the 390th Bomb Group.

Care of aircraft wasn't the part of combat flying that basked in fame. Yet the teamwork of this unseen army partnering with fliers made the difference between excellence and mediocrity in a group's operational record.

No matter how well armed or skillfully piloted, aircraft had to be kept in top condition in every way to outfly the enemy, perform in punishing weather conditions and get back home.

Aircraft that flew hour after hour through punishing skies required painstaking work of repairing battle damage and performing routine maintenance. In a group's engineering section, ground crews comprised of a crew chief, chief assistant and three air mechanics were assigned specific aircraft for which they assumed overall responsibility.

The crew chief was the ultimate authority for his assigned aircraft. It was his job to know the peculiarities of his plane, its temperamental weaknesses and the history of its ailments. Since most ground crewmen were stationed with a group for the duration—in contrast to the relatively short time for combat crews who flew their mission quota and went

Repairing the big bombers was a mammoth task. Even changing a tire took the cooperation of the whole crew. 8th Photo Tech Squadron

home—one aircraft could be used by a number of "generations" of aircrews. So the crew chief sometimes coached more than one aircrew about the quirks of a particular aircraft.

Ground crewmen were trained by the Army Air Forces Technical Training Command, whose motto was *Sustineo Alas*—"I sustain the wings."

"I felt comfortable with the training," asserted Charles Upright, 361st Fighter Group crew chief. "I went through mechanics school in Lincoln, Nebraska and went to Republic Aircraft in New York after that for more training. I had good schooling before I went overseas."

Even good training couldn't fully condition air mechanics and specialists for nearly incessant repair hours out on the line in a climate few of them were used to. An adversity not only to fliers, England's weather hampered the ground crews' work as well. Maintenance and repairs were usually performed in raw elements on the open hardstands, where there was seldom any respite from the wind that whisked across the tarmac.

Air mechanic Leroy Kuest said: "The hardest thing about our job was putting up with constant rain and fog. All our repair work was done out in the open. Tools would rust or mildew. Hands and feet were numb from constant cold and dampness."

Surrounded by scaffolding and replacement parts on open hardstands, combat aircraft reposed with the majesty of queen bees, their needs attended to by worker bees—ground crews on call twenty-four hours a day.

The men in green, grease-stained coveralls checked and double-checked; removed and replaced; repaired and despaired over the mechanical heartbeats of each aircraft assigned to them. "Our mission on the ground crew was to make damn sure our airplane was in the best condition possible—as good as if we'd be flying in it ourselves," said Joe Redden.

These individuals took fierce, personal pride in their work. Satisfaction came from tuning the cough of battle-ravaged engines to sweet song and watching their planes go for as many missions as possible without an abort due to mechanical malfunction.

"Their goal was to make sure their plane never had to abort for a mechanical failure," commented Ralph Price, 381st Bomb Group ball turret gunner. "I understand our plane had over a hundred missions without a single abort. That tells you something about our ground crew."

The work could be emotionally taxing to members of ground crews, who knew that lives depended on how well they did their jobs.

"When your plane didn't come back, it was an awfully empty feeling," said Upright. "I lost one fighter and we had no idea what happened to the pilot—until he showed up in the briefing room months later. He had come back through the underground. I was glad to see him and especially relieved to hear that the aircraft had performed well—it was flak that brought him down."

One flier wrote, "One can but wonder what the ground crew chief was thinking when his bird was one of the missing. My red-headed ground crew chief from North Carolina . . . cried the day someone taxied [his aircraft] into another aircraft and ended in a mass of flames and molten aluminum. What good had that 'midnight requisition of a part' from another squadron done? None! She was gone and so was a part of him."

Crew chief Carl Lose of the 94th Bomb Group denied developing sentiment for any particular aircraft, but commented, "The ones we like best were the good performers—as did the pilots."

Although sometimes ill-equipped, ground crews did the best they could with what they had. Occasionally, they resorted to "midnight requisitioning," when an otherwise unobtainable part was "absconded."

Replacement parts for aircraft, in short supply especially early in the war, were often removed from "hangar queens," aircraft that were cannibalized due to damage. Hangar queens promptly became engineless, often wingless, noseless and tailless—with only a battered fuselage remaining.

"My pilot, Captain Marony, came out often to check on the plane in his off-hours," said Al Giesting, 352nd Fighter Group crew chief. "He asked if work was going well and if we needed any parts that he could use his rank to help us get."

Some tools were scarce as well. "We didn't have all the proper tools," added Kuest. "We had to improvise, so a lot of things were done with brute strength and awkwardness."

Early in the war, each ground crew was assigned one plane to service. As the war effort went into full swing, and US

"Our crew chief's one ambition was to fly a mission. He wanted to see flak and fighters, but he wanted a written guarantee that he would get back. Unfortunately, we couldn't give him such a guarantee."
—Ralph Price, 381st Bomb Group (H)

"P-51s had a lot of spark plug trouble. The main reason seemed to be the fuel—150 octane fuel with a lot of additives that fouled the plugs. Especially the front two on the exhaust bank. If the motor had a miss in it, the first things you'd check were those two spark plugs. Often you'd put in a couple new ones, run 'er up again, and it'd be all right."
—Al Giesting, 352nd Fighter Group

production of warplanes skyrocketed, the Eighth Air Force received skyfuls of new aircraft. Strangely, however, ground crew numbers remained quite constant.

"Sometime in 1944, our group doubled its planes," Leroy Kuest continued. "Then we had to service two planes." One government publication of the day noted, "The reason that they are able to do twice the amount of work is because they have steadily stepped up their efficiency as they added to their experience." Kuest conciliated, "Somehow we managed."

"Sometimes planes were flown even if they were a little shaky because they wanted maximum effort," commented Giesting. "You'd give it the best maintenance you could with the time you had."

Toiling feverishly through the night to repair damage from the previous mission, mechanics sometimes were frustrated for hours by a malfunction whose source couldn't be pinpointed. Then, sometimes just before dawn when the crew chief would be forced to a red "X" (meaning the airplane was unflyable and in its own esoteric way, a sense of defeat on this side of the air front), the trouble was found and fixed.

Specialists

Along with the engineering section's crews, others performed an array of specialized tasks on a group's aircraft.

For instance, while it was the engineering section's mechanics who changed engines, it was the sub-depot's mechanics who rebuilt them. And there were others specially trained for maintaining radar, radio compasses, bombsights, and the rest of the aerial arsenal. Still others were charged with replenishing oxygen tanks, filling fuel tanks and patching holes in aircraft.

Sheet metal crews swiftly patched the hundreds of holes found in the metallic skins of aircraft—testimony to the hazards of flying over flak batteries. John Pendleton, 466th Bomb Group sheet metal specialist, recalled the precarious side of his work:

"Most of the time mechanics removed the parts and brought them to [the sheet metal/welding shack] for repair. But when the group needed every B-24 possible for the next mission, we did our work without taking the parts off. If I needed to weld aluminum cover plates over flak holes [close to wing gas tanks],

A Cletrac lowers worn radial engine while new Studebaker-made Cyclone engines in crates await as replacements in background. 94th BGMA

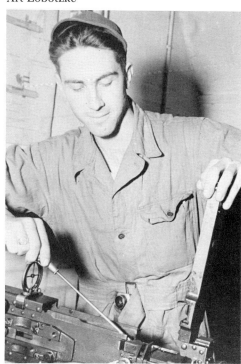

Engine overhaul and major repairs were done on an assembly-line-like process at air depots. Art Lobotzke

Gassers fill the tanks of a 352nd Fighter Group Mustang. John Campbell

everyone left the area. It was lonesome out there until I shut off the acetylene torch fire of the gas welder. Then everyone returned and resumed work. This saved pulling an engine and having the aircraft out of service for 24 to 36 hours."

Oliver La Rouche summarized his nightly routine with the 93rd Bomb Group by saying, "I . . . went around in a Jeep from 10 P.M. to 3 A.M. adjusting and repairing radar."

Bill Weith of the 357th Fighter Group worked in a unit of about twenty men, "mostly specialists in some phase of aircraft maintenance such as instruments, electrical systems, propellers, engines, etc." All these contributed to the effort that airmen would have every possible advantage in successfully completing their missions.

Like the mechanics, specialists often improvised in the face of shortages. "We were never advised [in the United States] about what or how much to take for supplies," explained Pendleton. "Assumed we'd be able to order from a central supply depot. But when we ran out of welding rod, we were out. We had to cut up pieces of the barbed wire entanglement surrounding the base. We removed the barbs and used it as welding rods."

In its operational lifetime, a bomber or fighter might return repeatedly from missions with hydraulic lines severed, an engine ailing, whole sections of wings and stabilizers torn away, bullet and flak holes scattered from nose to tail. Often that aircraft was back on line for the next mission, and it was due to the conscientious efforts of the men who worked all night on the flight line.

Gassing up

Based on distance to target, fuel loads had to be calculated and passed ultimately to "gassers," who drove 4,000 gallon tank trucks. The "big gas birds" typically were gassed up shortly after their arrival from the previous mission. But almost invariably, gassers were directed to remove a few hundred gallons, or if it was to be a deep penetration, pump more into the wings. Fighters were given a full measure of fuel in external belly or wing tanks to enable them to fly deep penetrations.

"On the long missions, wingtip tanks had to be filled," recalled Kuest. "Two ground crewman always assisted the gas truck driver as he went from plane to plane, as always, in the dark. Sometimes this would take two or three hours, depending on how many planes the group planned to put up that day."

An oxygen truck usually followed close behind the gasser. Oxygen was replenished in aircraft oxygen containers.

As aircraft preparations neared conclusion, a photo specialist arrived to install cameras. In bombers, he lifted radio room floor boards and installed the camera in mounts and activated an internal heater so that the shutter functioned at high altitude. In fighters, trigger-activated gun cameras in the wings were readied for action.

"One early morning, during routine preflight, our B-17's number three engine caught fire. Our crew chief shut all engines off and leaped out of the forward hatch. He didn't wait for the props to quit turning and stepped into one—killed him instantly."
—Leroy Kuest, 94th Bomb Group (H)

Driver and gas wagon with capacity of 4,000 US gallons fill the tanks of a 351st Bomb Group B-17. (B-17s and B-24s each held about 2,500 gallons.) Norm Schleitwiler

Preflight

Whether ground crew mechanics had spent an entire night with their aircraft or had the good fortune of tackling only minor routine maintenance, they needed to preflight the aircraft, completing a hundred last-minute checks as dawn was breaking.

Typical preflight procedures sounded like this:

"Set on preflight."
"Weight and balance."
"Check."
"Fuel transfer valves and switch."

"Right."
"Intercoolers."
"Check."
"Gyros."
"Check—left and right."
"Fuel shutoff switches."
"OK."
"Gear switch."
"Neutral."
"Cowl flaps—open right."
"Open left and locked."
"Idle cutoff."
"Check."
"Throttle."
"Check."
"High rpm."
"Check."
"Auto pilot."
"Off."
"De-icers and anti-icers, wing and prop."
"Off."
"Cabin heat."
"Off."
"Generators."
"Check."
"All set to fire up."
"Master switches."
"On."
"Battery switches and inverters."
"On and check."
"Reset."
"Booster pumps, pressure."
"On and check."
"Carburetor coolers."
"Open."

This morning one of the ships on a near by field blew up. It was started by a fire in the ball turret which exploded the oxygen which in turn exploded the gasoline & bomb load. One man was killed

—Leroy Kuest,
September 3, 1943
diary entry

"Fuel quantity."

"Check."

"Start engines."

"Energize."

"Mesh!"

Propellers rotated slowly through cold night air until, suddenly, the engine belched a cloud of blue exhaust as it clanked to life.

Pre-mission jitters

Ground personnel preparing for the next morning's mission weren't necessarily the only ones awake. Some fliers endured sleepless hours pondering a million possible (tragic) fates. "Nights before missions were anxious," said Preston Clark. "I resigned myself to the worst, but hoped for the best."

"The night before my first mission was rough," recalled Ray Patulski. "I got very little sleep. After I had a few missions under my belt, sleeping was a little better. Then, as I neared the end of my tour, I became more nervous again. . . ."

Lloyd Nelson said: "There was a lot of restlessness, especially if your previous mission was a rough one. I bunked next to my crew's engineer and by morning, there'd be a lot of cigarette butts on the floor between us. Past missions were glued in your head—you didn't forget any of them if they were bad."

G. W. Pederson commented: "On nights when a mission alert was on, I usually would not sleep at all. If I did it was just for a short three minutes at a time—not very restful sleep. What could happen the next day ran constantly through my mind."

Rude awakenings and preparation for flight

Bernarr Cresap recounted the details of wake-up on a mission morning:

"You will be rudely awakened by the squadron CQ (charge-of-quarters) standing over you and saying, 'Are you Bernarr Cresap?' He knows that you are Bernarr Cresap, but he wants to be sure you know it. At 3:30 A.M., who can be sure?

"You somewhat reluctantly discover that you are who you are and you finally admit it. He says, 'You know you are flying a mission today.' He knows it and you know it, but it's probably a good idea for the two of you to agree on it. You say, 'Yes, I know.' He says, 'Be sure to sign in at the orderly room before you leave the squadron area.'

—Harold Henslin,
February 10 and 18, 1944
letters to family

"He goes to the next bed. . . .

"You go to the washroom and you shave carefully and closely because you are going to be wearing an oxygen mask, probably for several hours. A stubble of beard under that mask can produce a torture of irritation you will remember for a long time."

Phil Garey described getting dressed, gunner-style:

"I dressed in long johns, two pairs of socks (cotton and wool), electric slippers, sheepskin-lined boots, an electric flying suit, a parka, chest high sheepskin pants, silk gloves, electric gloves, elbow high gauntlets, a scarf, a skull cap, and leather helmet.

"After I was in the aircraft, I donned my Mae West, my back pack parachute, and after I had crawled back to the tail and was in position, someone came back and helped me on with my armor, which consisted of back and chest sections with groin and thigh pieces attached and a steel helmet."

It was as a wartime editorial in the *New York Times* asserted about a former sword maker in London that specialized in body armor for airmen: "Thus the cycle rolls around again, and American fighters, like the Yank at King Arthur's Court, find themselves back in medieval armor. . . ."

Chow

Some fliers dabbled with their food and ate little—not necessarily because of its quality, but because of the imminent mission. If some looked like they hadn't slept a wink, they probably hadn't. Uncertainty gnawed at them.

"Briefings were often at three or four A.M.," said Fred Bartz, 306th Bomb Group cook, "so we were up and ready for them. Typically, we were at the mess hall at two o'clock and didn't leave until three in the afternoon. On each shift, we had a mess officer, a mess sergeant and eight cooks to feed three thousand."

And the breakfast cuisine? "Everything was either dehydrated or frozen," Bartz replied. "Once a month, we had 'fresh eggs'—eggs that had been in cold storage for three to four months." But, at least, they weren't the powdered eggs that many claim "could gag a buzzard."

"The cold storage eggs went over pretty well, compared to the powdered eggs. They didn't like them, but they ate them. We had a lot of English-grown foods, like brussels sprouts," which also were none too popular.

Along with eggs, real or powdered, was typically cold cereal, french toast or flapjacks, juice and strong coffee.

"You could eat pretty much all you wanted, but you had to eat all you took," Bartz continued. "Someone would check to see that you didn't leave anything on your plate. Most of the food was shipped over from the States and they didn't want waste."

Mission briefing

Military police stood on either side of the briefing room doors, while fliers began to congregate outside. They continued to mull among themselves the nagging question that's persisted since the mission alert was issued: "Where's the target?"

"Before briefing, fliers often pumped us [in the intelligence section] for information about the target," said Francis Cunningham, 466th Bomb Group intelligence NCO. "They were understandably anxious to find out about where they'd be going."

Lester Rentmeester recounted briefings:

"Our briefing room [at Bassingbourn] had a stage and seats like a small movie theater. You had to show your pass to MPs at the door, but you weren't allowed

An army moves on its stomach—whether "moves" means slithering inch by inch or flying at 25,000 feet. 94th BGMA

Oh yes, that's one thing about the days we go on missions. We always get a super breakfast—real storage eggs & sometimes wheat cakes. Also, along with our escape kit we are rationed one chocolate bar to each flight.

—Jack Kirschbraun,
March 15, 1944
letter to family

Hoisting bomb on sling—tense, dangerous work that often had to be undone when the *mission was cancelled.* 8th Photo Tech Squadron

to take any identification on the mission outside of dog tags and [evasion] photos."

As they entered the briefing room, eyes were drawn to the sheet-covered map. Some ventured guesses about the target, based on where the pinheads protruded in the cloth.

C. L. Anderson said: "When they pulled the curtain back and it was a major target, you'd hear *ooos* and *ahs*. Anyone who said he wasn't frightened of the missions either had something wrong mentally or they were the world's biggest liars."

"When they raised the curtain and the map was all red (with ribbon), you knew someone would die," said Ed Pickering.

Airmen were told what to expect on a mission: what the weather would be, where heavy concentrations of flak batteries were, where German fighters might attack, and for bomber crews, where and when escorts would join them, and for fighter pilots, where and when they would rendezvous with bombers or what zone they would cover.

Robert Bieck commented:

"During the winter months, almost everyone had a cold and coughed profusely during the briefing. The coughing was invariably heightened by crew member smoking.

"Briefings were always tense, regardless of the target. It was dramatic when the curtains were parted and we could see the huge map of Europe and the ribbon that ran from our base to the day's target. If the target was in northern France, it spawned some light-hearted cackling. If that ribbon ran all the way to Stettin, Brux, Munich, Posen, etc., you would hear a groan like a cow in labor.

"Some briefers came off better than others. Colonel Ramsey Potts [453rd Bomb Group CO], a genuine air hero, always came on strong and with a sense of humor. Concluding a briefing on Stettin, he announced that time was running short, and anyone who was late to his plane couldn't go. The crews actually laughed.

"I noted that chaplains never had much business if the raid was to northern France. But if we had a deep penetration, their little rooms simply weren't big enough."

"After we heard what weather was likely," said Bob Strehlow, "then our CO would walk on to the stage and deliver a pep talk: 'Give 'er hell—everything you've got!'"

Crucifixion painting on wall at Hethel, once the home of the 389th Bomb Group. Trevor Austin

"There was always fear in the cockpit and one time there was pure panic when we were under fighter attack and other B-17s in our squadron nearly rammed us. On the first couple of missions, I did all the flying and I noticed my copilot fidgeting. I realized he didn't have enough to do. Bombardiers and copilots had a greater tendency to want to stop flying than the rest—and I think it was because they had time to worry. After that we switched off flying every fifteen minutes. Concentrating on the task at hand definitely helps."
—Lester Rentmeester, 91st Bomb Group (H)

James Goodson recalled fighter pilot briefings: "Our briefings were short and to the point. A fighter pilot's actions depend on the situation at the time [in flight], to which he must react fast and often on his own initiative."

Briefing ended with a time-tick, as watches were synchronized. To help ease tensions, fliers found humor where they could. "We always laughed at the guy we called the 'Hack Officer,'" recalled Phil Garey. "We made up stories about him leaving his warm bed and girlfriend to rush down to briefing. Then he'd wait impatiently for his turn for glory to come up. At that moment he'd pop up in front of us and start the countdown to set our watches: 'In ten seconds it will be exactly 0450 hours. 9, 8, 7, 6, 5, 4, 3, 2, 1, HACK!' Then back to his warm bed. In reality, he had many duties. . . ."

Chaplains gave benediction after the briefing. At Flixton, John Gannon, 446th Bomb Group chaplain, did not stress in his message the idea of victory over an enemy, but reaffirmed the thought that God was with them always—on the ground and in the air.

To the hardstands

After briefings, fliers clambered aboard six-by-six trucks with group numbers stencilled on the tailgate and rode to their ships.

Garey said: "When we left our briefing and got to the aircraft, the ground crew would be there waiting for us, telling us this and that about the plane. We sometimes waited for takeoff in the ground crew's half-buried hut, drinking coffee and reading week-old British newspapers."

"The tenseness in crews really showed at the hardstands," Bieck said. "After we had checked all our equipment, we usually had about forty-five minutes to sit around and wait for the flare that signaled 'start engines.' One crew member I knew would vomit incessantly. Some would go into a shell of silence. And some would talk—too much."

Takeoff

Finally, around daybreak, ground crewmen pulled aside wheel-chocks. On bomber stations, a single, garish-colored, war-weary bomber started the procession, then other bombers lurched from their hardstands to line up single-file on perimeter tracks until the field reached a crescendo of roaring, taxiing aircraft. On fighter stations, aircraft lined up for takeoff, two or more abreast.

From the tower or checkered control vehicle, a flare or green wink of an Aldis lamp signaled the first plane to begin its

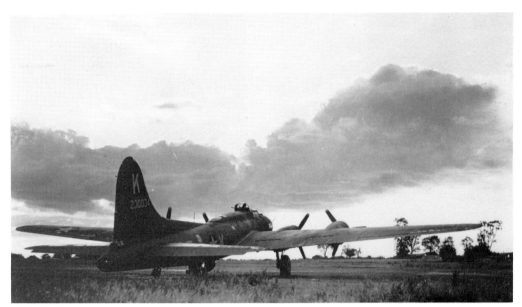

After the ground crews' night of work, a B-17F of the 379th Bomb Group awaits its aircrew. 8th Photo Tech Squadron

"My time of great fear in combat was from briefing until I got back! If someone said they were not afraid, they were either lying or something was wrong with them."
—C. L. Anderson, 390th Bomb Group (H)

trek down the runway—and the mission was under way.

Then it was the ground crews' time for rest. "After we watched our planes take off," Kuest commented, "we went to chow and then back to the barracks to get some sleep. We would usually know their ETA (estimated time of arrival) in the afternoon, so we would get back to the hardstand by then to sweat our planes in." Thus, the ground echelon sustained a perpetual cycle of all-out effort to "keep 'em flying."

Each bomber that lumbered down the runway, heaving its thirty-plus tons off the runway, and each fighter that lifted smoothly into the sky represented hundreds of man-hours in preparation. And every aircraft put in the air for a mission carried with it the hopes, anxieties, sweat, cursing, patience and ingenuity of hundreds of nameless men.

Crew of Messie Bessie *working off premission tension. The crew was the first 418th Squadron crew of the Bloody Hundredth to complete 25 missions.* 100th BG via Harry Crosby

The English

This happy breed of men, this little world,
This precious stone set in the silver sea. . . .

—William Shakespeare, *Richard II*

The Eighth Air Force was the vanguard for American forces in the European Theater. Before the Eighth's arrival, rural England's residents had scarcely seen an American, let alone these high-spirited Yanks eventually to number more than 200,000 at peak operating strength.

Squadron after squadron of American aircraft roared low over villages as they approached airfields. Convoys incessantly rumbled past houses and farms with loads of ordnance and aviation gasoline.

Eighth Air Force historian Roger Freeman noted, "In villages where an American airfield was created, the impact was severe because the newcomers outnumbered the villagers, perhaps a hundred to one."

Contrasting cultures

Suddenly, the countryside was inundated with young Americans "cutting a rug" and unconsciously subjecting the local populace to a crash course in American youth culture — or perhaps, culture *shock*. They brought with them a whole new set of manners, new catch phrases and a new lifestyle to an England gone drab and austere after several years of war.

Things acceptable in the United States sometimes were frowned upon here. Ruby Kranz, a teenager during the war, remembered with good humor how she was scandalized at the sight of airmen sitting on the steps of her church: "I was shocked. Sitting on our church steps was never done in High Wycombe. At the time it seemed like a desecration! When a girlfriend and I stopped to inquire about it, they explained, 'It's just something to do—a place where we can sit and look. And besides, there's no signs.'"

There is more than one report that artwork painted on the noses of aircraft got crews in trouble. In one incident involving a newly arrived bombardment group, a B-24 with nose-art depicting a gracefully posed lady, albeit naked, had flown low over a village in an approach to its home field after a mission. Aghast at the "abomination," townspeople protested emphatically, citing that it was in plain view of everyone. The group commander, sensitive about first impressions, ordered them to paint clothes on her. Of course, this order set no precedent. Thousands of aircraft would promulgate distinctive artwork, many of which involved the female form. Similar conflicts arose with artwork painted on the backs of flight jackets worn on liberty.

"My sisters and I woke up and went outside in the early morning. We found 'tinsel' hanging on everything—the trees, the fences, the house, and the wood pile. We also found what we called angel hair—like people sometimes put on Christmas trees. The morning was so pretty because there was a heavy dew. It looked like cobwebs glistening with dew drops. We picked up the stuff and wondered at first where it had come from. The adults told us that the Germans had flown over."
—Ruby Kranz, Buckinghamshire youth (referring to chaff dropped to confuse Allied radar)

Cambridge: Our Lady and the English Martyrs Church steeple.

This currency table is from A Short Guide To Great Britain. GIs were given this booklet, produced by the War and Navy departments, as they arrived in the United Kingdom. The booklet offered down-to-earth facts about the land they were entering.

TABLE OF BRITISH CURRENCY

Copper Coins

Symbol	Name	British value	American value (approximate)
¼d.	farthing (rare)	¼ penny	½ cent.
½d.	halfpenny ("hay-p'ny")	½ penny	1 cent.
1d.	penny	1 penny	2 cents.
3d.	threepence ("thruppence" or "thrup-'ny bit"; rare).	3 pence	5 cents.

Silver Coins

Symbol	Name	British value	American value (approximate)
3d.	threepence ("thruppence" or "thrup-'ny bit"; not common in cities).	3 pence	5 cents.
6d.	sixpence	6 pence	10 cents.
1s.	shilling (or "bob")	12 pence	20 cents.
2s.	florin (fairly rare)	2 shillings	40 cents.
2s. 6d.	half crown (or "two and six").	2½ shillings	50 cents.
5s.	crown (rare)	5 shillings	$1.00.

Paper Currency

Symbol	Name	British value	American value (approximate)
10s.	10-shilling note	10 shillings (or ½ pound).	$2.00
1	pound note	20 shillings	$4.00.
5	5-pound note	5 pounds	$20.00.

There were basic differences in nature between the British and Americans. The British had a tendency to be reserved and Americans were, well, the opposite. In an effort to bridge the culture gap, *Meet the Americans* (a publication produced by Britain's Army Bureau of Current Affairs) explains that Americans "... delight in tall tales, wordy battle full of cross-talk, wisecracks and jeering remarks which sound, and are meant to sound (but not to be) fantastically offensive." An inference was that "British people habitually understate," but that when an American wanted to be friendly, he talked about his home and about himself. The publication suggested that this type of conversation was perfectly natural in Americans' minds. But some conservative Englishmen took it as a sign of insolence.

Some Britons groused about Americans being "overpaid, overbearing, oversexed and over here." They did earn more money than their British counterparts. In fact, a USAAF sergeant on flight pay

There isn't a popular American song, actor, actress or NUT that these English don't know about. Their conception of the American way of life is absurdly funny. They still think the west is wild & that we *all* live out in the open air (that last is partly due to our complexion — we are 70 times as ruddy & dark in complexion due to the scarcity of sunshine? here, the English have white, pale faces — & when they do spend time out of doors - their faces look just as white but there's a red spot on their cheek which resembles poorly-applied rouge.) They believe what they see in the movies about us & look horrified when I tell them: "I'm from Chicago". I now begin a conversation like this: "I'm a gangster" — sure enough they know where I live, & it doesn't frighten them nearly so much waiting in suspense - to see whether I'll whip out a machine gun or not.

—Jack Kirschbraun,
March 18, 1944
letter to sister

"I didn't find that differences in British culture were a matter of inferiority or superiority. They were just differences."
—John Houk, 92nd Bomb Group (H)

"The English were by then well used to the many nationalities who were in their country. The most notable thing about American airmen [on initial impression] was that the uniform was far better tailored than those of British servicemen."
—Roger Freeman, Eighth Air Force historian

"I left a piece of potato and a slice of bread on my plate. The waitress asked what was wrong. When I told her that I had eaten all that I wanted, her immediate question was, 'Why did your order it if you were not going to eat it all?'"
—Wilton Fremaux, 379th Bomb Group (H)

"The closest village [the village of Eye] could almost be considered part of the base. I never spent much time in Eye, because there wasn't much there. If we had a few hours off, we'd bicycle up to Diss, on the main railway between Ipswich and Norwich, which took you into London. At Diss, you could always have fish and chips and beans and cheeses. And if you got [to] the pub early enough, you might be able to have a bitter or ale."
—Ray Patulski, 490th Bomb Group (H)

earned as much as a major in the British land army. (But what they'll tell you today is that Britain's soldiers simply weren't paid enough—not that Americans were overpaid.) And there was no doubt that Americans were "over here,"—eventually numbering over 1.5 million combined total forces prior to D-day. As for the other two, it was strictly a matter of opinion.

Even before Americans overcame the reputation of being "big talkers" and little doers, the general attitude was tolerance because the English were so accustomed to seeing a kaleidoscope of foreign uniforms. John Mills, then a youth living near Bedford, explained: "In the preceding three years, we had seen Poles, Frenchmen, Dutchmen, Norwegians, and Belgians. Americans arrived in larger numbers, but they were just more foreign servicemen. They were all, whatever nationality, our allies. They were welcomed as such."

Mere tolerance gave way to warm cordiality. Eventually few could resist their simplicity of heart. "They became *our* boys in just the same way as British

soldiers," Mills continued. "Losses were deplored, whether they were of USAAF or RAF."

"Around Christmastime," mused John Houk, "I sat in the Exchange Hotel in Wellingborough having a pint. I turned to someone next to me and asked, 'What is the significance of Boxing Day?' [In a nutshell, Boxing Day is the day after Christmas, when one gives away unneeded presents to the postman, barmaid, and so on—you *box* the gift.] This

SOME IMPORTANT DO'S AND DON'TS

BE FRIENDLY—but don't intrude anywhere it seems you are not wanted. You will find the British money system easier than you think. A little study beforehand on shipboard will make it still easier.

You are higher paid than the British "Tommy." Don't rub it in. Play fair with him. He can be a pal in need.

Don't show off or brag or bluster—"swank" as the British say. If somebody looks in your direction and says, "He's chucking his weight about," you can be pretty sure you're off base. That's the time to pull in your ears.

If you are invited to eat with a family don't eat too much. Otherwise you may eat up their weekly rations.

Don't make fun of British speech or accents. You sound just as funny to them but they will be too polite to show it.

Avoid comments on the British Government or politics.

Don't try to tell the British that America won the last war or make wisecracks about the war debts or about British defeats in this war.

NEVER criticize the King or Queen.

Don't criticize the food, beer, or cigarettes to the British. Remember they have been at war since 1939.

Use common sense on all occasions. By your conduct you have great power to bring about a better understanding between the two countries after the war is over.

You will soon find yourself among a kindly, quiet, hard-working people who have been living under a strain such as few people in the world have ever known. In your dealings with them, let this be your slogan:

*It is always impolite to criticize your hosts;
it is militarily stupid to criticize your allies.*

"Important do's and don'ts" page from A Short Guide To Great Britain.

question led to a wholesale examination of history and everybody in the pub was involved—something that wouldn't typically happen at home. It took several hours as everyone put in his contribution to the historical meaning of Boxing Day."

English youngsters: immediate, enthusiastic fans

While it might have taken time for the English men and women to become accustomed to their new neighbors, the local youngsters were instantly enamored by the Yanks, who became the subject of great mystique. They brought not only impressive aircraft, but also pockets filled with candy and gum and other treasures freely given. The omnipresent phrase, "Gum, chum?" spoken in the high and persistent voices of village urchins yielded various brands of gum: "Juicy Fruit, Beechnut, Dentyne, Beemans and later on, Orbit," as Englishman Gerry Darnell recalled.

A joke in England was that so much American chewing gum had been tossed in the fountains of London's Trafalgar Square that pigeons were laying rubber eggs.

Youngsters came to know the local airfield's planes by nickname and chose their favorites. To the youngsters, avidly

"At the beginning of the war, all the signposts disappeared and sometimes incorrect ones were put in place of them," said Rudy Kranz, a Buckinghamshire youth. 100th BG

observing the activity around the hardstands, the airmen and aircraft represented all the power and glamor in the world, in much the same way the airmen themselves had been caught up in the mystique of World War I and postwar aviation.

Darnell regularly cycled from school to watch bombers come back to Poding-

"The British are gutsy people. The hardships they suffered were unbelievable and yet they kept going." —Ralph Price, 381st Bomb Group (H)

General Doolittle converses with the King and Queen of England outside Eighth Air Force Headquarters at High Wycombe. 8th Photo Tech Squadron

An officer explains the workings of a B–17 engine to a group of local boys. 94th BGMA

"I went into the underground during a buzz bomb attack. The English were cheerful, singing. Whole families were huddled together making the best of it."
—Phil Garey, 94th Bomb Group (H)

"Morale was always high. Although it was obvious to everyone that Britain was completely unprepared for war and that Germany had superiority, particularly in the air, no one doubted that the Allies would win. This was true even in the darkest days of the Battle of Britain."
—James Goodson, 4th Fighter Group

"Sometimes we'd be awakened by earth-shaking explosions—accidents at the bases either in bombing up or taking off on missions."
—John Mills, Bedfordshire youth

"The noise over two or three hours in the early morning was incessant."
—Roger Freeman

"We often practice-fired our .45 caliber pistols on the range until a nearby farmer protested that [as a result] his cows stopped giving milk."
—Glen Lunde, 93rd Bomb Group (H)

A funny item that the English crave is gum, pronounced without the "U", making it sound like "oo" as in "you." When I visited Stone, the children there were particularly enthusiastic over the possibility of getting a stick of gum.

—Jack Kirschbraun,
February 16, 1944
letter to sister

ton. "When we counted the aircraft back in after a mission," he said, "we used to particularly look for those whose individual identification letters on the fin below the triangle-B coincided with the initials of our Christian names."

John Archer, fourteen years old during the American "invasion," commented:

"My most vivid memory of the war is the early morning takeoffs of the B–17s and B–24s, their forming up in formations, and then the lull after they had departed. The thought was always there—how many wouldn't return today?

"There were a ring of landing lights one mile from each base, which were turned on just before the mission returned. One such light, mounted on a pole, was located in our garden. From that, we always knew when to expect the group back.

"In high winds, I watched B–24s approach sideways, their noses too low for comfort. They'd land, burning rubber and trailing smoke.

"I would spend hours around the bases. There was an American base every few miles. One could bicycle around several on a Sunday afternoon. The closest to my home, Hardwick (93rd BG), was just twenty minutes up the road. I would watch the ground crews working on the B–24s named *Ball of Fire, Shoot Luke, Hellsapoppin'*, and others. . . . They became very much a part of our lives. Standing by the perimeter fence it was easy to see if a certain aircraft had failed to return."

Many English youngsters had never known anything but the lean living of

British children attend a party at Rougham. 94th BGMA

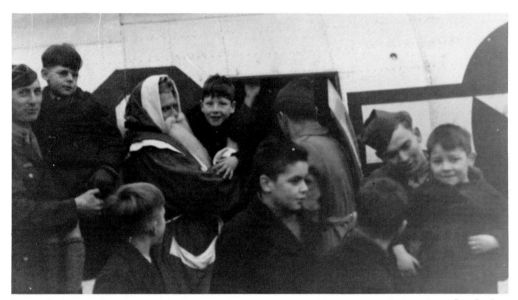

Instead of a reindeer-powered sleigh, Santa's mode of transportation in 1944 is a 94th Bomb Group's B-17. He arrived at other stations that year in many types of aircraft and vehicles, including B-24s, P-51s, P-47s and jeeps. 94th BGMA

"I was fascinated with England. California in the 1940s was less than 100 years from the Gold Rush. Here I was in England where the newer buildings were older than the oldest structure in California. I explored the ruins of the abbey at Bury St. Edmunds. I couldn't believe that this was the place where the knights had drawn up their demands to King John that had resulted in the Magna Carta. I returned from my explorations and said, 'Hey guys. What I saw today!' And the response shot back was, 'What'd she look like?'"
—Phil Garey, 94th Bomb Group (H)

war. Horham resident Alan Johnson said, "Before I went to parties on base at Horham, I had never seen oranges, apples, bananas, or ice cream."

Kinship flourishes

To the newcomers, the English looked threadbare—worn thin by years of rationing and shortages. Yanks shared everything they had, including their indefatigable, youthful spirit—youthful as America herself relative to her long-standing, war-weary, conservative sister, Great Britain. "Parachutes disappeared from air bases and reappeared in homes of civilians, whose clothing rations were severely restricted," observed Barbara Pathe of the Red Cross. "Butter, meat, sugar, chocolate, coal and other items unobtainable by civilians also found their way into the homes of grateful civilians."

Lloyd Nelson said: "Kids from Old Buckenham and Attleborough often would come to pay us a visit and we always gave them treats. We liked them very much—especially one particular family of kids, whose mother did our laundry. We always felt sorry for the kids, so we paid more than she wanted. They had never seen popcorn before. I remember how big their eyes got when they saw it popping at a base party for the first time."

But the English gave back a greater share than they received.

"This nice lady offered us tea, cookies and cheese that we consumed in a few minutes," said Wilton Fremaux. "Too late we learned we had eaten her month's supply of cheese."

Joe Kendrick of the 904th Signal Company, recounted his brief contact with a farmer who worked the field just outside Alconbury's fence. "I asked him if

"I lived next door to a pub. You can imagine the bicycles from the base parked around this favorite watering hole. . . . In our yard stood two nice rose bushes. Many a 'button hole' was snatched during a warm summer evening."
—John Archer, Suffolk youth

Perhaps the first square meal this British youngster has enjoyed in a long time, served at an air station somewhere in England. Note American candy in foreground. 94th BGMA

"Restrooms on the line were regularly serviced by English 'honey bucket' collectors who wore dress suits and ties while at work. We never really understood their attire."
—John Pendleton, 466th Bomb Group (H)

"My aunt opened her pub, called the Carpenter's Arm, at five o'clock and by six all the glasses were gone. The pub was filled with Americans from the Eighth Air Force."
—Audrey Darnell, Bedfordshire youth

British double-deck bus, pulling its own source of fuel. The unit burns coal and creates fuel oil that is transferred to the fuel system of the bus. *Photo taken in Manchester.* Robert Neel

he kept chickens, because I needed some feathers to reflight my darts. He said he did. He agreed to leave some feathers for me at the base of a certain fence post. I never saw the farmer again, but a day or two later I checked the post and found a good supply of perfect feathers. Just one of the many kindnesses shown me by those wonderful British people."

"My father would have me bicycle up to the lonely guard on duty at one of the security posts and take him some home-baked sausage rolls and a bottle of beer," recalled John Archer.

Perhaps the greatest gift given to an American by the English was acceptance as one of their own. Invaluable was the kinship amidst the horrors of war, friends lost and home sickness. The English couldn't always provide much in the way of extravagant meals and other tangibles, but they offered what they had: a quiet refuge away from the stress of their duties, a listening ear and hospitable treatment. In short, a place like home.

A Short Guide to Great Britain cautioned, "If you are invited into a British home and the host exhorts you to 'eat up—there's plenty on the table,' go easy. It may be the family's ration for a whole week spread out to show their hospitality."

Thousands of English families opened their homes to Eighth Air Force people, posting notices in Red Cross Aeroclubs. For Christmas 1943, Saul Kupferman responded to an invitation "... by Don and Dot Nicholl, who lived in Bedford. It was one of the best things I've ever done in my life! They became 'my' family for the nearly eight months I was

> Another thing thats in minus quantities is citrus fruit. One RAF lad in Stranrear, Scotland, told me he'd not seen an orange in four years. What burns me up — is that I came with three dozen of same, and gave them away before I knew their value. You should have seen the mad scramble when I released the bag — man alive, the men looked like starved beasts.
>
> —Jack Kirschbraun,
> February 11, 1944
> letter to sister

in England. They shared their very meager rations with me, which I complemented by bringing goodies from the base. My family in the States sent little gift packages of hair ribbons, storybooks, and such to their seven-year-old daughter, Cindy, who had very little in the way of those. Anytime I had a pass I had an open invitation to stay with them." Kupferman credits the home atmosphere shared by the Nicholls as a factor in his survival during thirty missions with the 306th Bomb Group.

Bernarr Cresap, too, relishes the memory of hospitality, English style:

"I met an Englishman who made a vivid impression upon me. His name was Albert Good, a name which fitted him well. Our meeting occurred one evening when my friend and fellow gunnery instructor Staff Sergeant Urban Florin and I borrowed bicycles and rode over to the pub at Bildeston, a crossroads village located just off the air base at Rattlesden in Suffolk County. Florin, who belonged to the 711th Squadron, was already acquainted with Albert.

"Albert was a farmer of the sturdy Anglo-Saxon type. His face was ruddy and the slightly thinning hair was sandy. He was a favorite in the area, as many people in the pub greeted with, 'Hello Albert,' or 'Goodnight, Albert.' At closing time Albert mounted his bicycle and we mounted ours and rode the short distance from Bildeston to Albert's farm. He was a bachelor and must have been the end of a long line of farmers of his name.

Typical English town, in this case Baldock, seen by rail on the route from Eighth Air Force country to London.

"Farm houses in East Anglia are old, and Albert's was no exception. Some have literally endured for centuries. Beneath their thatched roofs, the old houses have a framework of oak, mostly old ship's timbers. Between the old beams is wattle and daub. [Wattle: bunches of hedge sticks bound together. Daub: clay, water, and cow's dung well mixed and long since hardened.] I was struck by the fact that the interior of the house was neatly whitewashed.

"The class system was something I had been unfamiliar with. I was dating a (British) Red Cross volunteer. She worked as a maid for a wealthy family. When I met the family, I felt very much looked down upon. I was an American officer, but was dating their hired help."
—John Ziebell, 357th Fighter Group

The glossary from A Short Guide To Great Britain.

GLOSSARY OF TERMS

aisle (theatre)—*gangway*
alcohol lamp—*spirit lamp*
ale—*beer, or bitter*
apartment—*flat*
apartment house—*block of flats*
ash can—*dust bin*
ashman—*dustman*
atomizer—*scent spray*
automobile—*motor car, or car*
baby carriage—*perambulator, or pram*
baggage—*luggage*
baggage car—*luggage van*
bakery—*baker's shop*
bathrobe—*dressing gown*
bartender—*barman, or potman*
bathtub—*bath*
battery (automobile)—*accumulator*
beach—*seaside*
beer—*lager*
bill (money)—*banknote, or note*
billboard—*hoarding*
biscuit—*scone, or tea cake*
bouncer—*chucker out*
bowling alley—*skittle alley*
broiled (meat)—*grilled*
business suit—*lounge suit*
call up—*ring up*
candy (hard)—*boiled sweets*

candy store—*sweet shop*
cane—*stick*
can opener—*tin opener, or key*
carom (billiards)—*cannon*
chain store—*multiple shop*
check baggage—*register luggage*
checkers (game)—*draughts*
chickenyard—*fowl run*
cigarette butt—*cigarette end*
closed season (for game)—*close season*
conductor—*guard*
closet—*cupboard*
coal oil—*paraffin*
collar button—*collar stud*
cookie—*biscuit*
cop—*bobby*
corn—*maize, or Indian corn*
cornmeal—*Indian meal*
cotton (absorbent)—*cotton wool*
cracker—*biscuit (unsweetened)*
daylight-saving time—*summer time*
deck (of cards)—*pack*
derby (hat)—*bowler, or hard hat*
dessert—*sweet*
dishpan—*washing-up bowl*
drawers (men's)—*pants*
druggist—*chemist*

drug store—*chemist's shop*
drygoods store—*draper's shop*
elevator—*lift*
fender (automobile)—*wing, or mudguard*
fish dealer—*fishmonger*
five-and-ten (store)—*bazaar*
floorwalker—*shopwalker*
frame house—*wooden house*
fruit seller (or dealer)—*fruiterer*
fruit store—*fruiterer's*
fresh fruit—*dessert (at the end of a meal)*
french fried potatoes—*chips*
freight car—*goods wagon*
garters (men's)—*sock suspenders*
gasoline, or gas—*petrol*
gear shift (automobile)—*gear lever*
generator (automobile)—*dynamo*
ground wire (radio)—*earth wire*
guv—*bloke, fellow*
haberdashery—*men's wear*
hardware—*ironmongery*
headliner (vaudeville)—*topliner*
highball—*whiskey and soda*
hood (automobile)—*bonnet*
huckster—*coster, or hawker*
hunting—*shooting*
ill, sick—*ill, queer*
instalment plan—*hire-purchase system, or hire system*
intermission—*interval*
janitor—*caretaker, or porter*
junk—*rubbish*

lawyer—*solicitor*
legal holiday—*bank holiday*
line up—*queue up*
living room—*sitting room*
lobby (theatre)—*foyer, or entrance hall*
long distance (telephone)—*trunks*
low gear (automobile)—*first speed*
mail a letter—*post a letter*
mail box—*pillar box*
marriage certificate—*marriage lines*
molasses—*black treacle*
monkey wrench—*screw spanner*
movie house—*cinema*
movies—*flicks*
mucilage—*gum*
muffler (automobile)—*silencer*
necktie—*tie*
newsstand—*kiosk*
oatmeal (boiled)—*porridge*
oil pan (automobile)—*sump*
okay—*righto*
orchestra seats—*stalls*
package—*parcel*
pebbly beach—*shingle*
phonograph—*gramophone*
pie (fruit)—*tart*
pitcher—*jug*
poolroom—*billiards saloon*
potato chips—*crisps*
private hospital—*nursing home*
push cart—*barrow*
race track—*race course*

radio—*wireless*
railway car—*railway carriage*
raincoat—*mackintosh, or mac, or waterproof*
roadster (automobile)—*two-seater*
roast (of meat)—*joint*
roller coaster—*switchback-railway*
rolling grasslands—*downs*
round trip—*return trip*
roomer—*lodger*
rooster—*cock, or cockerel*
rubbers—*galoshes*
rumble seat—*dickey*
run (in a stocking)—*ladder*
saloon—*public house, or pub*
scallion—*spring onion*
scrambled eggs—*buttered eggs*
second floor—*first floor*
sedan (automobile)—*saloon car*
sewerage (house)—*drains*
shoestring—*bootlace, or shoelace*
shot (athletics)—*weight*
shoulder (of road)—*verge*
rubberneck wagon—*char-a-banc*
silverware—*plate*
slacks—*bags*
sled—*sledge*
smoked herring—*kipper*
soda biscuit (or cracker)—*cream-cracker*
soft drinks—*minerals*
spark plug—*sparking-plug*
spigot (or faucet)—*tap*
squash—*vegetable marrow*

stairway—*staircase, or stairs*
string bean—*French-bean*
store—*shop*
subway—*underground*
sugar-bowl—*sugar-basin*
suspenders (men's)—*braces*
sweater—*pull-over*
syrup—*treacle*
taffy—*toffee*
taxi stand—*cab rank*
telegram—*wire*
tenderloin (of beef)—*under-cut, or fillet*
ten pins—*nine pins*
thumb-tack—*drawing pin*
ticket office—*booking office*
toilet—*lavatory, closet*
top (automobile)—*hood*
transom (of door)—*fanlight*
trolley—*tram*
truck—*lorry*
undershirt—*vest, or singlet*
union-suit—*combinations*
vaudeville—*variety*
vaudeville theatre—*music hall*
vest—*waistcoat*
vomit—*be sick*
washbowl—*washbasin*
washrag—*face cloth*
washstand—*wash-hand stand*
water heater—*geyser*
window shade—*blind*
"you're connected"—"you're through" (telephone)*
windshield (automobile)—*windscreen*

"The first thing was more ale, several bottles of which Albert had secured by special dispensation of the innkeeper. After all, Albert had guests.

"While Florin and I talked and drank, our host set about to prepare a late evening snack for us. In short order we had before us delicious fried eggs and toast and, of course, more ale to wash it down. Fresh eggs were a delicacy, quite in contrast with our regular GI fare of powdered eggs.

"Albert talked and Florin and I were quite content to listen. His goodwill toward us strangers in his native land was genuine. He was best acquainted with members of the 711th Bomb Squadron, and he spoke of many of them by name. Some whom he had entertained had since been shot down over Germany.

"He was justifiably proud of having been the host to high officers of the squadron in the same manner in which he entertained Florin and me. I felt warm inside that he might consider myself at least on the periphery of Albert's many American friends."

Vivid memories: inescapable noise and formations that filled the sky

Of all the changes accompanying the Eighth Air Force invasion, noise is perhaps the most prevalent memory. "Thundering noise is what first comes to mind," said Percy Kindred, a Framlingham farmer. "The middle of the day was the only quiet time we had."

Constant noise could not be escaped anywhere in East Anglia as squadron after squadron of fighters and bombers warmed up, thundered down the runway and droned high in the morning skies, flocking into wild-goose V-formations that faded behind fleecy cloud banks.

"Beginning in the early hours of the morning, five o'clock perhaps, we could hear the Wright Cyclones running up before takeoff," John Mills said. "Then the group flew overhead as it gathered into formation—finally flying away to be followed by other groups of aircraft in the hundreds. I stood outside my house and counted five or six hundred B-17s and B-24s flying over on their way out to a mission. The noise they created was impressive to say the least."

"The most spectacular spectacle was that of 1,000 bombers going to war on one cold and frosty morning in 1945," said Roger Freeman. "I could not actually count 1,000 bombers but I could see twenty-eight contrailing groups converging on a coastal departure point. In fact, two parallel streams with the two horizons. I was looking at 10,000 young men going to war."

The sights and sounds of a typical 1944 day were recorded in the diary of John Archer, then a fourteen-year-old English boy:

"0700. It's still dark. The engines of B-17s are being run to a constant pitch all around the countryside. Lights are flashing everywhere from vehicles on the move round the perimeter to the hardstands.

"0715. Engine noise has dropped, being replaced by the sound of screeching brakes, reminding me that once again the B-17s are on the move for position, ready for take-off for another mission.

"0720. Just daybreak. The lead B-17 is airborne with the rest of the group following at regular intervals.

"0730. In the south the 95th Bomb Group (Horham) are already forming, with tail-end Charlies still trying to catch up.

"0800. The sky is alive with B-17s and B-24s, all forming up in a racetrack fashion over their own bases. Hundreds of different colored flares are seen giving a sight never to be forgotten.

"0830. The Groups are now formed up in Wing position, and make a last big circuit round the area eventually heading out eastward for the coast.

"0835. A B-17 heads in from the opposite direction with one engine dead. He has aborted the mission.

"0900. The last of the various groups disappears into the distance, shining in the sun's rays, their outlines getting smaller, and the noise dying away.

"0930. After two hours or so of continuous activity the surrounding countryside settles down to the daily routine once again. Loaded gasoline tankers rumble by. Air Force trucks loaded with bombs, fuses, fins, etc., make their way to the base to replenish the stocks which are now used up as they bring them in.

"1030. A single B-17 takes off, does several passes over the field, two or three touch and goes, and then finally lands. I assume this was a training flight or test.

"1100. Dozens of P-47s in formations of fours streak out towards the coast.

"1115. Another single B-17 comes to land. It looks like a new one, as no markings are seen. Probably a replacement.

"1200. Another single B–17 takes off, goes through the same routine as the earlier one.

"1215. Hazy sunshine turning to overcast skies, visibility down to about one mile.

"1245. During my lunch I hear a B–17. I run outside to find it above the overcast. It must be from another group stationed farther inland.

"1330. Getting a bit uneasy as I observe the weather is closing in, knowing the group is still out, and the conditions will be against them on the return to base.

"1400. Almost without warning a group of B–17s appears to the north of the base, still looking good after their long haul over Germany; with strained eyes I observe they are from the 388th Bomb Group, "K" on fins. The 100th won't be long now, I guess.

"1420. At last the Square D group comes into view. I count 26 . . . 27 . . . a lone one—28—yes, I could say they've had a good day. I never do hear how many fail to return on these occasions, but I guess many empty beds would be at Thorpe Abbotts on some days.

"1500. I assume everybody is now safely down, although one of two had to make two or three passes. As I cycle round the base, I observe the *The All-American Girl* has made it back once again, but *Hang the Expense* has made a mess of Farmer Draper's barn! Pausing to talk awhile with the lonely Air Policemen on sentry watch, we exchange a few stories and, as it starts to rain, I bid him farewell and make for my home which is a short distance from the base."

This is all that was left after a B-17 exploded. USAF via Karen Laws

To anyone who watched a group's return, a vivid memory is bombers coming in, to use vernacular phrasing of the day, on a wing and a prayer, "with two burning and two turning" and half a horizontal stabilizer missing and gaping holes in the wings large enough to drop a desk through. To both the aviation-minded and those who were not, there was amazement that aircraft could take enormous punishment and get back, usually still in formation.

"On base, there was a newsstand where we could buy a copy of Stars and Stripes, *the armed forces' newspaper. All the amenities of home—in olive drab. We even had a shuttle bus running throughout the day from our [barracks site] around the airfield perimeter and back."* —Bill Weith, 357th Fighter Group

Chapter 8

The paradox of the commuting GI

Who can be wise, amazed, temperate and furious,
Loyal and neutral, in a moment?

—William Shakespeare, *Macbeth* Act II, Scene iii

It was a puzzle of troubling, inordinate contrasts: jigsaw pieces of fear, horror and exhilaration in air combat, somehow connecting with that of serene landscape beyond the White Cliffs of Dover. Itinerant GIs boarded their morning shuttles, fighters or heavy bombers—like so many businessmen living in secure, tree-lined suburbs hopped on commuter trains—and traveled to their work in an inner city of Pandemonium.

It was all a part of the paradox: a contradictory world tucked away in the peaceful English countryside that was at once the heart of the aerial assault on Germany. The countryside itself was transformed into an integral cog for the vast war machine, as Great Britain became "a giant aircraft carrier anchored off the shores of Fortress Europe."

The paradoxical scene had contrasting sights: a convoy of ordnance trucks held to a snail's pace by a hay wagon wobbling toward a 300 year old thatched-roof farmhouse, a stone's throw away from an airfield's perimeter track. Stray cows occasionally finding their way onto a runway and hoofing in astonishment at a pasture made of concrete instead of sweet grass. And stalks of grain waving in the shadows of combat aircraft wings.

There were also contrasting sounds: breathless quiet, once interrupted only by the peals of bells in ancient church towers, routinely shattered by the sharp reports of fighters' six fifty-caliber wing guns test-fired into not-so-distant gun butts. Heart-rending airfield explosions sending shock waves through the peaceful countryside. And the healthy bellow of aircraft embarking on early morning flight—a reverberating, pummeling, angry sound that reached every crevice in East Anglia—followed by conspicuous silence.

There were even contrasting smells: the delicious scent of warm bread fresh from the oven wafting from farmhouses to nearby hardstands. Native smells of clover and new-mown hay perfuming the wet, fresh sea air blown across eastern England. Mingling with these, the odors of war: gun powder; burned cordite from spent shells; uniforms damp with perspiration from hours of nervousness and toil; and the potent exhale of huge motors breathing high-octane fuel.

And for those who flew, contrasts not directly perceptible by sense organs were even more striking. Commuting GIs lived with the standard comforts of home—a bed to sleep in, a roof overhead, and hot meals—in the safety afforded by their rural England home. Then suddenly they were catapulted into hostile, punishing skies, to face bleak odds of survival

MARCH 7, 1944
SOMEWHERE IN
ENGLAND

DEAR FOLKS,

I recall the day, away back when, that home meant to me the house in which I lived. Then, when I went to College, home was the town in which I lived. When the Army took over home spread out about 300 miles in every direction. "Home" since I have been overseas has been the whole United States. Well, let me tell you right here & now that the shores of this island looming up thru the haze of the Channel is the most welcome, beautiful sight I have ever encountered. Boy, that is home to me!

—Jack Kirschbraun,
March 7, 1944
letter to parents

against an enemy who skillfully attacked from above and below.

The faceless enemy

Strange, too, was the fact that this enemy was largely unseen—an enemy seemingly devoid of human form and instead delineated by muzzle flashes on the ground and fleeting machines slashing like razor blades through formations.

Perhaps that's why seeing a Nazi-uniformed individual at liberty even on an American air station would cause no particular alarm—it was just another part of the surreal peaceful surroundings: "One day while riding my bike I saw a person dressed in a German uniform," recalled Hiram Drache. "I thought it was unusual, but did nothing about it. At 4:00 P.M. that day all personnel were called for assembly. The person in German uniform was marched across the stage. The commanding officer gave us a real chewing out about security because that 'German soldier' had walked around the base all day and had been ignored by everyone."

While their patriotism was unquestionable and feelings were strong that

Hitler must be stopped, American fliers did not have the vendetta of the Poles, Russians and others, who witnessed first-hand the vast Nazi atrocities. The fliers' perception was more that of a deadly joust against lead-spitting machinery with an operator who was merely a small extension of the machine. And the ultimate objective of strategic bombing was to deliver bombs to a faceless target.

Bernarr Cresap commented:

"I was struck by the impersonal nature of the war in the sense that the airman has little feel for the results of what he is doing. The bombs go, you watch those of neighboring aircraft fall, and then they disappear from sight. Most of the time you have little or no concept of the destruction. This is especially true when bombing by radar and the bombs simply disappear into the clouds below. The war became personal only when flak bangs into the metal of the airplane and when a German fighter flashes by. Otherwise, it's a strange, isolated setting four and a half miles above the earth—detached and unreal.

"My surprise at being shot at for the first time [over the Nuremberg railroad yards on Feb. 20, 1945] was curious as I look back upon it. I seemed to be saying to myself, 'Why are they shooting at innocent me? I'm the finest fellow you'll ever meet anywhere.' Of course, this overlooked the fact that I was a party to a lot of destruction down below."

G. W. Pederson (who suffered eighteen months as a POW) echoed the sentiment: "I had no feeling of hatred for Germans. [Aerial combat] was more like fighting a machine than a person. It was a very impersonal war. I had difficulty connecting it with people actually firing at me."

Living day to day

"The early combat crews lived day to day," said Carl Lose. "The early going was especially tough."

Shortly after Glen Lunde's arrival to England, the crew who shared quarters had crashed. All but one had been killed. The crew's sole survivor, a gunner who suffered a flak wound in the leg, lost control. "He kept screaming, 'I gotta see my buddies! Gotta help them!'" recounted Lunde. "He kept falling out of his bunk, reinjuring the wound on his thigh. He became so frantic that they had to give him a hypo."

"I was taken to the First Army's bivouac in the woods. They were waiting around in the mud and had to construct little levies around their tents to keep the water out. . . . The infantrymen said, 'Boy we wouldn't trade places with you guys up there. We see you up there being shot at and there's no place to hide. Down here on the ground, if it gets too tough, we dig a hole and we can get away from it.'"
—C. L. Anderson, 390th Bomb Group (H)

"The barracks always reminded me of living in a huge culvert. . . . It had semi-circular walls, two windows on each end and a vestibule complete with blackout curtains."
—Bill Weith, 357th Fighter Group

"At nine o'clock in the morning, we'd be bombing Berlin and at midnight we'd be at a fancy dance in London."
—Harry Crosby, 100th Bomb Group (H)

"For a while, we had more casualties from bicycles than the enemy," according to Harry Crosby. "It was often dark when we rode. And Americans were accustomed to coaster brakes—braking by reversing the pedals. British bikes had brakes on the handlebars and you had to learn to coordinate your right hand with the front brake and left with the rear brake. If you hit the front brake too hard, you go right over the front wheel." 94th BGMA*

Escaping the tumult

Strangely, almost supernaturally, the peaceful English countryside harbored dark traces of man's age-old tumultuous annals.

"My favorite diversion was to get on my bike and ride, usually along the sea through the little villages," said Bill Weith. "There were ruins of abbeys built in the eighth century, an old Roman burial ground washing out to sea. As I walked through an old church graveyard near Therbeton, I once found the graves of German crewmen of a Zeppelin that had been shot down during World War I."

Robert Bieck said, "I rode my bike everywhere and more often than not, I saw churches. Inside the churches invariably there was a small memorial chapel devoted exclusively to the fallen in the Great War. It was in these chapels that it impacted on me the enormous loss of life that struck British young men. The walls of these chapels were lined from the floor to a height of eight feet with small brass plaques, each containing the name of a fallen member from the country regiments."

"The worst time was when the crew sharing our hut was lost and they brought in no one to replace them for weeks," recalled Thomas O'Brien. "I'd come into that hut with a whole side vacant and think about it. If a crew had replaced them right away, it wouldn't have picked at me so bad."

Contrast to life in the trenches

It was an entirely different existence than the land army facing combat around the clock. "We'd fly over the front lines and see them shooting at each other," said Harry Crosby. "We'd go on to Berlin and come back—and they'd still be there. We always thought the infantry had it harder and we were very respectful of them."

When they returned from a mission—*if* they returned from a mission—an evening of liberty usually followed. "It was like returning to . . . a safe nest at which you could laugh and play—until the next misison," noted Carroll Lewis, pilot for the 379th Group. Another pilot implied that it was something like standing with one foot in hell and the other in heaven.

Familiar comforts often included an ice cream maker. 94th BGMA

Comforts only wished for by the GIs in the foxholes—the first American soda fountain this side of the Atlantic, located at Bury St. Edmunds (Rougham). 94th BGMA

This morning as I PX-ed for my weekly rations, I counted-off ninety men & then backed up the line. It seems that they got a shipment of candy in stock & were permitting one 1 pound box per person. They had only 100 boxes. I guess I was lucky to hit things right & certainly was happy to stand in line for an hour. I tucked the box under my arm & sneaked it into the barrack. The crew had a picnic & now it's all gone.

—Jack Kirschbraun,
March 15, 1944
letter to family

The 94th Bomb Group's PX. PXs were often stocked with candy and gum. 94th BGMA

"Strange to me was that we could have a savage air battle over Germany," said G. W. Pederson. "Then come back to the base, go into town—and live an almost normal civilian life."

Life at England's Army Air Force stations was perhaps as close to "normal civilian life" as the wartime US military had yet come. It was a different world than the land army. John Houk affirmed: "Life on the base was laid back. Military discipline was not followed closely."

It was close to civilian life, although conditions in quarters sometimes left

something to be desired. Coming from well-equipped, modern bases in the United States, new arrivals were always a little shocked at the spartan quarters of British air stations.

Robert Bieck recalled: "We had come from nice barracks, where you could take a shower right inside. The first few weeks, we were miserable." It gradually became evident that this was a besieged land where creature comforts were not priorities. "We grew to the fact that the English people were existing on meager rations and suffered shortages of all types."

A wall of victories for the 362nd Fighter Squadron (357th Fighter Group) marked above the fireplace at Leiston. John Ziebell

One-armed bandit at the 94th Bomb Group's enlisted men's club. 94th BGMA

When military duties permitted, station personnel often assisted with harvest and other farming chores. With the critical shortage of manpower due to Great Britain's war efforts, the GI's assistance helped not only relieve the manpower shortage, it also served as "therapy," a good diversion from the stresses of airfield duties.

Living in a culvert: Nissen huts and the struggle to keep warm

Nissen huts were metal structures used for a wide variety of purposes. Though versatile, Nissens' heating capabilities, or lack thereof, were a topic of great notoriety.

The weather was the biggest factor not only for missions and the ground crews' preparation for missions, but for living conditions. For most of the year in England's damp, cool climate, it took extraordinary measures to stay warm in the thinly insulated Nissens. The accommodations, combined with a perpetual shortage of any type of heating fuel and the great distances between essential facilities like latrines, made for less than convenient living conditions.

"I lived in a Nissen hut," Fred Bartz said. "They were cool, 'air conditioned' in fact. And we had to walk a half a block to the latrine."

When Bernarr Cresap was the newest arrival to the 709th Bomb Squadron, he inherited the only available bunk—"just inside the front door of a Nissen hut. It was the least desirable spot in the hut, since the occupant received a cold blast of air with every opening of the door and, after all, this was England in the wintertime. But it was the only vacant place, and seniority is seniority. I was the last man in and that was that."

"English weather was not only awful for flying," Robert Bieck noted, "it was not pleasant for living at certain times of the year. It was very cold, not cold like in the severe Nebraska winters I used to know—but damp, raw penetrating cold. Of course, the problem was made worse by inability to heat our huts."

"Coal was delivered once a week and dumped in a pile," said Lloyd Nelson. "Everyone had a container of some sort. You had to run like hell to get some

Sometimes there was even time for a ball-game. 94th BGMA

Baseball at Bury St. Edmunds in 1944. 94th BGMA

or you were out of luck until the next week."

"They stored coal in a compound with gates chained together," explained Frank Halm. "If you had a long enough shovel you could tickle the bottom of the pile and tease some of the coal down. Then you could slide out a half a shovelful at a time to put in your bucket."

"We would go so far as to waylay the coal trucks coming to the base," continued Bieck. "We would ride our bikes alongside the truck and knock chunks of coal to the road and one of our own would follow with a barracks bag and scoop up the droppings.

Others resorted to chopping down "the King's wood," until an authority—local police or group commander—pointed out you needed the king's permission to chop it down. And without the king's permission, it was fines, and in extreme cases, a court-martial.

"At first we had good sized heaters stamped out of sheet metal," Ralph Ballinger said. "Then before D-day, they took those away and gave us little English heaters. Had a fire chamber the size of a tea pot. You can imagine what kind of heat you got out of those things. They gave the bigger ones to the infantry troops in the field. But I didn't argue at all about that, or when they took our buckle overshoes away and gave them to the combat troops preparing for D-day."

This area was once the tennis courts of the Ridgewell-based 381st Bomb Group. Andrew Morland

A party for 331st Squadron of the 94th Bomb Group with officers, enlisted men and British women in attendance. 94th BGMA

"Most huts had a radio and everyone wanted a bedside light that you could reach from the bed. Every time the fuses started to blow, they'd come on a security sweep and confiscate the illegal electrical devices."
—Frank Halm, 94th Bomb Group (H)

Many airfield buildings were Nissen or prefabricated huts (other makes of huts were Hall, Janes, Laing, Orlit, Seco and Thorne). Nissen huts, the most common, were half-cylinders of corrugated steel set on a concrete slab. The huts were named for Peter N. Nissen, a British mining engineer, who had devised them in the early 1930s. Sometimes

called Quonset huts in American, Nissen huts were all-purpose structures serving as everything from living quarters to headquarters. Pictured is a dispensary at High Wycombe. The huts came in a variety of sizes and configurations—often joined together, depending on their uses. 8th Photo Tech Squadron

Little Walden during the war. There is a haphazard air about the winding roads and clusters of buildings, yet they form a careful economical pattern. As much as possible, airfields were laid out to minimize disruption to farm production, which was also crucial to the outcome of the war. Structures often were built within groves of trees on the borders of farming acreage. Also, the stations were planned and built when there was greater likelihood of enemy air attack. Thus, buildings were widely dispersed. USAF

Present-day aerial view of Little Walden. Andrew Morland

95

However, compared to the conditions faced by the ground forces on the continent, accommodations of English air stations were heavenly. Edwin Lundell recalled the infantry troops, who had been injured and could not return to ground fighting, were delighted to be assigned to an airfield in England. Many worked in his armament section. He said, "When men who had been at the airfield all along complained of the conditions, these infantrymen who had been on Continental Europe told them what was really rough."

The songs

Songs were a big part of life for those stationed at the airfields. Aeroclub phonographs were often playing Glenn Miller. Many songs popular among Americans seemed tailor-made for the Eighth Air Force. For instance, "The White Cliffs of Dover" with the line, "There'll be blue-birds over . . ." (although those who were there knew no Dover resident ever saw a bluebird anywhere in those parts). And many of the song titles appeared on noses of aircraft, like *Shoo-Shoo Baby*, *I'll Be Around* and *Jersey Bounce*, to name a few.

Top hits of 1942–1945 were as follows:

1942

"Army Air Corps Song" (originally released in 1939)
"Be Careful It's My Heart"
"Be Honest with Me"
"Blues in the Night"
"Can't Get Out of This Mood"
"Cowboy Serenade"
"Dearly Beloved"
"Don't Sit Under the Apple Tree with Anyone Else But Me"
"Easy Street"
"Elmer's Tune"
"Happiness is Just a Thing Called Joe"
"He Wears a Pair of Silver Wings"
"I Had the Craziest Dream"
"I Left My Heart at the Stage Door Canteen"
"Idaho"
"I'll Be Around"
"In the Blue of Evening"
"It Can't Be Wrong"
"I've Got a Gal in Kalamazoo"
"Jersey Bounce"
"Jingle Jangle Jingle"
"The Lamplighter's Serenade"
"Moonlight Cocktail"
"My Devotion"

"One Dozen Roses"
"Paper Doll"
"Perdido"
"Praise the Lord and Pass the Ammunition"
"Rose O'Day"
"Seranade in Blue"
"A String of Pearls"
"Tangerine"
"That Old Black Magic"
"There Are Such Things"
"There Will Never Be Another You"
"This Is Worth Fighting For"
"Warsaw Concerto"
"When the Lights Go On Again All Over the World"
"(There'll Be Blue Birds Over) The White Cliffs of Dover"
"Who Wouldn't Love You"
"With My Head in the Clouds"
"You Were Never Lovelier"
"You'd Be So Nice To Come Home To"

"We listened to Armed Forces Radio, Axis Sally or the BBC Nine O'clock News. The BBC program was interesting because it was beamed overseas and contained a great many encrypted messages to the French underground and other Allied undercover groups."
—Barbara Pathe, Red Cross volunteer

POPULAR SONGS
WORLD WAR - NUMBER TWO

"White Cliffs of Dover"
"The Japs Won't Have a Ghost of a Chance"
"Remember Pearl Harbor"
"You're A Sap, Mr. Jap"
"Let's Take A Rap at the Japs"
"Those Nasty, Nasty Nazis"
"I'm Buying a Bond for Baby"
"He's 1-A in the Army, but He's A-1 in My Heart"
"Goodbye Mama, I'm on My Way to Yokohama"
"Keep 'Em Flying"
"Let's Put the Axe to the Axis"
"Let's All Remember Kelly"
"They Started Something and We're Going to End It"
"We Did It Before and We Can Do It Again"

ADDITIONAL SONGS I WISH TO REMEMBER

Army Air Corps
Black Magic (sheppard Field Texas)
Pistol Packing Momma (Knoxville Tenn)
Paper Doll (Lafayette La.)
People Will Say We're IN Love (Lafayette La)
Sunday. Monday or Always (Maxwell Field)
Dont Cry Baby (walnut Ridge)
I'll Be Around (Walnut Ridge)
Do. Nothing 'Til You Hear From Me (pence)

—John Ziebell
diary

In color: East Anglia today

Eighth Air Force Country tour

No matter where you travel in East Anglia and eastern Midlands in the United Kingdom, you're never more than a few miles from traces of the World War II Eighth Air Force. Even after the nearly half century since the war, everywhere are tangible and intangible reminders—in the form of expansive concrete brick and steel installations, or ineradicable memories attached to a certain place.

Bungay, 446th BG

Members of the 446th Bomb Group, nicknamed the "Bungay Buckeroos," painted many murals inside this building, well maintained by the resident farmer, Mr. Hensley. Andrew Morland

Airfields that were once on the cutting edge of the Allied strategic bombing offensive now bloom with foliage—and history. The 446th Bomb Group dining hall is part of Mr. Hensley's farmyard at Bungay airfield (also known as Flixton airfield). Bungay, along with Seething (448th Bomb Group) and Hardwick (93rd Bomb Group), were the three stations of the 20th Combat Wing. Andrew Morland

This sailor and mermaid mural may suggest parallelism between a sailor drawn irresistibly to the sea by sirens and an airman drawn to the sky. Andrew Morland

This propeller assembly found near Bungay was possibly once an object of meticulous work by propeller specialists of the 446th Bomb Group. Andrew Morland

The overgrowth of peaceful decades envelopes this roofless, stucco building at Bungay. Andrew Morland

Wistful thoughts of home perhaps inspired this mural of a United States map at Bungay. Andrew Morland

Bury St. Edmunds (Rougham) 94th BG

Old English Rose Garden, located on the abbey grounds at Bury St. Edmunds, pays homage to those lost in service with the 94th Bomb Group. Andrew Morland

SUFFOLK SUMMER
ON SALE AT
BOWLS HUT

BOROUGH OF BURY ST. EDMUNDS

Old English Rose Garden

THE CONSTRUCTION OF THIS OLD ENGLISH ROSE GARDEN IS DUE TO THE GENEROSITY OF AN AMERICAN FRIEND OF THIS BOROUGH, MR. JOHN T. APPLEBY, WHO WAS STATIONED NEAR BURY ST. EDMUNDS DURING THE WAR WHILST A MEMBER OF THE UNITED STATES 8TH AIR FORCE.

MR. APPLEBY became very attached to this old town and its historic associations and also to the surrounding countryside with its numerous picturesque villages and fine churches. His regard and affection for this portion of England and its people is portrayed in his book "Suffolk Summer" written after his return to the United States. The Royalties from the sales of this book have been generously given to the Borough for making and effecting improvements in this Rose Garden.

The 94th Bomb Group memorial stands amid the delicate beauty of Old English Rose Garden. Andrew Morland

Just to the side of the control tower, a Nissen hut offers a window to the vividly green world of England. Andrew Morland

At Bury St. Edmunds airfield, the 94th Bomb Group's control tower was occupied as a residence after the war. Now vacant, the tower is surrounded by an industrial park. It was for sale at the time this photo was taken. Andrew Morland

Decades later, English amity toward the Eighth Air Force remains strong. On December 8, 1988, The Flying Fortress Pub was opened in a building at Bury St. Edmunds, once used by the 94th Bomb Group for engineering stores and offices. Andrew Morland

Original instructions for emergency dropping of ball turret persevere inside a B-17 on display at Duxford England. D. A. Lande

A Belfast-type hangar, built in 1917–1918, was used by the 78th Fighter Group at Duxford. The 78th was the only fighter group in the Eighth Air Force to fly all three primary fighter types: the P–38, P–47 and P–51. Duxford is now an aviation museum where many aircraft are stored and displayed. D. A. Lande

Duxford's modernized control tower is very active today. D. A. Lande

Eight restored B-17s from France, England and the United States were used in filming Memphis Belle *at Duxford in 1989. John Mills*

Silhouetted against a summer evening sky, P-51 Mustangs repose at Duxford in 1989, when they were assembled for filming of Memphis Belle. *John Mills*

Framlingham (Parham), 390th BG

Percy Kindred of Crabbs Farm welcomes guests (particularly Eighth veterans) to Framlingham control tower, which he purchased and helped restore. Old Glory still flies proudly on the roof of Framlingham's control tower, thanks to the Friends of the Eighth. The restored tower reopened as a museum in August 1980. Andrew Morland

Squadron insignia for the 385th Fighter Squadron, part of the 364th Fighter Group based at Honington, is displayed at Framlingham's control tower museum. Andrew Morland

The control tower's watch office, complete with original equipment, overlooks a cultivated field where a runway once stretched across gentle undulations. Andrew Morland

101

A small city of Nissens, located on Moat Farm, owned by John Gray, was used by the 371st Squadron of the 390th Bomb Group. Andrew Morland

Adjacent to a chicken farm stand partially restored remains of the Red Feather Club of Horham airfield, home to the Red Feather Group, the 95th Bomb Group. On the far west side of the airfield the large station hospital has been annexed by another farm. Inside the hospital, stenciled doors still mark passage to the main ward, nurse's station, linen closet, and so on. Andrew Morland

Unlike the mind's eye that is capable of viewing past events with astonishing clarity, this now opaque window at Framlingham allows no vision into a Nissen hut interior that once was a scene of bunkbeds and enlisted men gathered closely around a small coke stove. Andrew Morland

Walls of fairy tale characters carry a medieval theme inside the Red Feather Club. Still discernible Old English lettering appears throughout—as over the latrine, designated "Gents." Andrew Morland

Still awaiting mail. . . . Framlingham door bears stenciled markings of "mail room." Andrew Morland

The Horham guard house is now used as a community center.
Andrew Morland

A knight and his charger on Red Feather Club wall. Note the
faded red feather on the knight's shield. Andrew Morland

Horham memorial with the Square-B for the 95th Bomb
Group, known as the "Big B." The 95th Bomb Group was the
first American unit to bomb Berlin. Andrew Morland

Troupe of minstrels and other medieval characters on Red
Feather Club wall. Note that the strings of the cello are
actually electrical wires. Andrew Morland

Lavenham, 487th BG

Little Walden, 361st FG

On the walls of the Swan Hotel, known previously as the Swan Inn, hangs a portrait of Brig. Gen. Frederick Castle. Andrew Morland

The control tower at Little Walden airfield, former home to the 361st Fighter Group, is now an immaculate architecture office. Its restoration preserved the integrity of the structure's original design. Atop the tower, a station 165 flag still flies. The 361st Fighter Group had occupied nearby Bottisham until September 1944. They moved to Little Walden when a Ninth Air Force group vacated. The 493rd Bomb Group flew briefly from here when Debach airfield was temporarily closed for repair in March 1945. Andrew Morland

Viewed through the shattered window of a rescue-vehicle garage is Lavenham's control tower. On the tower's front side is a plaque commemorating the 487th Bomb Group. The group's first commander was Lt. Col. Beirne Lay, Jr., author of Twelve O'clock High. *Andrew Morland*

Architects now occupy work areas where air controllers once watched yellow-nosed Mustangs of the 361st Fighter Group take flight. Andrew Morland

Church of St. Peter and St. Paul, built between 1485 and 1525, at Lavenham. Andrew Morland

Just southeast of Little Walden's control tower, a T2 hangar is now leased for heavy equipment storage. Andrew Morland

Near Little Walden's other T2 hangar, located at the field's northernmost site, an air raid shelter entrance still offers refuge from aerial attack. Andrew Morland

Its corrugated metal panels gone, a Nissen hut's skeleton stands at the technical site on eastern side of Little Walden airfield. Andrew Morland

Circular debris gives a whirlwind effect inside a derelict Nissen hut at Little Walden technical site. Andrew Morland

A memorial to the 361st Fighter Group is a permanent fixture on the second floor of Little Walden's control tower. Displayed with the memorial are aerial photographs of Little Walden airfield during and after the war, and wartime photos of the fighter group. Andrew Morland

IN MEMORY OF THE AIRMEN OF THE
361st FIGHTER GROUP
US 8th AIR FORCE WHO GAVE THEIR
LIVES IN THE DEFENCE OF FREEDOM
1943 ~ 1945

Henwick House, owned by the Orlebar family for ten generations, is adjacent to Podington airfield. Members of the 92nd Bomb Group, based at Podington, fondly recall being invited to the house for parties and tea. Much of the land for the airfield was requisitioned from the Orlebar estate. On a number of former Eighth airfields, you can look through the hazy glass of a Nissen's rickety window cheek across a meadow to see a country house. D. A. Lande

The poignant memorial for the 34th Bomb Group, erected in 1949, is just a few steps off the A140 road near Mendlesham. Mendlesham airfield served as an RAF fighter station until April 1944 when the 34th Bomb Group moved in. The group flew 170 missions, 62 of them with B-24s and the rest with B-17s. It lost no aircraft due to enemy action over enemy territory, but several bombers fell victim to Luftwaffe attack over Mendlesham airfield itself. Andrew Morland

Podington control tower, once completely derelict, now stands renovated as a residence, complete with brick patio. The land around it still reverberates from the bellow of powerful piston engines, but no longer from the Wright Cyclone engines of 92nd Bomb Group B-17s—and instead from engines powering cars raced at Santa Pod Raceway. Santa Pod began using a section of the old main runway in 1966 for its dragstrip. D. A. Lande

A service for returning veterans of the 92nd Bomb Group is held at St. Mary's Church at Podington in June 1989. Conducting the memorial service are the local minister and a US Air Force chaplain based in England. D. A. Lande

Eighth Air Force memorials take many forms, among them the 92nd Bomb Group's unique one inside St. Mary's Church. The group paid for restoration of this organ with inscribed casing. D. A. Lande

This B–17 mural at Podington, once home to the Eighth Air Force's oldest group, the 92nd Bomb Group, has since been extricated by EWACS (Eighth War Art Conservation Society) and moved intact to Duxford museum. The talented artist who painted the mural was Staff Sergeant Waldsmidt. Gerry Darnell

Crews of the 381st Bomb Group walked through dampness and darkness to this entrance of Ridgewell's mess hall, now used as a shop for farm work. The airfield originally was home to RAF Short Stirling bombers when it was completed in 1942. On June 31, 1943, the 381st Bomb Group moved in for the duration. Andrew Morland

Through the projector holes at Ridgewell's cinema once flickered movies like Mrs. Miniver, Sergeant York *and* In Which We Serve. Andrew Morland

Ridgewell's morgue is now a single-stall garage in the backyard of a postwar house. Andrew Morland

The interior of a large Nissen located at Ridgewell. Andrew Morland

381st Bomb Group memorial at Ridgewell is located near the station hospital. The 381st suffered the highest losses of all groups during the first Schweinfurt raid (August 17, 1943). Andrew Morland

Seething's control tower is now restored as a museum. Above the door is the 448th Bomb Group's insignia, which also was painted on the vertical stabilizers of its aircraft. Andrew Morland

The headquarters complex stands dark and empty. The absence of windows (a wartime precaution) makes passage through its inner rooms difficult without lamps. Andrew Morland

B-24s adorn the 448th Bomb Group memorial at Seething airfield. Andrew Morland

Sudbury, 486th BG

Aircraft art embellishes drab billet walls: (clockwise from lower left) American P-61 Black Widow, B-26 Marauder, P-40 Warhawk, P-38 Lightning, and (center) German Heinkel He 111. Andrew Morland

B-24s and later B-17s of the 486th Bomb Group once lurched into line on this perimeter track at Sudbury airfield. Only the base of the control tower remains, but the perimeter track and loop hardstands remain largely intact. Andrew Morland

Seething's runway is still active as a flying club airfield. This view looks southeast. D. A. Lande

In the apse behind the High Altar inside St. Pauls Cathedral, London, the morning sun blazes through a fantastic stained glass window containing the emblems of every state. Multicolored beams fall symbolically onto the Roll of Honor, a book containing the names of 28,000 Americans who lost their lives while based in Great Britain during World War II. Each day, a page in the Roll is turned. D. A. Lande

111

White caps in a sea of graves at Cambridge American Ceme-tery. Andrew Morland

1943

"Amor"
"Besame Mucho"
"Comin' in on a Wing and a Prayer"
"Do Nothin' Till You Hear from Me"
"Don't Get Around Much Anymore"
"Don't Sweetheart Me"
"A Gay Ranchero"
"Goodbye, Sue"
"Holiday for Strings"
"How Many Hearts Have You Broken"
"I Couldn't Sleep a Wink Last Night"
"I Had the Craziest Dream"
"I'll Be Seeing You"
"In My Arms"
"It's Love, Love, Love"
"(It Seems to Me) I've Heard That Song Before"
"Let's Get Lost"
"(This Is) A Lovely Way to Spend an Evening"
"Mairzy Doats"
"My Heart Tells Me"
"My Shining Hour"
"Oh, What a Beautiful Morning"
"Oklahoma!"
"People Will Say We're in Love"
"Pistol Packing Mama"
"Shoo-Shoo Baby"
"Speak Low"
"Star Eyes"
"Sunday, Monday or Always"
"The Surrey with the Fringe on Top"
"Take It Easy"
"Taking a Chance on Love"
"They're Either Too Young or Too Old"
"Tico Tico"
"Walking the Floor Over You"
"What Do You Do in the Infantry?"
"You Keep Coming Back Like a Song"
"You'll Never Know"

1944

"Ac-cent-tchu-ate the Positive"
"All of a Sudden"
"Candy"
"Don't Fence Me In"
"Down in the Valley"
"Dream"
"Evalina"
"Going My Way"
"Holiday for Strings"
"How Blue the Night"
"I Dream of You"
"I Hear Music"
"I Love You"
"I Should Care"
"I'll Get By"

"I'll Walk Along"
"I'm Making Believe"
"Is You Is or Is You Ain't My Baby?"
"It Could Happen to You"
"Jealous Heart"
"Lili Marlene"
"Long Ago and Far Away"
"My Heart Tells Me"
"Right as the Rain"
"Roll Me Over"
"Rum and Coca-Cola"
"San Fernando Valley"
"Saturday Night Is the Loneliest Night of the Week"
"Sentimental Journey"
"Spring Will Be a Little Late This Year"
"Swinging on a Star"
"Till Then"
"Time Waits for No One"
"The Trolley Song"
"Twilight Time"
"You Always Hurt the One You Love"

1945

"All of My Life"
"Along the Navajo Trail"
"Aren't You Glad You're You"
"Autumn Serenade"
"Chickery Chick"
"Close as Pages in a Book"
"Cruising Down the River"
"Doctor, Lawyer, Indian Chief"
"Dream (When You're Feeling Blue)"
"For Sentimental Reasons"
"Give Me the Simple Life"
"I Can't Begin to Tell You"
"I Should Care"
"I Wish I Knew"
"If I Loved You"
"I'll Be Yours"
"I'll Close My Eyes"
"I'm Beginning to See the Light"
"It Might As Well Be Spring"
"It's a Grand Night for Singing"
"It's Been a Long, Long Time"
"J'Attendrai"
"June Is Bustin' Out All Over"
"Just a Little Fond Affection"
"Laura"
"Let It Snow, Let It Snow, Let It Snow"
"The More I See You"
"My Dreams Are Getting Better All the Time"
"Oh What It Seemed to Be"
"On the Atchison, Topeka, and the Santa Fe"
"(You Came Along from) Out of Nowhere"

The Glenn Miller Band, led here by Sgt. Ray McKinley, plays for the 94th Bomb Group's 200th mission celebration. 94th BGMA

"I heard Glenn Miller at Podington a month before he was lost. They set up flatbed trucks in front of headquarters and people stood around to listen. Everyone enjoyed that more than you can imagine."
—Edwin Lundell, 92nd Bomb Group (H)

"Seems Like Old Times"
"Symphony"
"That's for Me"
"There, I've Said It Again"
"While the Angelus Was Ringing"
"You'll Never Walk Alone"
For the English and former GIs alike, these great songs are a strong link to their common past.

In the loft of a barn near Old Buckenham, it sat—under forty years' accumulation of dust. A cardboard box containing dusty 78 rpm records: "Tuxedo Junction," "In the Mood," "The Jersey Bounce" and "Pennsylvania 6-5000" among them. Written on the box were dozens of GI signatures, all from the 735th Squadron of the 453rd Bomb Group stationed at Old Buckenham.

Evidently left for the enjoyment of an English friend at war's end, the box of records was discovered by a young couple who had recently purchased an old farmhouse and adjoining buildings. The records now have a place in Norwich's Second Air Division Memorial Library.

Liberty

To many stationed "somewhere in England," a forty-eight-hour pass to London was the dream escape from weeks at

A GI five-piece band at officer's 94th Bomb Group party on July 2, 1943. 94th BGMA

a mist-bound airfield. And the prospect of an evening spent at a nearby liberty town was an incentive that helped spur performance during the day.

"If we weren't flying the next day, we'd usually take a liberty run to Cambridge," said Bill Blackmon. "I 'stayed gone' as much as I could, just to escape the drone of airplanes. Mechanics had to

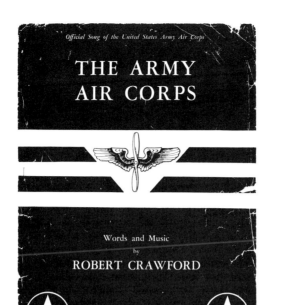

Merry Christmas from the mess personnel of 2nd Air Depot. Art Lobotzke

Dinner on-station wasn't always this extravagant at Bury St. Edmunds (Rougham). The 94th Bomb Group is celebrating its 200th mission. 94th BGMA

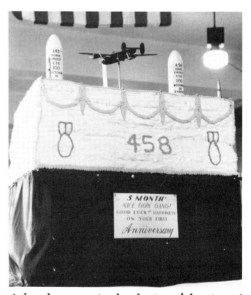

A bomb-group-sized cake in celebration of the 458th Bomb Group's five-month anniversary. Robert Neel

test them day and night. We'd drink 'hot beer'—I never saw an ice cube in England. Or we'd go to Cambridge University and find a date."

"A favorite place to visit was Cambridge, mainly because it could be reached so easily from Rattlesden," said Bernarr Cresap. "One popular recreation there was 'punting on the Cam.' A punt is an open, flat-bottomed boat with squared ends and propelled by a pole."

A 325th Reconnaissance chow hall pass.

Piccadilly Circus in London. 8th Photo Tech Squadron

The movie, The Bridge of San Luis Rey, *played in London in 1944. "In the course of the show an air raid signal was flashed on the screen," said Bernarr Cresap. "Nobody in the theater bothered to get up and go to an air raid shelter."* 8th Photo Tech Squadron

"At our 200th mission party we gathered around under the wings of a B–17 to hear the Century Bombers and Glenn Miller's band." —Roger Lyons, 100th Bomb Group (H)

"We had a few dances, but usually when the ground crews were working. However, we did get to see Glenn Miller in the hangar." —Carl Lose, 94th Bomb Group (H)

"[In combat] I did a lot of praying—a ten-minute prayer as we started the bomb run. Of course, I didn't always make good on the promises I'd made during those ten minutes. In London, I suppose I got into trouble as much as any of them. That seemed to be the way we got uncorked—go to London and turn everything loose." —C. L. Anderson, 390th Bomb Group (H)

"We forgot the pain and lived for the fun. That's all I want to remember." —Ed Pickering, 401st Bomb Group (H)

From a Briton's perspective in Bedford, John Mills commented: "If you went into Bedford in the evenings and weekends, a large percentage of the people were GIs and nearly all from the Eighth Air Force. To people who had already endured two or three years of total war, they were impressive. They were well-dressed, certainly by comparison with our service men. They were generous, liked children and wanted to be liked themselves."

John Archer of Suffolk recalled observing GIs on "liberty runs into Bungay, Norwich, and other nearby towns. Most pubs ran dry after two or three days as

116

beer was in short supply at certain times. But not all men were drinkers—some made for the cinema, dance halls, and church functions."

But whatever means of recreation chosen, they lived life to the fullest. It's a common observation of the English that Americans conducted themselves with a live-as-if-there's-no-tomorrow attitude. But then, omnipresent was the possibility that there *was* no tomorrow.

Laughing the fear away

"All of us were scared," said Joe Curley. "But there were some hilarious times. In wartime, your sense of humor is accentuated—you laugh at things that as a civilian in peacetime, you would not."

Esoteric jokes originated from difficult circumstances. For instance:

"An East Anglian farmer stood with a crew chief in a field near a runway watching a B–17 in test maneuvers. The bomber did a low pass with all four engines running. The pilot shut down one engine, made a pass. He shut down another, made another pass. He shut down another and made a pass with a single engine running. Finally, the farmer said, 'That's really something.' The crew chief responded, 'That ain't nothing. Next he'll make a pass with only the windshield wipers running.'"

The English reacted to the invasion of their American neighbors with a characteristically restrained story that summarized the troubles of the day:

"A farmer suddenly found his farm enveloped by an American airfield. The farmer went to market one day and ran into a friend, who asked, 'How are you getting along with them Yankees?' The farmer nearly exploded in his response: 'Getting on? I'll tell you how I'm getting on. Since they've been here, my cat was run over by a lorrie. My dog has been enticed away. My hens have been going off to lay. My apples have been stolen. My daughter is pregnant. My wife has run off with one of them. And I can't drown me sorrows because they've drunk all the pubs dry.'"

"Morale was good because of the guys you were with," said Lloyd Nelson. "They were the best—lots of joking and making the best of what we had."

The women

Squarely in the middle of the paradox were English women. Few other circumstances mixed the inordinate ingredients

357th Fighter Group pilot at the controls of a tamer mode of transportation at the Bridge of Sighs, St. John's College in Cambridge. John Ziebell

of war's carnage and the sweetness of romance. And perhaps because of the strange combination, love's potion was double-dosed.

In Great Britain, Americans quickly established a reputation for pursuing any female who appeared remotely available. Initially, American servicemen met with a cool reception from the women. It was considered bad form to be seen with a GI in the eyes of the conservative British.

Many an English mother forbade, in no uncertain terms, association with the Americans at the local airfield. Ruby

Two air policemen and a British "bobby" stand at entrance of train station. Art Lobotzke

Aerial attacks

Germany never made a serious effort to attack East Anglian airfields. However, East Anglia presented a convenient target for France-based enemy aircraft.

Often launched from France, V-weapons (V for *Vergeltungswaffe*, meaning vengeance weapons) were pilotless aircraft carrying explosives. Launched from a ski-ramp, a V-1 flew toward the target and crashed a ton of explosives when its engine stopped. "They were not accurate," Bernarr Cresap recalled. "We could hear them going over our base at night. The sound of the engine was unmistakable. It was comparable to a Model T Ford, rough and noisy."

Audrey Darnell remembered the "doodle bugs" that occasionally streaked across even the sky of her rural Bedfordshire homeland: "I hid in the pantry."

V-1s were slow enough that the faster Allied fighters often could intercept and shoot them down in the Channel.

The V-2 was a different matter. It was a thirteen-ton rocket with great speed. Consequently, there was little defense against it at the time.

Relatively safe as it was, one never knew when a stray V-1 or V-2 (probably intended for London or other major city) or an arbitrary attack from German aircraft might come at any time of day or night.

"A Jerry plane we called Bed-check Charlie came over at the same time each night," said Bill Blackmon. "You could tell by the sound that it was German. About ten o'clock he'd drop his bombs. Another came over about two A.M.—I won't mention what we called him. Sometimes the bombs exploded so close that our bicycles leaning against the Nissen hut fell over."

"Prior to D-day, I was on the station defense team," said Ralph Ballinger. "If we were attacked I was to be among the first out when the air raid siren blew. For a while I slept separately from the rest of my unit. If there was an air raid, I was supposed to run through the gate, off the base, up the road to a church cemetery in Great Stukely, where I could see over the entire valley and observe."

Bill Weith, stationed at Leiston, said: "Our airfield was attacked only once. A single German twin-engined aircraft came up the coast about midnight, probably on a recon mission. He made one pass at the field, putting a few holes in the mess hall, which our crew had just left. Then he sprayed one runway with gunfire and was on his way home."

Frequent transient V-1s, however, were observed from Leiston, located about seventy miles northeast of London. Weith continued: "The Germans were launching them over the North Sea, aimed at London. We watched

"My usual bicycle ride around the nearby Eighth Air Force bases ended with a visit to Hardwick, home of the 93rd Bomb Group. After watching the activities around the airfield, I started for home, just twenty minutes down the road. On nearing my final mile I heard a thunderous explosion to the northwest— Hardwick's direction. Windows shattered over a wide area and blast waves rent through the countryside—a weird sensation. The nearest buildings, including the base hospital at Hardwick airfield, were just yards from the crater, left by a V-2. To think back, if I had delayed my return just a few minutes I would have passed the impact point of the V-2 at a very bad time."
—John Archer, Suffolk youth

"There was a war bond drive to create a 'victory squadron' for the Eighth Air Force. The bonds paid for that squadron of planes. If a barracks passed a certain figure, they got a 24-hour pass. If an individual bought a certain amount, he got a 24-hour pass. Our barracks surpassed the figure, so we went to Edinburgh."
—Ralph Ballinger, 904th Signal Company (at Alconbury)

St. Pauls Cathedral in wartime. Note scaffolding to repair blitz damage. 8th Photo Tech Squadron

"I saw local girls you'd least expect to have American boyfriends, and some even married them!"
—John Archer, Suffolk youth

"Hollywood made the life look glamorous. I've laughed at their portrayals. Here's what it was like in a ball turret: At 25,000 feet, it was fifty degrees below zero. There was a relief tube under the seat. It was a plastic line funnel, chamois-lined, that ran outside the turret. I learned early not to drink that last two or three cups of coffee before I left, because once you climbed into the turret, you didn't leave it until out of enemy territory. Using the tube at that altitude, the hose would freeze up and back up to the funnel. If it spilled on the sighting glass, it would turn instantly to ice and obscure vision."
—C. L. Anderson, 390th Bomb Group (H)

Aerial attacks continued

them rumble over—sometimes so low they rattled the tile roof of the latrine."

Horsham St. Faith, located near Norwich, was the target of repeated V–2 attacks, but according to Robert C. Neel: "A direct hit was never made. After several failed efforts, the rockets ceased and the attack concentrated on London."

On leave in London, GIs experienced more frequent and more effective attacks. "You'd hear the sirens go off and see a buzz bomb go over," L. G. Spillman said. "The English people seemed to disappear into the walls. Only GIs were left on the streets. Finally, we'd find a crowded air raid shelter."

"One of our crew members got a Purple Heart for a buzz bomb attack," said Spillman. "He was in a bathtub and a buzz bomb exploded close enough so that the windows blew out a piece of glass and cut his leg. Of all the things that can happen on aircrews, that's how he rated the Purple Heart."

However, even attacks in London became less frightening and more routine. Buildings shook and curtains billowed from a blast, but "the show went on." Early in the war, theater operators interrupted movies to flash warnings. Later they superimposed the warning over the film to avoid interruption. Bernarr Cresap recalled attending a movie in London: "In the course of the show an air raid signal was flashed on the screen. Nobody in the theater bothered to get up and go to an air raid shelter."

Kranz experienced an introduction to an American stationed at High Wycombe that was perhaps an epitome of the larger picture of Anglo-American, male-female relationships. She ran into him—literally—when exiting a movie theater and was knocked to the ground. After helping her up, he asked her name, which she refused to give—partly from the fluster of the moment and partly from her mother's stern warnings about getting involved with GIs. He walked her home, but still she refused to give her name. Suspecting that he might seek her out later, she half-dreaded the day of his return:

"Through the frosted glass of the door, I could see the shape of the peaked military cap. I knew I'd really be in trouble if my mother found that I had become involved in any way with a GI, so I didn't answer the door. But Mother did. He explained that he wanted to see me. In the meantime I had slipped into my room. She brought him in and made him sit for the longest time, drilling him with questions.

"He won her over that afternoon. And from that point on he was part of the family. He came every night and my mother would save the best pieces of meat for him, since male members of a family always got the best cut."

Eventually, there was a decided willingness on the part of British women to get to know the GIs.

"As a whole, the British may have considered us brash," said Harry Crosby.

"But the women in general found Americans very courteous. Americans treated the English women well—and they *liked* it."

"Americans were anxious to please us," said Lalli Coppinger, a British volunteer hostess at a Red Cross club in London. "They were generous to a fault, but we were satisfied with far less. Most girls were price-conscious on their behalf, which the fellows didn't quite understand. But they noticed and appreciated it."

C. L. Anderson said: 'You know, we were those 'rich Yanks' that British girls really went for. We had more money and I think we were more gentlemanly toward the women than some Englishmen were. We would take them to the very best [restaurants] and they would keep the menu or something to prove to their friends that they had been in the Lion's Corner House or other nice London restaurants."

There were surprises on both sides of Anglo-American relationships. "Americans definitely were not used to English girls," continued Lalli Coppinger. "Americans found them far less demanding than most American girls. They were surprised when English girls gave them the prerogative of taking the lead on a date."

But both sides caught on very quickly.

Wartime had a way of inspiring romance. "They were young, lonely, and living from day to day," noted Barbara Pathe. The war affected everything in

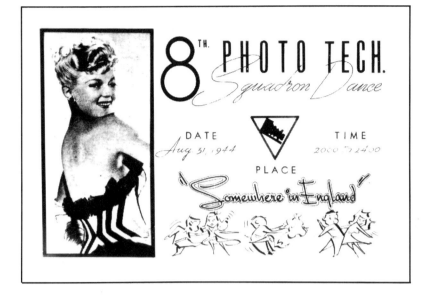

England, including courtship—or perhaps, especially courtship. For instance, one could walk a girl through nighttime London streets bustling with people in uniform or go with her to the park—although the latter offered no more privacy than the former: "Hyde Park was an encampment of searchlights, barrage balloons, and anti-aircraft guns," mused Don Morse. "In total darkness, you could sit on a park bench and listen to the buzz bombs."

One didn't have to leave the station to meet women. They were brought in by the truckload for special occasions. "Our group was holding a celebration of our 100th mission," said Clyde Coenen. "Trucks were sent to pick up gals at nearby villages. They liked to be around Americans and they liked ice cream. I knew a Colchester girl, who I asked to the celebration. She said she couldn't make it without a perm, so I gave her a handful of British pounds. She came to the party and I didn't even recognize her at first—she was done up like I'd never seen her. I wanted her to join me at the bar, but all she wanted to do was go to the mess hall and eat ice cream. By the end of the evening, the group CO had cornered her and my 'investment' was *lost*."

And if they weren't trucked in, it was just as easy to go to the nearby liberty towns they came from. "Bedford was

A welcoming conductress aboard a double-deck bus. Art Lobotzke

almost a soldier's paradise," said G. W. Pederson. "There was all the things a soldier likes: pubs, restaurants, movies, dance hall, and a live stage show. Best of all the women. There was a WAAF (Women's Auxiliary Air Force) training base just three miles south of Bedford with thousands of WAAFs there. Besides all the service women, there were thousands of civilian women, too."

Warbrides

Lloyd Hoeft recalled how "the power went off at a dance on base and when power was restored, we saw each other and got together. I married her

"Some films, like Twelve O'Clock High *were pretty close to capturing the way it was. Others, like* Fighter Squadron *overdid the glamor and fun image—it looked like a perpetual party time at a Harvard frat house."*
—Preston Clark, Jr., 94th Bomb Group (H)

"There was nothing glamorous about ground crews. We just hung in there doing the best we could to keep 'em flying."
—John Pendleton, 466th Bomb Group (H)

"Hollywood's depictions of fighter pilots were accurate to a point. But not all were the heavy-drinking, hell-raising types. Some were very conservative, very down to earth. But all had to be aggressive when they got in the air."
—Robert Powell, Jr., 352nd Fighter Group

"The [1990 movie] Memphis Belle *was embellished, of course, to make for good theater. But generally speaking, it was a good job of capturing the time. [The movie was made by the daughter of William Wyler, maker of the award-winning* Memphis Belle *documentary in 1943].*
—Harold Loch, 91st Bomb Group (H), Memphis Belle *gunner*

A wartime wedding: Doyle and Lalli Coppinger

"Ours was a typical wartime wedding," said Lalli Coppinger, English warbride. "No frills, but plenty of noise, goodwill and jollity, with food and clothing coupons contributed by relatives and neighbors. A close neighbor made the wedding cake. I didn't wear white—too proud to rent a dress from the American Red Cross. There were many guests including a truckload of GIs who (I was told later) didn't find their way back to camp for a couple of days. Doyle [Coppinger, a radio operator, and later radio section chief for the 94th Bomb Group] and I had a brief honeymoon in Edinburgh, Scotland, a very cold place in that wartime October. It was dark and raining hard when we made our way on foot to the hotel from the railway station. The hotel had run out of food for the day, so our honeymoon dinner consisted of a Spam sandwich washed down with a bottle of rum (a gift from a wedding guest) that Doyle had brought along. As we were getting ready for bed two detectives banged on the door demanding to see our marriage license. If we hadn't been married, it would have been *out*."

---

before I came back to the States." He voiced typical problems faced by British women immigrating. "She had quite a time when she came over, because she couldn't come when I did in September 1945. She went to London to help cut through the paperwork. But then the first boat she was on had trouble and had to go back. She had quite a time and didn't reach the States until April 1946."

British *Good Housekeeping* and the United States Office of War Information collaborated on a booklet, *A Bride's Guide to the U.S.A.*, that offered suggestions to help ease the transition to America: 'Keep your accent while you can; most English accents, especially when spoken by a girl, are regarded in America as charming.'

Special legislation—the War Brides Act, and the Fiancees or Sweethearts Act—was eventually enacted to override restrictive immigration laws and expedite the passage of warbrides. But there were still the rigors of a transoceanic voyage. "We sat on our luggage, stamped our feet to keep them from getting numb, while the mothers of the crying babies tried with help from all of us to comfort them," recalled Lalli Coppinger. "Finally, we were herded into trucks and taken to a covered boarding dock at Southampton.

Many English girlfriends became warbrides.
Leroy Kuest

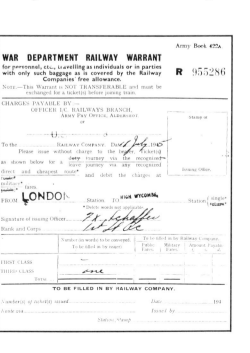

A woman's view

British writer Pat Garrod wrote:

"There's an extraordinary feeling about coming back to East Anglia . . . we can't help but escape the feeling that we and hundreds of our generation of women are reminded of the Yanks who dropped out of the sky in 1942-43, churning our countryside into oceans of mud; smothering the gold of our corn with grey airstrip concrete.

"It's almost as if those of us who knew the invading Yanks when they were young, secretly scared because they could die tomorrow, have momentarily slipped out of our fifty-plus-plus skins and become the 'chicks' the boys from over there knew.

"We are back in the Doughnut or Red Cross clubs that sprang up overnight.

"When you enter, you are in a world where there is no war on, no shortages, no rationing.

"The guys say: 'Gimme five!' and grab one of your hands; 'Gimme ten!' and grab two hands and haul you on the dance floor. They christen you 'Peaches' or 'Honey' or 'Chicken.' They treat you as if you are a queen, sliding your chair under you when you sit down.

"They help you into or out of your often pathetic, certainly coupon-costly coat as carefully as if it were mink. They bring you a corsage of violets, and write your name and 'I love you' in smoke on the club walls.

" 'Aw! Let your hair down, Honey!' they say. You learn that 'Cut a rug, Baby!' means 'C'mon and dance!' You jive and jitterbug and do a slow cheek-to-cheek shuffle, 'dancing on a dime.'

"It was all so very long ago. Why should we still feel guilty when we remember those guys who often had to cut short a wise-cracking evening with us to 'hit the hay' early because at dawn they'd be on a daylight raid deep into Germany?

"Why didn't our folds understand that we had to hang about the airfield and try (from the vantage point our guys expected to see us on when they landed) to count the B–17s coming back?

"We turned colder than the scything wind when we read the flare that signalled there were dead or wounded on board, and saw the 'meat wagons' closing in to take the wounded to the hospital and the dead to the mortuary.

"Some of those guys never made it back across the Atlantic. Some were never found and now are only names on the Wall of the Missing at Cambridge. Even now, some of us can't admit that when we're nearby we spend a little time in the American Military Cemetery there, with its crew-cut grass, immaculately kept paths and quiet pool.

"A name can call up the ghost of some pilot or ball-turret gunner with a broad grin, still barely twenty; dishing out candy and gum to every kid he sees; kissing the ground when he returns to safety from a mission; finding you and hugging you without speaking or kissing, so that your tears fall on to his sheepskin flying jacket and his tears end up in your ear.

" . . . Haven't most of us one-time 'Peaches' and 'Honeys' and 'Chickens' enjoyed thirty-five to forty years—bonus years—that some of our Yanks were denied? . . . sometimes when the East Anglian sky seems like one vast, soaring airplane, we remember a summer time in 1944 when planes . . . passed over in an unending stream . . . in perfect formation. It's then that we tremble."

"Unlike in some movies, there wasn't a girl waiting for you on the runway when you got back from a mission. And movies don't show the boredom—there was a lot of sitting around in a cold barracks without much light."
—John Wood, 381st Bomb Group (H)

"Some of the people who wrote stories . . . were in my group and one wonders how they could distort reality so. However, it wouldn't have made a very good movie if all you heard was disembodied voices, flak and machine guns, and all you saw was goggles and oxygen masks."
—Lester Rentmeester, 91st Bomb Group (H)

"I do not watch war movies. I had my oxygen knocked out twice by flak and it was very cold . . . and you were constantly on the lookout—very scared. My ears got black on the tip from frostbite. Bothers me to this day. I wet my pants a couple of times and was worried about you know what."
—Ed Pickering, 401st Bomb Group (H)

We didn't know what ship we would be sailing on. We were unloaded beside what appeared to be a tall building but what, in reality, was the world-famous ocean liner, *Queen Mary*. This was a thrill and bonus we hadn't expected."

Chapter 9

Ammunition for the heart and spirit

The doughnut was not just diet. Served by cheerful Red Cross girls, it was also ammunition for the heart and spirit.

—George Korson, *At His Side*

To members of the Eighth Air Force, the American Red Cross (ARC) was more than just doughnuts and coffee. Its work was intertwined in Eighth Air Force life—on station through Aeroclubs and clubmobiles, and off station through combat rest homes (commonly known as "flak farms" or "flak homes") and in service clubs that served as hotels, like the Rainbow Club and Eagle Club in London. And to downed airmen in prisoner of war camps, the red-stenciled crosses on ARC parcels and provisions were more than merely a welcome sight.

Rest homes

At a not-too-early hour of the morning, a dozen or so sleepy-eyed guests gathered at the breakfast table of an English country house, where the aroma of bacon and real eggs wafted from the kitchen. No one here grumbled about slogging through darkness and a hundred yards of mud to get to a latrine. No one speculated about targets for the day or if weather would delay them again.

Dressed in herringbone sport coats or sweaters and slacks of neither khaki nor olive drab, the guests were incognito combat fliers. On civilian hours and in civilian attire, the airmen enjoyed their first real respite since arrival in England.

During the previous months, they had been roused from never-adequate slumber at infernal hours and herded off through the icy dampness of blacked-out avenues to a mess hall, where they gulped down a GI breakfast before rushing to briefing. Then after a hurry-up-and-wait typical of the military and further accentuated by the English weather, they faced

Knightshayes Court, located at Tiverton, Devonshire. Owned by Lord and Lady Amory. USAF via R. C. Harris

"Homes provided civilian clothing which often caused the wearer to look relaxed whether he was or not."
—R. C. Harris, adjutant at Station 523, Coombe House

Ebrington Manor, located at Chipping Camden, Gloucester. USAF via R. C. Harris

the day's most traumatic event—the punishing and perilous flight to and (hopefully) from target. They were sent to combat rest homes to break that stressful routine: to tune out and tune up.

Usually after the mid-point of their missions or after a particularly harrowing combat experience, a squadron's flight surgeon recommended individuals or crews for a week of R-and-R at lavish rest homes.

"We made *recommendations* about sending people to rest homes," emphasized Dr. Clifford Kinder, flight surgeon for the 100th Bomb Group's 351st Squadron. "But we didn't have final authority on the decision. I once wanted to ground a crew that had flown three missions in three days. But the group's command staff confided that the next day's mission was so important that, unless it was absolutely necessary, I should withdraw the recommendation." Nonetheless, most combat fliers were eventually granted the week-long respite.

At first, the rest home program was entirely under the authority of the USAAF. In military terminology, "a Rest Home system provid[ed] rest and recuperative facilities for large numbers of fatigued air crew members." The very rigidness of that statement gives some clue to why, after the first two rest homes

were established in 1943, responsibility for the program was delegated largely to the American Red Cross—the rationale being to make them as *un-military* as possible. Control became an "Air Force–Red Cross partnership" according to a July 18, 1945 letter from Barbara Graves, director of the Rest and Convalescent Home Division. "This program was an experiment without precedent in either military or Red Cross procedures."

"Lack of Army demands and freedom from regulations help create the free and easy tempo of the place," noted David Wright, then a captain and psychiatric consultant for the Eighth Air Force. Quoted in the *Red Cross Courier*, Wright explained:

". . . after the Red Cross began shaping a new rest home pattern, the results in terms of rehabilitating fliers are to me impressive and surprising.

"I can say now the rest homes are saving lives—and badly needed airmen—by returning them to combat as more efficient fliers. That efficiency has been developed by making them individuals again—men with feeling of stability and a renewed sense of belonging to a world they knew before.

"It is hard to tell you just how Red Cross women are accomplishing this. I found many intangibles. The girls make

"In this unreal world, a man came to think of his plane, his flying mates and his own skill or endurance as the only familiar elements he has to hold on to. He attaches a tremendous importance to them and suffers when anything happens to them."
—letter to Eighth Air Force Command from Barbara Graves, Director of the Rest and Convalescent Home Division

Phyllis Court, located at Henley-on-Thames, Oxfordshire. USAF via R. C. Harris

each newcomer feel himself a welcome addition to the household. The atmosphere of so many things 'just like home' reawakens a feeling of some real security for him—the comfort of a chair by an open fire, games to play in the living room, home-cooked meals by candlelight, and good, natural, happy companionship.

". . . statistics show that a remarkable percentage of the men who finish their missions have had a chance to be in a Rest Home sometime during their combat tour."

An excerpt from a rest home manual offered the following insights behind the mission of rest homes:

"Men succumb to the shattering impact of combat because they have lost the impact of things which make them stronger than their fear. Based on that knowledge of the men we are dealing with, what we can do for them is easy to give. What they need most to restore them is a renewed impact of the things that mattered to them. They need to be reminded of the things which made them choose to fly and fight. The stronger their desire to live *for* something, the greater their ability to face their jobs.

"If you want to make these men better fitted to win their own battles, surround them with as many as possible of the symbols (like civilian clothes or base-

ball) and qualities (like laughter), which take them back to their own homes, their own memories of America, even their own interpretations of democracy. Though it may sound fantastic to you, if they can live for a week as they once lived, with freedom to think and act as normal individuals they can better face their unreal, chaotic, over-disciplined combat world. They will benefit from every opportunity you give them to live as free human beings. Your efforts must never be apparent if they are to reach the man. The chances are that neither you nor they will never know how much or how little you accomplish. But if the impact is sharp enough it will make a difference."

Saving airmen was top priority in war strategy at the time. Consequently, very special privileges were accorded the program. Rest homes were authorized hospital rations that afforded them food a few cuts above mess hall fare: fresh meat (steaks, fried chicken, and ham); fresh-squeezed fruit juice; ice cream; and other rare wartime delicacies, all "excellently prepared," according to one flight surgeon's firsthand judgment.

Cecil Carnes stated that, as director of a rest home, she "was given carte blanche in carrying out directions from our superior headquarters. The thrust was to provide good food, comfort,

Three Red Cross hostesses at Eynsham Hall.
Barbara Graves

Fliers from the 44th, 92nd and 381st Bomb Groups having tea and "hangar-flying" at Coombe House on Feb. 2, 1944. R. C. Harris

ambience, rest, rehabilitation with the facilities. . . ."

Facilities were of the elegant kind one might associate with a Noel Coward play. British owners of country houses generously offered use of them to their American Allies in a reverse lend-lease. The amenities afforded by the great houses were "just what the doctor ordered" for escaping the severe stresses of combat.

Some of the rest homes were stately Jacobean- or Queen Anne-style manors on estates of vast acreage. Others were formerly resorts and hotels. Clyde Coenen recalled the rest home he visited as "the castle at Blackpool. It was an actual castle—moat, gate and all."

On staff were gardeners, porters, cooks, waiters, and maids—each contributing to the ultimate objectives of putting their guests at ease and reminding them of the "good life" outside of war.

Typical activities included country fox hunts, archery, golf, skeet shooting, and tennis—possibly all before lunch. The afternoon was filled to capacity with the same, but all at the guest's decision. After that, guests often preferred more subdued entertainment, like a game of

billiards or bridge. Or dancing in the estate's grand ballroom, which at some rest homes doubled as a badminton court by day. And perhaps as a cap on an active morning and afternoon, a quiet evening in the study, writing home or browsing through the first civilian US newspaper available to them in months.

A station diary highlighted the agenda and services of one day out of the life

Dinner at a "flak home"—the only time one dressed in formal military attire. USAF via R. C. Harris

Returning to the stables at Coombe House, located at Shaftesbury, Dorset. USAF via R. C. Harris

Shooting skeet on flak leave. USAF via R. C. Harris

at AAF Station 523, better known as Coombe House:

"Cablegrams and EFMs may be sent from the office.

Movie tonight in the lounge at 2030: "Winter Time" with Sonja Heinie.

Tennis in Shaftesbury every day. Bicycles available in the motor pool for riding to the courts.

Leave your shoes outside your door at night for the best shine in the ETO.

Dance in the Ball Room tomorrow night."

But true to the nature of wartime conditions, not all regulations could be dispensed with. A notation on the agenda stipulated "Blackout hours: 2252 to 0532."

In an August 1944 report about Coombe House, flight surgeon Howard P. Wheeler wrote: "The location of Coombe House is such that the occupants need not be worried over the probability of raids by enemy aircraft . . . this, in itself, is productive of a feeling of security and well being that can be acquired in few other places. The landscaping and surroundings are all conducive to rest and relaxation. . . . The Red Cross girls ably round out the score of entertainment and recreation with the feminine touch that the army cannot supply. . . ."

Red Cross staff member Marjorie Kuhl commented: "Our central effort was to divert the combat fliers' minds as far away from the awesomeness of war as possible. . . . This we did with both planned and spontaneous activities . . . and perhaps most important of all, doing away with rank."

"They made everyone feel at home," said George E. Swanson, 94th Bomb Group bombardier. "The main room [at Eynsham Hall] was huge, with fireplaces at each end, and each fireplace large enough to hold a car. There was a Steinway grand piano in the main hall on which I played Chopin's 'Polonaise in A-flat' which was then popular because of the movie, *A Song to Remember*. P–51s sometimes buzzed the place, probably flown by pilots who had stayed there. Each morning we were awakened by a British manservant with tomato juice, then down to the dining room for a big breakfast."

"It was a complete change of pace," said Frank Halm, who stayed at the

Palace Hotel Rest Home in Southport. "We had a nice time, because they had all kinds of relaxing things, like horses to ride, pool tables and ping pong, and girls to dance with. The officers and enlisted crewmen all went together."

"That was the best opportunity we had to spend time with the enlisted members of the crew," said Clyde Coenen, who was granted flak leave after his fifteenth mission. "On the base they were housed separately and due to miltary protocol, we had little contact with them except on missions. It was a good break from the routine, and I didn't think much about the missions to come."

Some, however, did think about the missions they had yet to face. Like the long weather delays spent waiting for the takeoff flare, flak leave gave them an interlude to contemplate what lay ahead after they returned to operational status. "I had time to think about combat," said William Blackmon, Jr. "Then, really for the first time, I got scared. After we discussed it between ourselves, I became skittish—realizing that flak wasn't just smoke going by. It was frightening just to lay there five days and think about it. The very next mission I had, I was truly frightened—and hadn't been before."

And some subtle comments may indicate that flak leave sometimes may have put combat fliers back in a civilian state of mind just a little too soon. One visiting officer wrote in a letter of thanks: "I do wish that I could have stolen that bed and brought it back with me, as mine doesn't seem so good now." Ralph Price said his two weeks of R-and-R at Southport helped him remember "what it was like to lead a normal life. And it did make it pretty tough to go back and fly again."

However, on the whole, the outcome was positive. Fliers returned from flak leave with a renewed fighting spirit they had during their earlier combat missions. "They didn't necessarily come back cheerful," said Dr. Kinder, "but they were visibly more alert and rested."

Flak leave itself stands out clearly to many fliers as a threshold of sorts, a sense of having "reached the hump and it's all down hill from here on," as one flier put it.

"I found that the wonderful American fliers had a marvelous sense of humor," said Red Cross staff member Freda Scharman. "Even though they had been through ghastly stress, they were able to relax and were so funny that I

Rested and in good spirits after week-long stay at a flak house. Barbara Graves

laughed myself sick for two years. This humor enabled them to go back to the skies refreshed and strong enough to handle their next missions."

Rest homes in the U.K. were as follows:

Rest home, location
Aylesfield House, Alton, Hampshire
Bucklands Hotel, Wallingford, Berkshire
Coombe House, Shaftesbury, Dorset
Ebrington Manor, Chipping Campden, Gloucestershire
Eynsham Hall, Whitney, Oxfordshire
Furz Down House, Kings Somborne, Hampshire
Keythorpe Hall, Tugby, Leicestershire
Knightshayes Court, Tiverton, Devon
Moulsford Manor, Wallingford, Oxfordshire
Palace Hotel, Southport, Lancashire
Pangbourne House, Pangborne, Berkshire
Phyllis Court, Henley-on-Thames, Oxfordshire
Roke Manor, Romsey, Hampshire
Spetchley Park, Worcester
Stanbridge Earls, Romsey, Hampshire
Walhampton House, Lymington, Hampshire

Aeroclubs

"Aeroclubs . . . were a home away from home," said Hiram Drache. Located on station, clubs typically provided a

To Ruth and the ARC
This rest this week I've spent without a care,
Has been a God-sent gift—a moment rare
That shall forever be remembered.
You cannot know—you cannot understand
The thanks we feel. Your helping hand
Has put us once again upon our feet;
Endowed us with that strength we need to meet
The foe once more, upon his ground.
Perhaps because of what you've done,
Someday, somewhere, some battle will be won
Above the earth, where on each bated breath
There lurks the thought that sudden death
Is near.

You cannot know, nor realize the worth
Of what you're doing here.
But I have ridden in the sky,
And I have seen my comrades die

In bullet-spattered planes that fly
On God-knows what!
And I have seen that sky explode,
In all the horror Mars has ever known.
With death on either side I've flown
The trackless, German sky.
That's why I know—how much this really means.
Here in this verse (though crude it be)
I offered my thanks. For me
This rest—this week—will ever be
An unforgotten one.

May God see fit to bless thee,
In all the things you do
Accept thou, then my humble thanks—
And the thanks of a grateful crew.

Staff Sergeant Roy E. Joyner
3 December 1944

The Aeroclub located at the 2nd Base Air Depot at Warton. Art Lobotzke

game room with ping pong and pool tables, a library, and most popular, a snack bar. They weren't necessarily granted the same "carte blanche" priority that rest homes enjoyed. However, staff members used what they had to do what they could to keep up the morale of station personnel. When better furniture was unavailable, for instance, GI cots and mattresses were covered with cretonne to serve as couches. Clubs were housed often in large Nissen huts or several connected together. The first club was

opened in February 1943, and eventually most American airfields in East Anglia had one.

Aeroclubs provided an alternative to an airfield's other clubs. "A difference was that no alcohol was allowed in the Aeroclub," explained Hilda Kinder, director of Thorpe Abbotts Aeroclub.

During evenings when a mission alert was on for the next morning, Bob Strehlow remembered, "We lounged around at the club—bought Cokes and read magazines and newspapers."

Aeroclubs, usually staffed by a director and two Red Cross girls aided by British volunteers, catered to air station personnel in off-duty hours. Kinder continued: "We had everything from dances to current events programs put on by the intelligence officers. We had an older, motherly British woman who sat in the library two mornings a week mending uniforms and sewing on buttons."

The staff members were stationed at the airfields by the Red Cross according to the same largely random assignment process the military used. And like their military guests, they shared the same anxiety and hope in sweating out a group during a mission, and lived in the same conditions.

Aeroclub staff were also on hand after a mission in the debriefing room. Ready with a smile, coffee and doughnuts, they welcomed the crews back from raids.

Am at the Aero Club now drinking a "coke" — the first in three weeks. The first available too. I eat & drink heavily but never fill the cavity

I spend a lot of time at the Red Cross Club here, in spite of the fact that I could go to town. I do a lot of reading — smoke my pipe & sip cocoa—

—Jack Kirschtraun,
February 28, 1944
and March 7, 1944

An ARC hostess. 8th Photo Tech Squadron

"I remember a particular waist gunner who underwent a personality change. When I first came to know him, he was outspoken and outgoing. By the time he got to his last few missions, he was a walking zombie—wild-eyed, withdrawn, spoke rarely about anything to anyone."
—William Blackmon, Jr., 381st Bomb Group (H)

A club's snack bar was available to satisfy the late evening hunger resulting from the irregular hours inherent to a station's operation. "Traditionally, the army supper is served very early," continued Kinder. So the men were often hungry around ten or eleven at night. At those hours, the snack bar became a very popular place." Food was sold for a nominal sum, as ordered by Secretary of War, Henry L. Stimson, who laid down the policy of charging for items: "It is believed advisable that American soldiers be required to pay at least the actual cost of meals and lodging furninshed for their convenience. . . ."

But perhaps the greatest value of the Red Cross in Aeroclubs were intangibles they provided, often unconsciously. The Red Cross staff lifted spirits in ways they could not be aware of at the time. At a reunion forty-four years after the war, a former 100th Bomb Group crew chief said to Hilda Kinder:

"You don't remember me—I rarely went to the Aeroclub. But I'll always remember the way you picked up my spirits one day when I was feeling low. My B–17 had to abort that day for mechanical problems. I had just spent hours in the rain and cold without being able to figure out the problem. Plus, I had just received a letter from my wife, who wrote about our two little daughters' birthday parties—and I thought about how I had missed another year of their lives. I was becoming very depressed.

"You and another Red Cross girl were laughing—I don't know what for— but you were laughing. It just picked me up. I thought, 'If these two American girls can stand it here, then I can, too.'"

Clubmobiles

Doughnuts served by the mobile Red Cross units were a strong attraction. They were almost like Mom used to make, but in numbers that were a factorial of her family-size batch. Equipment aboard a clubmobile was capable of producing 5000 "sinkers" daily. And doughnuts were an item one would be hard-pressed to find anywhere else in the doughnut-desolate UK (one Englishman described doughnuts as an "ethnic food" largely foreign to the English).

Clubmobiles, the early ones converted from Green Line coaches belonging to London Transport and later ones custom-built American vehicles, traveled to air stations, as much as possible to coincide with mission days, to serve coffee and doughnuts. In addition to tremendous quantities of doughnuts and coffee, they carried a phonograph, a stock of records, cases of cigarettes, and for viewing in the clubmobile's lounge, magazines and newspapers.

Parking preferably near a station's mess hall where an electrical outlet and water spigot were accessible, the three-member staff filled their urns with water and started the coffee brewing. They set

An ARC clubmobile stops in front of a Thorpe Abbotts hangar and the men take a welcome break to have coffee and doughnuts. 100th BG

This noon, after lunch we had a mobile Red Cross outfit here. They served some coffee and real live do-nuts. I figured that the first five samples were too good to be overlooked — so I went back for more. (There was quite a mob fighting to get near the window) Darn it, though, after my eighteenth doughnut, they decided to serve in an orderly manner. Naturally I didn't want to sweat-out a line so I gave up and went back to work.

It is awfully hard for me to write unless I hear from you occasionally. Please write often. I guess you'll have to bear with me & hear

—Jack Kirschbraun,
February 23, 1944
letter to parents

out the doughnuts on serving trays, cranked up the Victrola and prepared for the onslaught of anxious guests.

Serving usually became hectic, according to Barbara Pathe, staff assistant on a clubmobile based in Bury St. Edmunds in 1944. And every day brought new adventures as varied as their colorful guests. In September of that year, she wrote to her family: "We draw coffee, grab cups from the dishwasher who stood behind working steadily and frantically, keep an eye on the doughnut trays and replenish them, lift down empty urns and get the boys to lift full ones onto the counter, chat with GIs, replenish the cigarette supply, keep an ear on the Victrola to hear when [it] runs down, collect dirty cups and keep an eye on the men in the lounge [section of the vehicle]. . . ."

And describing one particular episode, she wrote:

"All at once a GI took the dish mop . . . another took to fishing out the cups, another took over Dotty's coffee urn and a fourth took over mine. After that, things went from mad to madder. The boys seemed to know everyone who came up to the serving hatches, and if a friend asked for black coffee he got cream, and vice versa. For particular buddies they mixed up horrible potions or refused to serve them anything.

"All the time they urged everyone to take more and more and more doughnuts, though our ration is two. . . .

"When it was all over, they flipped a coin for the task of mopping up. The loser

"It hurt, of course, when we learned they had gone down. We thought about the families they had told us about . . . But you couldn't break down. Breaking down can cause a chain reaction. There was little time to spend grieving—and much need for us to be cheerful with the troops. . . ."
—Hilda Kinder, Thorpe Abbotts Aeroclub

poured gallons of water on the floor and mopped. . . ."

Of course, the overall objective was not to fatten up GIs with doughnuts. Morale was the primary focus. The doughnut was the symbol of that focus.

To a Red Cross worker like Pathe, the most painful moments came when "hurt was suffered by GIs you knew and there wasn't a whole lot you could do about it. There were things like 'Dear John' letters, rejections by peers, hopes that were dashed, friends who were lost, loneliness in the midst of people whose interests differed—and all you could do was listen."

Maybe listening was enough. Homesick boys, plucked from families and whisked away by the military to a foreign land, found comfort in a quiet moment and a listening ear. Pathe commented: "There were some who rejected [Red Cross's] 'good clean fun' and 'girl next door' approach, but to most of them it fulfilled its role as a provider of respite and reminder of caring folks at home. They . . . have countless friends among

131

This ticket cost about fifty cents and was good for one night's lodging at an ARC Service Club.

An ARC hostess outside the White Swan Service Club. USAF via R. C. Harris

those of us who were privileged to have served with them."

Service clubs

Service clubs functioning as hotels, plus much more, were available throughout the British Isles for American personnel on leave. The best known were in London.

When it opened in April 1942, the Eagle Club, on Charing Cross Road in London, became the first American Red Cross club in England and the haunt of many in the Eighth Air Force.

A bed cost the British equivalent of fifty cents per night. Typically there were two bunkbeds (sleeping four to a room)—not that much time was spent in the room.

On Piccadilly Circus in London, at the Rainbow Corner Cub (the largest club with 450 full-time and volunteer staff) activity never ceased.

Rainbow Corner was a piece of America set down in England. The basement, called Dunker's Den, was the precise replica of a corner drugstore on Main Street back home. Gramophone records played around the clock, sodas were served ice-cold for "thrippence." The families of many Eighth Air Force men

London's Rainbow Corner Red Cross Club bustles with activity both night and day. 94th BGMA

received letters written by Adele Astaire, sister of Fred. She and others wrote for any GI who asked. Upstairs was a ballroom where volunteer hostesses danced nightly. Other floors were devoted to hobbies and a library containing well-thumbed papers from the States. No matter what time of day or night they arrived from air stations north of London, they found welcoming staff on duty.

The clubs were often the pivot they revolved from during liberty. "The most fun I had was staying at a place run by the Red Cross in London," said Ray Patulski, who enjoyed the prime locations of the clubs. "I spent a couple nights in Piccadilly seeing the theater shows."

POW

If a pass to London with accommodations at a Red Cross club was the best time to be had, the precise opposite had to be bailing out of a stricken airplane at 25,000 feet and parachuting into enemy territory. For those captured and thrown in a prison camp, perhaps the singular thread connecting POWs to a sane, civilized world was a parcel with a Red Cross stencil.

The Red Cross served as an instrument of the government for assisting to captured Americans. Mail and cablegrams were sent via the International Red Cross Committee. Funded by the US Army, eleven-pound Red Cross food packages were sent weekly to downed Eighth Air Force fliers. Other parcels included medical, dental and garden supplies.

"We were starved," said William Blackmon, who was interred at Stalag 17 in Austria. "We ate dandelions, insects, anything we could find. By the time the Red Cross parcels got to us, there wasn't [much left] that the guards didn't take. . . . But once in awhile, maybe once in a month and a half, we'd get . . . crackers . . . or a chocolate D-bar, as they called it."

"When I was a prisoner of war," said G. W. Pederson, "the Red Cross food parcels were a welcome sight. . . . They kept us from starving over there."

"Parcels were given to us usually about once every four weeks," said Stan Rames, 361st Fighter Group pilot and POW for eleven and a half months.

Ironically, when Red Cross shipments tapered off severely toward the end of the war, it was not due to interception by desperate people in a defeated nation. It was the Eighth Air Force's methodical devastation of Germany's lines of transportation. "I knew our boys were strafing the hell out of the trains carrying the parcels," said Rames. "I wished I could still be flying to help with the job."

"Lean living became leaner in 1945," said Pederson. "When the Eighth began concentrating on the railyards, the bad had to come with the good." As the phrase goes, the darkest hour came just before dawn.

Mayday!

Alone over no man's land

Spence's crew faced perhaps the most crucial decision of their combat careers. Damaged badly by flak, their bomber, christened *Homesick Angel*, was forced to drop out of the relative safety of the First Bombardment Division formation prior to the targets of a Mercedes complex and Sindelfinger Aircraft Engine factory at Stuttgart, Germany.

It wasn't a decision about whether to bail out or not. Rather, it was simply a decision of when and where to bail out. Allied/German lines were changing daily, in some cases hourly, in September 1944. Lt. Gen. George Patton's Third Army had been steadily pushing back the Germans. *Homesick Angel*'s navigator, Lt. S. J. Abelman, determined a heading that would take them back in the general direction of Allied lines.

As they plodded along, gradually losing precious altitude, the bombardier, Lt. Harry McCrossan, spotted a target of opportunity, a large Germany army warehouse, and called for a bomb run. As he tripped the bomb release, *Homesick Angel* jumped as its three tons of explosive cargo dropped free. Despite its lightened load, the stricken plane continued to lose altitude. Pilot Horace Spencer gave the order to jettison ammunition, guns, flak suits—in short, everything that could be heaved out.

"We tried to jettison the ball turret," recalled John Houk, "but the wrench normally supplied for that purpose wasn't there. We attempted to break the turret's gear ring by pounding on it with the barrels of our guns, but to no avail. If nothing else, at least that activity kept us busy and out of mischief."

Trailing a finger of dirty gray smoke and limping along now at about eight hundred feet, the bomber drew a hail of small arms fire as it crossed the Seigfried Line. Lieutenant Spencer was coaxing every inch out of the failing aircraft, two engines out and a third alternately running and on fire. Staying with the airplane just another minute or two could make the difference between parachuting into the German side or the American side.

Word went out over the interphone that they would ride as long as the aircraft was able to maintain enough speed to prevent stalling. Once that was no longer possible, they would bail out—hoping desperately they happened to be over Allied territory at the time.

"Our pilot, 'Spence' Spencer, was superb," continued Houk. "He nosed the aircraft down to create just enough airspeed to keep us airborne and moving in the direction of friendly lines. He called me forward and said, 'When we bail out, we have to do it quick, because we're going to be low,'" The plan was set: Navigator S. J. Abelman would come through and dive out the waist hatch. When he did, those in the aft section were to follow in close order—Houk being last in line. The pilots and bombardier would go out the nose hatch. "My mind was fixed on things going as they were supposed to—that it would happen as the pilot directed. That's what you do in a situation like that—you latch on to the small things."

"Believe it or not, my most vivid memory is not the day we were shot down and decorated by Patton. It was when we came back on one engine halfway from the English coast to our base. It was difficult to fly, naturally. And what made matters worse, we didn't get lined up just right with the runway. I was braced in crash position and listening on the interphone. When they told us to go around again, I frankly didn't think we had much of a chance. We skimmed the trees coming around and had to pull that one engine so hard. Fortunately on touchdown, we hit evenly on the two front wheels. We bounced two or three times and settled down."
—L. G. Spillman, 92nd Bomb Group (H)

"We knew flak was the greatest danger, but we did not hesitate to strafe airfields, which is how I got shot down. I accepted fear as a healthy and normal reaction."
—James Goodson, 4th Fighter Group

"Since there wasn't room for my parachute in the turret, I was afraid that if something happened to the plane, I would just have to ride it down. . . . After a while, a sense of resignation sets in and you decide that what is to be will be. I remember on a specific occasion when we were deep in Germany, I made up my mind that I was not going to leave the plane no matter what happened. A sense of calm came over me that I know if we had been shot down, I would not be here today."
—Ralph Price, 381st Bomb Group (H)

The crew's confidence in their pilot was unshakable. Since their first days of training together in Dalhart, Texas, they had been known as "Spence's crew." Diverse and determined as the nation they came from, Spence's crew—Abelman, Bupp, Hensley, Houk, Jenkins, McCrossan, Spillman and Spratt—was an all-American miscellany of ancestry hailing from across the United States, from California to Kentucky.

They were also a cohesive, disciplined fighting team and knew from several perilous experiences in their previous missions—including once flying on a single engine halfway from the English coast to Podington at treetop level.

Suddenly, Abelman came back through the waist and pulled the latch on the waist door, which automatically yanked the hinge pins free. The entire door disappeared from its frame.

Anxious as the moments were, bail-out was conducted in an orderly fashion, everyone exiting the appropriate hatch in the planned order.

Ball turret gunner Jack Spratt recounted:

"The plane was only about six hundred feet when I jumped out. John (Houk) was right after me. We'd been trained to look back at the airplane and count to ten before pulling the rip cord. I looked to see I was clear of the tail and pulled it. The little pilot chute came out on a tether cord and was supposed to pull the full chest chute—but the rest didn't follow. I found out later that either the gunfire from the ground or flak had gone through the chute when it was hanging on hooks in the fuselage. The chute was fan-folded and in an accordion pleat so that normally it pulls out easily and unfurls. The hot projectile evidently went through the chute and sealed the silk between the folds. The hole it made wasn't the issue.

"When I realized the rest wouldn't come out on its own, I started pulling it out by hand. Only parts of it were out and it never fully blossomed. I always thought I passed everybody else on the way down, but that might have been my imagination. During those scant seconds while I was falling, the subconscious seemed to come forward and I thought of things I had done and shouldn't have done during my life. The flashback of that stayed with me for years. I started to pray and then—boom . . . I hit a seventy-five foot tree. My chute draped over the tree and I was flung back upward and then down again,

ending up dangling five feet off the ground.

"There was no way I could get the harness unhooked with my own weight pulling down on it. If I pulled myself up with one hand, then I didn't have the hand to unhook the harness. I tried to flip over and get out that way, but the lines were too fouled in the branches."

"Lt. Spencer, the last to bail out, put the plane into a condition to cause a stall only a few hundred feet from the ground," commented flight engineer Thomas Jenkins. Spencer's chute had just fully opened as he hit the ground, but he was unhurt. Simultaneously, the plane crashed and exploded with an earthshaking boom.

"Where the first one out landed to where the pilot landed, there wasn't a football field of distance between," said Spratt.

All landed miraculously without serious injury, but they found themselves in no man's land—squarely between American and German forces. The crewmen had heard ground fire as they plummeted to earth and didn't know what kind of reception awaited them on the ground.

"We hadn't had radio contact with the infantry," said radio operator Houk. "We were too busy and a Mayday call wouldn't have done any good at all in those circumstances."

"We tried to find out where we were," continued Jenkins. "There was visibility for a long way and we saw a man on a bicycle about two hundred yards from us. No one else was in sight. McCrossan and I ran over to him, not knowing whether he would be German or French or what, but we were ready for whatever we had to cope with. As luck would have it, he was a young French boy about fifteen or sixteen, and he told us that the Germans were one way and the Americans were the other way."

P-51s began to buzz them. Jenkins noted, "They had apparently been furnishing us cover and one by one, they buzzed us, all in the same direction of the American forces, but we didn't realize it."

They found and untangled Spratt from his puppet's perch in the tree. And they walked to the burning wreckage of the plane, where a wheel strut was the largest piece remaining.

A Piper Cub with US insignia landed in a clearing nearby and a lieutenant colonel from Third Army Headquarters ambled to them. He explained to the

The 92nd Bomb Group crew that bailed out into no man's land on Sept. 10, 1944, pictured with Lt. Gen. George Patton, Jr. Left to right: 2nd Lt. Paul K. Bupp; 1st Lt. Horace L. Spencer; Sgt. John P. Hensley; 2nd Lt. Harry J. McCrossan, Jr.; Sgt. L. G. Spillman; Lt. Gen. George S. Patton, Jr.; Staff Sgt. John L. Houk; Staff Sgt. Thomas F. Jenkins; Staff Sgt. Jack Spratt; and 2nd Lt. Sargent J. Abelman. US Army Signal Corps via Jack Spratt

"The pilot, Jim Wheat, was a farm boy from Texas. As a youngster, I had visited farms and was impressed that the kids there drove tractors, operated all types of farm equipment and anything you could think of. I came away with the impression they could do anything. It was the same with Jim—I marvelled at his know-how. To him, the B-17 was just another piece of machinery. When ditching like that, the objective was to keep the nose as high as possible and let the tail hit first— then drag and slow you down. He accomplished that masterfully. The fact that we survived was a credit to the way he operated the aircraft."
—William Sullivan, 379th Bomb Group (H)

crew where they were and that vehicles would be sent to pick them up.

It was arranged that they would wait at a French family's home nearby. The family was ecstatic for being liberated by American forces. "They offered us cognac and champagne," said Spratt.

They were taken to General Patton's headquarters, just outside of Metz, France. The Third Army was on the verge of crossing the Mozelle River at the time.

Then General Patton summoned the crew to his command trailer. "To see a gentleman as tall as Patton, a big-boned, stocky man, come down off those steps toward us was quite a sensation," commented Spratt. "And what does a staff sergeant or lieutenant say to a man like this?" Illustrative of army aviators' lesser inurement to military formalities than their infantry counterparts, he added, "I wondered, do we come to attention, salute, or what?"

The general told them to stand at ease and commended them on their action of bombing the German warehouse despite their battle damage. But an awkward few minutes followed when no one knew what to say. Finally, Sergeant Spratt broke the silence: "Sir, will you sign our short snorter bills?"

"This broke the ice," said Houk. "The general signed our bills."

"Once you started talking with him," recalled Spratt, "he became just like an old country gentleman, a grandfather type you could easily converse with. He didn't look like his pictures and he didn't act like his reputation. He was glad to meet us because of the air support we were giving the Third Army." General Patton chatted with each of them, asking where they were from and other generally expected questions. But unexpectedly, the general turned to his aide and said, "Get me nine Bronze Stars." The aide explained that couldn't be done, because the Bronze Star is for ground personnel—not to mention the fact the aircrew was not under his command. Patton repeated, "Get me nine Bronze Stars."

Like all good soldiers do, the aide obeyed. After an impromptu ceremony in which a Bronze Star medal was pinned on each man, the general said that he would provide them transportation back to England on his private C-47—"a limousine-type Cadillac," in which their hosts loaded "a case each of cognac and champagne," noted Jenkins.

"When we landed, the pilot gave his call sign and the tower recognized it as Patton's," said Spratt. "Naturally, they

"I'd describe myself as fatalistic. I was of the feeling that if there was a bullet with my name on it, I would get it and there wasn't anything I could do about it. Of course, I didn't do anything stupid to tempt fate. Those of us who were fatalistic had it easier than the others."
—Frank Halm, 94th Bomb Group (H)

"To say there was fear while flying a mission is an understatement. People up there were shooting at you. And of course, the people downstairs didn't like you either."
—John Ziebell, 357th Fighter Group

"All of a sudden, we were going straight down in a tight spin. Oil lines had been hit by flak and the engines froze instantaneously. I found myself standing in a horizontal position, looking straight down at the earth. I couldn't move. In my mind, I saw my folks' house and my hometown. My thoughts were 'Gee, it's too bad my folks are going to get this telegram saying I'm missing in action.' I knew I was going to die and that telegram is what I felt most badly about. Then, at about 4,000 feet, the pilot was able to pull us out of the dive. After we got on the ground in England, they told us it was aerodynamically impossible. I got the feeling I was destined to lead a long, productive life, because we had faced sure death and had survived."
—Hiram Drache, 457th Bomb Group (H)

"They said you couldn't go in a vertical dive in a B-17 and pull it out. On two occasions I saw B-17s do it. One of them was hit, an engine out. He went into a vertical dive and on the way down I saw one parachute open, but then the pilot was able to pull it out of the dive and joined the formation again as tail-end charlie. I always wondered what that bailed out crewman thought when he saw it recover."
—Harold Loch, 91st Bomb Group (H), *Memphis Belle* gunner

assumed Patton was on board and a number of command cars came zooming out to meet him. But instead, a group of grungy looking sergeants and lieutenants came out. A group administrative officer immediately said, 'You're not allowed to wear that Bronze Star.'"

Houk asserted, "Jack [Spratt] was the saucy one of the bunch. He said, 'Until General Patton tells me not to wear it, I'm going to wear it.'"

General Order 58, dated Sept. 12, 1944, stated the following notation by the name of each member of Spence's crew: "By direction of the President . . . a Bronze Star is awarded . . . for meritorious achievement in connection with military operations against an enemy of the United States in France on 10 September 1944." And to make award of the medal legitimate, the crew was assigned administratively to General Patton's Third Army for three days.

An evader's story

Twenty thousand feet over Nazi-held Holland, Lt. Howard Moebius put his bullet-riddled P–51 in a tight right turn deliberately causing a stall, and vaulted out of the cockpit over the right wing to avoid hitting the horizontal stabilizer and rudder.

His emergency actions were based largely on the advice of another 357th Fighter Group pilot who had faced similar circumstances. "Not long before, a young pilot by the name of Chuck Yeager had given us some tips on bailing out of a P–51, how not to pull the chute too soon, and what to do on the ground in enemy territory," Moebius explained. "But since I didn't think I would ever be shot down, I didn't pay close attention."

However, in the desperation of the moment, the memory of it all came quickly to him, as his every resource as pilot came into play. Just as Yeager recommended, he had stalled the aircraft in a tight turn to help avoid deadly impact with the tail as he bailed out. Another point by Yeager was that if you open your chute too soon ". . . the whole German army will be under you and shoot you before you get to the ground." The advice likely contributed to Moebius' survival.

Moebius free-fell thousands of feet before finally opening his chute at about 1,500 feet. But even then, he was strafed and narrowly missed by a German fighter. He pulled the toggle straps to spill air from the chute and quicken his descent.

Evasion photos of Ken Stone. "After the war, Hans Scharff, a master German interrogator, stated that they kept files on shirts and ties. By looking at my photo they could easily tell that I was from the 381st Bomb Group, because the photographers used the same shirts and ties to photograph all its personnel," according to Stone. Ken Stone

Just the previous day the young American pilot had shot down an FW 190, his third kill. But this day, Sept. 19, 1944, he was on the receiving end as he witnessed his Mustang, spewing flames, plummet to earth and smash into a bog.

Landing on a newly plowed field, he quickly gathered up his chute and hid under large tobacco leaves. Hearing sounds of distant machine gun fire, Moebius decided to move on from his landing site. But as he stood, a little boy appeared and motioned frantically for him to get back down. Moebius slid into a deep ditch at the edge of the field, removed his G-suit and waited.

That night a local civilian, Gys Van Beek, having heard from the little boy that an American pilot was downed near his small village of Angeren, Netherlands, slipped out into the darkness to help.

Van Beek recalled: "After walking around in the dark for a while, I decided to risk whistling the Victory Code and called softly, 'Pilot, I am your friend and will help you.' Out came a figure who stood in front of me with a .45 caliber pistol in hand."

"He didn't pay any attention to the gun," Moebius commented. "He simply said, 'Follow me.'" The pilot was to find out later that this Dutchman, active with the Underground, had helped a number of Allied fliers escape.

The two traveled a circuitous and unobtrusive route to a local church, where they climbed to the highest floor in the steeple.

"Sleeping, under the circumstances, was impossible for me," said Van Beek, "but somehow my new friend had dozed on the hard wooden floor." Moebius thrashed around, mumbling barely discernible phrases about the trauma of the day, until he was roused by loud knocks on the door far below. Impatient knocks became louder on the sturdy church door that was bolted inside.

They stayed silent, hoping trouble would pass. Finally, they heard a German soldier shout in the churchyard, "Lass die Schweinhunde sehlafen wir gehen weiter," meaning "Let the dirty dogs sleep—we'll go further."

Unaware that the "dirty dogs" were an American fighter pilot and a member of the Dutch Underground, the soldiers returned to their vehicle and went on, but ominous sounds of German traffic, mostly motorcycles on the road by the church, persisted the rest of the night.

In fall 1944, fighting was heavy around the bridge at nearby Arnhem, the bridge made famous in *A Bridge Too Far* by Cornelius Ryan. "Everybody presumed that the war for us would be over in a matter of days," said Van Beek. "For the previous two or three weeks we had watched thousands of German troops withdraw, very much in disorder."

In the morning, Van Beek and Moebius went to a nearby farm, where a large family lived. Moebius gave all his chocolate candy bars to the children, who hadn't seen chocolate for two years.

The pair traveled on stealthily through fenced and flooded backcountry to avoid contact with the retreating Germans. At Angeren, located between the Rhine and Waal Rivers, they contacted a village policeman named Stevens, who was aware of Van Beek's Underground activities and was willing to hide the American pilot.

Van Beek went on his way, but returned a few days later with a cake—a chocolate birthday cake. Moebius had

"After the second bounce, the wing hit a tree and a fire started," said John Ziebell. "The machine guns went off—and the approaching rescue crew hit the deck on the far end of the runway. They found me a little while later in the woods, where I had wandered off dazed. I was going into shock, but I heard someone yell, 'Here he is!' As they carried me away, they did a Humphrey Bogart on me—put a cigarette in my mouth whether I needed it or not." USAF via John Ziebell

mentioned wistfully that his birthday was September 23, four days after his bail-out on the nineteenth. The farm family used the chocolate candy bars given by Moebius to concoct it.

The pilot was outfitted in civilian clothes and the policeman forged a false ID using the pilot's evasion photo. As a precaution, the identification papers indicated their bearer was deaf and dumb, since Moebius was not fluent in either Dutch or German.

Van Beek noted they rehearsed the deaf and dumb facade, ". . . and to our amusement he could play this role masterfully."

Hope of quick liberation ended abruptly in mid-October. Van Beek continued: "The feldgendarmes ordered everyone to evacuate within two hours. . . . We still did not want to leave town and decided to hide for a few more days on a small farm behind Stevens' house, hoping to be liberated."

Van Beek was arrested and brutally interrogated by the German SS. He admitted to no Underground participation, even though they threatened to shoot him unless he confessed that he was a spy. He confessed nothing and the SS eventually released him.

"A plane in front of us took a direct flak burst in the bomb bay over France and exploded. There was no way anyone could have gotten out. Part of the plane went over the top of us and part underneath. As tail gunner, I watched the tail section, which had remained intact, fall all the way to the ground. With the long horizontal stabilizer of a '17, it just floated like a bird, in a downward circle. I reported it to the navigator to mark the coordinates. I watched for a parachute, but none came. It didn't break apart even when it hit the ground. And I experienced the miracle, before I left England, of seeing the tail gunner from the ship. Unconscious during the fall, he survived and was picked up by the French Underground, nursed back to health and returned to England."
—L. G. Spillman, 92nd Bomb Group (H)

"They generally advised bailing out over riding in a disabled fighter. Trying to land in water, for instance, was tricky. The scoop [of the P-51] would grab the water. If you had to touch down on water, you kicked the rudder hard just before hitting water, to turn the aircraft sideways."
—John Ziebell, 357th Fighter Group

"There was a fellow in our Nissen who had to bail out four times. We called him 'Shroud Lines.' When he came in, we'd say to him, 'Pull your shroud lines in—don't get them caught in the door.'"
—Clyde Coenen, 487th Bomb Group (H)

"Ewart, our pilot, had a watch, a nice watch. I always used to kid him, 'You really think you should fly with that watch? Why don't you leave it here while you fly.' He would always laugh. One day we watched all the aircraft come in and he wasn't with them. We waited and waited. Finally it got dark and still no one knew what happened to him. He had been knocked down. It really hit me hard. And I felt guilty—I hoped he realized that I was never serious about the watch."
—Joe Redden, 361st Fighter Group

Amongst themselves, they decided that Van Beek and Stevens would leave as ordered and Moebius would hide in a shed with blankets and food—still hoping liberation was soon to follow. "It was not easy to say good-by to him," said Van Beek, "but I promised to come back as soon as possible if Angeren was not liberated in the coming few days."

As the front moved closer, artillery shellings rocked the area, arbitrarily decimating farmyards, fields and houses. "One day, another farmer rushed me out of there and took me to the second floor of his house," said Moebius. "He hid me in a cubby hole measuring two by one-and-a-half feet, and only four feet deep." The farmer remained very nervous about the American's presence and finally moved him again, this time to a ditch near the farmhouse.

In the meantime, since liberation had not come, Van Beek returned as promised to get Moebius at the shed where he had stayed behind. Van Beek recounted: ". . . in an Old Red Cross truck . . . we entered no man's land. Practically no civilians were there anymore—only German soldiers and all kinds of cattle running loose. When I arrived at the shed . . . it was empty."

The many weeks of evasion, in which the pilot was constantly on the move and without proper food and shelter, began to take a toll. Moebius suffered from dysentery. And at one point, he was picked up by German soldiers. But with his fake identification and very real gaunt appearance combined with an effective deaf and dumb act, he fooled the German soldiers. The soldiers felt sorry for him and took him to a Dutch family who, because of old and sick family members, had been granted permission to remain temporarily in the evacuation zone.

The family in turn evacuated him to Hummelo, Netherlands, where the Underground helped him move farther north. Still, England was a world away and no sign of liberation was in sight.

Weakened by illness and trudging in wooden shoes toward the Rhine River, Moebius felt he could go no farther. Just as he was contemplating turning himself in to the Germans, he spotted by chance a farmer who Van Beek had introduced to him soon after bailing out.

This farmer took him to the home of a young married couple, both of whom were doctors and much involved in the Underground. "I got my first bath in forty-five days and breakfast in bed," said Moebius. "They nursed me back to health." He stayed with the couple for three months.

In February, he was teamed up with two other pilots, three Belgians and an individual called the "exterminator." "The exterminator," Moebius explained, "killed anyone suspected of telling the Germans about their [Underground] organization. He was getting well known for his mission and they wanted to get him out of there."

Early one morning the group set out in an iron boat down the Rhine River, which forks off into the Waal and Rhine. The Germans had blown up many dams, making navigation difficult. And being in unfamiliar territory, no one in the group knew for sure where they were. "We needed to go down the Waal," said Moebius, "because that was held by the Allies. If we accidentally continued down the Rhine, we would go to Arnhem and 'a bridge too far'—held by the Germans."

After paddling all day and into the night, they saw lights shining on the water ahead. They hesitated, wondering if the lights were from an Allied or German encampment. Cautiously making their way on to shore, they hid until morning. Two motorcyclists drove by and it was evident they were British. Liberating forces had come!

Five months after being shot down, Lieutenant Moebius returned to the 357th Fighter Group at Leiston, Suffolk. Since the rule was that downed fliers who came back through the Underground were not allowed to resume their combat flying tour (except by permission at a very high level), Moebius was reassigned to the States. But before he left, Eighth Air Force Fighter Command had one last mission for him: Like Chuck Yeager, he would share his firsthand experience of evasion with other Eighth fliers who might face similar circumstances.

Yankee ingenuity

The wings of Lieutenant Spiegel's B-17G gave lift through the icy air of dawn, Feb. 3, 1945. The target for today: the Big B, Berlin.

Irving Spiegel's crew anticipated returning to their station at Eye, England, along with the rest of the 490th Bomb Group, after the ten-or-so round-trip hours it took to fly the roughly 500 miles to Berlin. But as fate had it, they would not return until after an adventuresome

---

The ultimate war souvenir

Howard Moebius wanted to be alone when he pried open the wooden crate recently shipped from the Netherlands.

"I opened the crate and saw everything was covered with straw," said Moebius. "I felt underneath the straw and felt undefinable parts of metal."

In the crate were parts of his P-51 Mustang that he had last seen—as a "detached observer"—in embattled skies over Holland thirty-six years before. Now, incredibly, pieces of that same airplane were in his hands: one of four propeller blades, a six-foot length of steel twisted like an Arabian sword; a nose cone; and an assortment of other parts not readily identifiable.

Thirty-five years after the incident, Gys Van Beek called him to say that a Huissen (Netherlands) newspaper printed a picture of a road construction crew removing parts of the aircraft at the site of the crash and a picture of Moebius as a young fighter pilot.

"Naturally, few people get pieces of their crashed aircraft," Moebius commented. Still, for inexplicable reasons that went beyond sentimentality, he decided to ask for the parts. But after two months of waiting with no response, he took a long shot—and went right to the top. "I decided to write to Queen Julianna and asked her to use her influence in getting permission to receive it."

After another delay, he found Queen Julianna was stepping down and her daughter, Beatrix, would take the throne. He wrote again, and this time the long shot paid off. Within a week, a letter from the US Embassy at The Hague informed him that the Dutch government had pledged their full cooperation.

Friends from the old Underground had carefully packed the parts in straw and shipped them.

"It was an extraordinary feeling to see them, hold them in my hands," said Moebius. "It brought back those feelings, those emotions, everything that went into that day and those years."

"When B-24s were fatally struck and erupted in flame, invariably they would turn turtle and fly for a short period of time upside down before plunging straight down to earth."
—Robert Bieck, 453rd Bomb Group (H)

seven weeks and a 3,500 mile circle of Hitler's Europe. The adventure included an extended stay with the Russians, who shared "vodka that tasted like gasoline," and a display of Yankee ingenuity that resulted in two flyable aircraft—a Flying Fortress and Mustang—made from the components of disabled aircraft.

At the Initial Point (IP), Spiegel's number one engine shivered to a stop with mechanical problems. Soon they were over Berlin and as expected, black blossoms of flak were everywhere around them. Everyone watched the unreal, floating cotton slip ineffectually past, wings sometimes bisecting them. Watching was all they could do.

Suddenly, the plane shuddered as a flak burst tore into the right wing. Number four engine sent tremors through the plane as a flak-disfigured propeller began to bash wildly against the engine cowling. Sheered-away metal was cast into the slipstream. Slowly losing altitude as they exited the target, Spiegel conferred with navigator Ray Patulski about their options. Struggling against a stiff headwind, England seemed unreachably distant. Realizing that the ailing ship could not keep up with the formation, the decision was made to plot a course toward Russian lines instead of England.

"We left our formation when they turned for home and headed east," the pilot noted in an interrogation report. "Our object was to reach an airfield we believed to be intact at Warsaw."

In a shallow dive, but with the wind behind them, they flew uneventfully on two engines over farmland divided not by the familiar, welcoming hedgerows of England, but by troublesome trenches and tanktraps. They spotted a makeshift Russian airfield near Torun, Poland, and made several passes to determine if they could set down there.

Togglier Charles Sandusky reported: "We took a look at the field. . . . It looked like a series of landing strips with a hay stack in between each. At the end of the field there was a shack with something on a pole that looked like a wind sock. In back of the shack was a tree-lined road, a brick wall, and a small village."

The crew braced themselves for a crash-landing as the pilot came around again, this time touching down on the frozen-mud airfield. He applied the

"The plane suffered a direct hit [over the oil refinery at Wesseling, Germany, a suburb of Cologne] and went into a violent spin and exploded. I was knocked unconscious in the plane but was blown out of the plexiglas nose. The severe cold brought me to long enough to pull my rip cord—and then I passed out again. I had been advised by a major, a navigator from Milwaukee, to always wear the chest chute even if it's hooked only on one side. I owe my life to that man."
—Arvid Anderson, 303rd Bomb Group (H)

"I found one thing in combat that I hadn't known before. Religion."
—Howard Moebius, 357th Fighter Group

"Friends' deaths didn't affect my performance. I deliberately made myself a fatalist. I knew it could happen to me. I half expected it to happen to me. But I wasn't worried about it."
—John Houk, 92nd Bomb Group (H)

Membership Certificate
This is to certify that

Carl L. Anderson

Is a member of the Caterpillar Club whose life was spared the 25th day of September, 1944 because of an emergency parachute jump from an aircraft. This certificate is bestowed to the end that this safety medium in the art of flying may be furthered.

PRESENTED THROUGH

Switlik Parachute Co.

Harold L. Foster
PRESIDENT

Richard Switlik
SECRETARY

CATERPILLAR CLUB

brakes immediately to avoid the hard realities at the end of the runway. Sandusky continued, "We were still going too fast and sliding sideways as the trees approached."

The careening bomber continued on collision course until its pilot took the emergency action of a ground loop to the left—tearing the right wing away at number four engine, shearing off the horizontal stabilizer, and twisting the fuselage and wings out of the alignment carefully engineered at Boeing's plant in Seattle.

Emerging from the ship unhurt, the crew was promptly surrounded by a group of enthusiastic Poles "standing around jabbering and saying 'Ben Zine,'" according to the togglier. Gas was pouring out of the ruptured wing tanks and the Poles quickly grabbed buckets to catch the precious fuel. The field, near Plock, Poland, had been captured from the Germans thirteen days before by the Red Army.

Ray Patulski said, "The Russians at the field took us sixty miles in 1931 Ford trucks to what had been a Nazi experimental airfield at Torun [Poland]."

At Torun they met two P-51 pilots and a 384th Bomb Group crew headed by Lt. George Ruckman. The Ruckman crew had suffered similar problems over Berlin and landed with two engines out the same day Torun had been captured from the Germans. The two P-51s had flown an

escort mission on February 14 to Dresden, Germany. The two were flying together, one an element lead and the other his wing man. The lead Mustang's electrical system went out, leaving no compass, radio or coolant for the engine. They landed together, but the undamaged Mustang ground looped and was damaged beyond repair.

Their Russian hosts radioed the whereabouts of the fliers to US authorities and told them that a transport aircraft would be dispatched as soon as possible.

During the wait, "Russian pilots gave sources excellent treatment," in the words of the interrogator's report. "Other Russian officers were mainly tolerant and made no special effort to get them evacuated." The crews were housed in a vacated Luftwaffe mess hall described as "clean but not luxurious."

The Russians offered them "large steaks . . . as well as quantities of vodka, which had the consistence (sic) of gasoline. [Sources noted that, when short of liquor, the Russian would drink a mixture of fifty percent petrol and fifty percent water.]"

Air transport never came. "For a while we were waiting for a C–47 to haul us away," noted the togglier. "Then we lost hope and started in earnest to repair the ship the other crew had brought." Ruckman's B–17 had landed without additional damage, except a blown tire from the pocked runway left by the Germans. One engine was completely destroyed by flak, but the other engine had an oil leak that was repairable.

"After discovering that the other B–17 was almost flyable," noted Spiegel, "we decided to repair it with working parts from ours. What we needed was a wheel and an engine."

The group of fliers possessed some highly applicable talents. Among them were a peacetime aircraft mechanic, a pattern maker, a welder, two auto mechanics, farmers and construction workers. In a truck borrowed from the Russians, four of the fliers, accompanied by a Russian officer, crossed the frozen ice of the Vistula River to return to the crash site near Plock.

With "the help of two telephone poles and eighteen civilian Poles," according to a group newspaper, they went about the task of removing a 1,350 pound engine. Charles Sandusky explained:

"They had no winches or cranes or anything to do any lifting. The Polish

This 490th Bomb Group crew carried with them many souvenirs from their extended stay in Poland. Front row, left to right: Staff Sgt. Dale C. Tyler, Staff Sgt. Charles Sandusky, Sgt. Frank Stockton and Staff Sgt. Salvitor M.

Novarra. Back row, left to right: Tech. Sgt. Maurice Carpenter, 2nd Lt. Raymond Patulski, 1st Lt. William Hole, Sgt. Jack Caffrey and 1st Lt. Irving Spiegel. USAF via Ray Patulski

"We bailed out at 22,000 feet [on the first mission to Berlin, Mar. 6, 1944] and were trained to delay opening our chute until near the ground. This would enhance our ability to get away. However, as there was ground cover, I pulled my ripcord almost immediately. I had crash-landed two days prior to this mission and my parachute harness was messed up. The new harness I was wearing had not been fitted. Consequently, when the chute opened I was pulled to a stop with such force that I thought I would be an eunuch. The pain was so intense that I raised my legs over my head and was floating down seat first. About this time a German fighter flew up to look me over. I imagined he thought, 'That poor fellow will never make it down, he has no legs.' And he flew by with hardly a passing shot. . . ."
—Gilbert Falck, 91st Bomb Group (H)

people did all the labor. They lifted the engine off its mounts by means of poles. The wheel was taken off by placing a homemade horse affair under the wing, then digging a hole big enough under the wheel. The ground was frozen plenty hard, too.

"Meanwhile the remainder of the boys scouted around the air base at Torun for equipment to take the engine off and wheel off the ship we were to go home in. We found a crane, a tool box and a bunch of airplane jacks. They'd all been in a fire so there was a chance the jacks or the cable on the crane had crystallized. At least that's what the Russians said. Anyway . . . we all pitched in and got all the work done. After all the repairs were made the two pilots, a Russian pilot, and a few of the other guys test flew the ship, and it worked."

They were ready to leave, but were not granted clearance to take off. In the three weeks they waited for clearance, they cannibalized the ground-looped

P–51 to make flyable the P–51 with damaged electrical system. In test flights, Sandusky noted that the American fighter pilot "entertained the Russians by coming down the runway at fifty feet and at 400 [mph] plus. . . ." Then, not to be outdone, "The Russian fighters [Yak 9s] did better. They'd buzz, then climb straight up and do four rolls, still going up."

When the Americans finally departed, aboard the B–17 were two nine-man bomber crews and one P–51 pilot, and an array of German swords, rifles, helmets, pistols and beer steins—compliments of the Russians. The other P–51 pilot remained on the ground until he could convince the Russians he could return to England safely.

They set a course for Foggia, Italy, and a Fifteenth Air Force station, where mechanics—"other than tightening a few bolts"—declared the engine and wheel change well done. And they made the hop to England, the end of a 3,500 mile odyssey.

"They were marching us [to a German POW camp] . . . on the way there, these women came running over with long sling purses and were hitting us and kicking us on the shins. We were trying to get behind the guards. Old men were hitting us with canes . . . and cursing us in German. And the guards were using their gun butts to keep them off of us. Yet they kept coming anyway . . . I think . . . because they had loved ones that were killed in war, too."
—William Blackmon, Jr., 381st Bomb Group (H)

"I saw parachutes falling through our formation. . . . I saw a bail out that didn't work. A man jumped from a flaming, spinning B-17 and his chute caught on the tail. I don't know what happened to him—I didn't have time to worry about it. I saw airplanes blow up, some run together, some go down spinning. It all seemed so detached."
—Phil Garey, 94th Bomb Group (H)

"We were halfway across the North Sea when we were met by a Ju 88, which followed us all the way to Germany just out of range of our guns. We were met by a large force of fighters over the German coast. They held off their attacks until we were at the IP and then they attacked in force. They continued attacking right through the flak—the only mission I was on that this happened. We had an engine on fire on the way in, so we made the bomb run on three engines. We were hit by flak shortly after we dropped the bombs. The four men in the midsection of the plane—the radio operator, the ball turret and waist gunners—were killed. We lost another engine and couldn't keep up with the formation. After we dropped out of formation, eight or ten German fighters attacked us. They put another engine out of commission and set the plane on fire. The pilot ordered us to bail out and the six of us remaining got out. I always had a fear of making a parachute jump, but it came very automatically. It took about twenty minutes to make the descent from altitude. I made a soft landing in soft ground close to a river [and was captured]."
—G. W. Pederson, 306th Bomb Group (H)

Ruckman gets reimbursed

In May 1953, Lt. George Ruckman was reimbursed by Congress for money spent from his own pocket during the stay in Poland. Dry wording of the bill proffered the appropriation of $250 "in full satisfaction of the claim of the said George F. Ruckman." Ruckman's claim explained that he spent the money for food, shelter, clothing and labor while in Poland. He also had bartered his wristwatch and a fountain pen in order to borrow a Russian major's truck. He bribed Russian military police to overlook the cutting down of two telephone poles needed as hoists. And he gave his revolver to a Russian officer. The House of Representatives had approved Ruckman's claim and sent it to the White House for President Eisenhower's signature.

An air-sea rescue story

Ditching an aircraft in open sea is hazardous business, even under "controlled" conditions. For a pilot fighting the yoke of a writhing aircraft—engines out, and gashes and holes in control surfaces—the challenge went from hazardous to deadly.

Even though water and air share some of the same qualities of fluidity, water makes considerably greater demands on transients passing through it. Durable as some of the bombers and fighters were, aircraft are designed to fly through air. Passage through water offers far greater resistance. And destruction is the penalty for attempting to breach water's inviolable rules of physics. Many aircraft—after surviving flak and fighters—limped on only to succumb to the stringent demands of the unforgiving sea. Some split wide open on impact with churning waves. Others managed to set down as smooth as a bird settling into a nest.

But even if fliers escaped a ditched aircraft, the harshest of elements awaited them: high winds and waves and water temperatures survivable for only a short time. That's why air-sea rescuers had to be constantly ready and fast.

The Anglo-American rescue service has been aptly described as a "masterpiece of coordination." While P-47s canvassed the seascape searching for aircraft in trouble, RAF aircraft carried large wooden lifeboats dropped by parachute to survivors. The English had made air-sea rescue a precise science. American controllers joined in, plotting the data to cover Eighth Air Force operations. By triangulating fixes of downed fliers, Royal Navy and Coastal Command crews could be dispatched so quickly that fast motor launches sometimes raced parallel as an aircraft skimmed the water and splashed to a stop.

Unlike the death throes of a torpedoed ship, an aircraft generally plummets quickly to the bottom. Its crew must flee the machine as frigid, mountainous waves surge through a shattered fuselage. Then they must contend with vicious surf and frigid water, hoping help was on the way.

One such rescue comes from the diary of William J. Sullivan, 379th Bomb Group ball turret gunner:

"June 20, 1944 Hamburg, Germany 25,000 ft.—22.7 hrs. Heavy Flak (Acc.) Oil Refinery

"The boys had been here a few days before, while we were on a pass, and told us about the flak. So we expected a rough time in that regard but not quite as much as we did receive. Procedure was normal until we turned on our I.P. and number one started to act up. We just about feathered it and started on the bomb run when all Hell broke loose. The flak was the severest we had ever encountered and each burst seemed to be aimed at our particular squadron. After a few close bursts number two started to burn and number three was knocked out. We tried to feather number three but no soap, so we just had to let it windmill. The pilot told us to put on our chutes, for he thought it was all over for us. We fell out of formation after dropping our bombs and started in the general direction of home. The smoke had stopped coming out of number two but it was pouring oil. We were losing altitude but everything seemed to be under control. The pilot got in touch with Air Sea Rescue and told them of our plight. At about ten thousand we started throwing out equipment when the pilot informed us that we would probably have to ditch. The radio room was cleared of all unnecessary equipment

Miss Donna Mae
of the 94th Bomb Group

On May 19, 1944, twenty-one aircraft from the 94th Bomb Group flew a mission against railroad yards at Berlin. The 94th was leading the 4th Combat Wing.

Over Germany they encountered heavy contrails, making navigation and formation flying very difficult. On the bomb run the group made several "S" turns for proper spacing and alignment. At bombs away one of the lead element's 1000 pound bombs hit and severed the tail of the number two aircraft in the second element—*Miss Donna Mae.* The aircraft manned by Lt. M. U. Reid and crew of the 331st Squadron, went into a steep dive after the tail separated. The aircraft never recovered, and when at 13,000 feet a wing came off, it spun crazily to the ground. Abe Dolim, flying navigator on Lieutenant McMakin's crew,

watched in horror as the aircraft went down. Abe yelled, cursed and prayed for opening chutes, but his every plea was in vain.

"We cleared the [B–24J], pulled our ripcords—and the plane blew up. I was alone as I floated out of the clouds close to the ground . . . headed right at two military figures with rifles—and the longest fixed bayonets I had ever seen. I touched down . . . and then realized I really hurt. My flying suit was still smoldering. The Germans put down their guns and helped me beat out the embers. That done, they picked up their rifles, and began to search me. They . . . helped me pull off my burned gloves. And there it was—my West Point 1942 class ring. They motioned me to take it off. . . . [After several days of interrogation], the guard was opening my cell, and in came a German flying officer. His left arm was mangled, and heavily bandaged. In excellent English, with a British accent . . . he said he was sorry for me as an airplane pilot—for me the war was over. But he added he would never fly again either. There was more small talk, and then he arose to leave. He walked to the door, and then came back to me. His good hand was in his pocket. He pulled it out and dropped my class ring inside my clothes. Simply he said, 'I am sure this means something to you, and it means nothing to them. Hide it and do not wear it until you are free!'"
—Andrew Low, 453rd Bomb Group (H)

and we prepared to take our stations. While still descending, we went over our duties and ditching procedure, each man making sure of what he was to do. The radioman remained on interphone, informing us of our altitude and distance from shore. When about six miles out the pilot told them that it would be any minute now. Everybody braced themselves as we could feel the plane slowing down for the attempted landing. The first crash was slight as it was only the tail hitting the water. Then in a few seconds the big

impact came. Water came in from everywhere and we were tossed about like corks. I landed face down in the water, in the opposite direction from which I had been sitting. The floor of the radio room gave way and we all went down. When I regained my senses I was under water but soon came up as we all had half of our 'Mae Wests' inflated. I grabbed for an oxygen hose and some wires on the right side and tried to pull myself up. I could feel someone's body underneath me as I started to climb out the hatch. The tail

"Our group command, Colonel Thomas J. J. Christian, Jr., was one of the finest men I'd ever known, and also one of the finer pilots. When he went down, I began to worry, 'If it can happen to him, it can happen to anyone.' Getting knocked down was a constant worry after that."
—Charles Cummins, 361st Fighter Group

"We were flying on engines one and two only. The pilot was flying the plane as slowly as possible, trying not to overload those two engines since you gain a little speed with relaxed engines. But then number two engine began throwing oil and running a little rough, and the pilot feathered the propeller. The pilot asked me how much distance we had left to [England's] shore and I told him. Fortunately, we weren't far. The British had cleared the beachline back quite a ways so that planes in trouble could land on the coast. We came down, just touched water and slid on our belly up on to the beach."
—Hiram Drache, 457th Bomb Group (H)

"My greatest fear was getting shot down. But you always hope, or are foolish enough to think, 'This isn't my day for it.' The time for worry was before you got into the plane. After take off, you were so busy that you had no time to sit and create fears for yourself."
—Ray Patulski, 490th Bomb Group (H)

gunner was partly out and trying to pull the life raft release. He told me to step on his arm and when I did he gave another yank and the first raft popped out. The plane had broken in two at the ball turret and was sinking fast. The second raft appeared and I jumped into the water and grabbed a rope on it. The first one was washed away before anyone could get to it, so we all held on to the other one. A K-dingy floated into the pilot's arms and he inflated that. I kicked myself away from the wing of the plane as I thought there might be a suction created, but it just slid out of sight slowly. The bombardier was floundering around so we managed to get him in the large raft. Then the copilot and waist gunner climbed in, followed by the radioman. That left the engineer, the navigator and myself in the water, as the pilot had climbed in the one-man raft. By this time the sea had become quite rough and both rafts were shipping water. The ones in the raft attempted to bail out some of the water but each wave would seem to fill it again. With the pump in the raft, they tried to pump up the seats so that another man could enter, but the position of the bombardier made it difficult. We saw a buoy about fifty yards away and attempted to paddle towards it but were swept by too quickly. Between the swells we could see the top of a tower and a beacon on land, so we knew we weren't too far out. After about forty minutes someone spotted a launch heading our way and everyone felt better. My arms were quite tired from holding on and my body was shivering from the cold water but the sight of the boat seemed to give me strength and I knew it would only be a matter of minutes before we were picked up. As the boat came by, they threw over a net and lines and pulled us towards them. In no time we were all aboard, exhausted but happy, and shaking hands with all the crew who seemed as happy to see us."

Few people have heard of Spence's crew or that an Eighth Air Force bomber crew was decorated by Lt. Gen. George Patton. Few know of a flier who evaded capture for five months in Nazi-held Holland, where people he never met before risked their lives to save him. (He was reluctant to share his story because "so many guys—especially POWs—had it so much worse.") Or the ingenuity of a group of guys who were thrown together on a Polish field without proper tools, but who repaired two aircraft and flew them hundreds of miles home. Or a pilot who pancaked his bomber, shot to ribbons, into the North Sea without killing or even injuring a single crewman on board.

Each one was just another mission.

Chapter 11

Swords beaten into plowshares

*They shall beat their swords into plowshares
and their spears into pruning hooks.*

—Micah 4:3

The final Eighth Air Force combat mission of World War II was flown on Apr. 25, 1945. At 2:41 A.M. on Monday, May 7, 1945, in a red-brick schoolhouse in Rheims, France, Col. Gen. Alfred Jodl, the German chief of staff, signed the document of Germany's unconditional surrender.

VE-day, Victory in Europe Day, was proclaimed on Tuesday, May 8, 1945. Spontaneous celebrations erupted as soon as the news broke.

John Mills of Bedford recalled:

"May 8th was a fine, sunny and warm spring day—rather rare in this country, where the Eighth Air Force remembers the cold and rain. Although American servicemen were supposed to be confined to their bases (heaven knows why), many had obviously avoided that confinement and were in town celebrating. There were crowds all about, civilians and service people. We saw a couple parked Jeeps with Americans, who had brought from their bases a good supply of pyrotechnics and Vary flare pistols. They were putting up quite a good fireworks display. Wherever you went, celebratory bonfires were being lit."

Blackout curtains were raked aside for good. Lights snapped on everywhere. And across East Anglia, over villages and the Eighth's airfields, flares of all colors splashed across the sky. Loudspeaker systems barked out commands to cease all firing of pyrotechnics—and immediately another salvo of flares flew skyward.

VE-day, May 8, 1945: "Finally, around dusk we went home," said John Mills, then a Bedfordshire youth. "There was a bonfire in the street around which we all sat and sang patriotic songs and pop songs of the period. We went to bed later than usual feeling, 'Well that's a chapter of our lives over. No more V-1s or V-2s. Peace at last. Now let's look ahead and rebuild and plan for our happier future.'" 100th BG via Harry Crosby

*"After their final mission, some [bomber] pilots became quite exuberant—dipped a wing and acted like a fighter. As we came into the field after our final mission, our flight engineer called the pilot and said, 'Roll this thing in there.' The pilot said, 'Go to hell. I flew thirty-five missions and I'm going to get down safe.' And he brought it down to a beautiful landing."
—Joe Curley, 486th Bomb Group (H)*

146

The High Wycombe exchange on the day the lights came on again. 8th Photo Tech Squadron

Meanwhile, Cologne, Germany, lies in rubble. 7th Photo Recon Group

Trolley missions

Those not on flight crews, but who had toiled day and night to help write "Unconditional Surrender" across the German sky, were given the opportunity to see the damage wreaked on the Third Reich. In early May 1945, "trolley missions" were arranged for armament and ordnance crews, air mechanics, administrative staff and others interested from both bomber and fighter stations. More than 30,000 people from the ground echelon were taken on low-level aerial tours over Germany.

"We went sightseeing, flying at 2,000 feet so that everyone could get an idea of what had happened and what our efforts had accomplished," said Ray Patulski, serving then as a flight crew "host."

"It was worse than I expected to see," said "passenger" Al Giesting. "We saw the devastation at Merseburg and in the Ruhr Valley."

"We flew low over Cologne," added Francis Cunningham. "We saw the cathedral still standing—standing alone. I tried to imagine what it was like to have been on the ground during the bombing."

A devastated people

For those on the receiving end of the raids it was all as terrible as one might imagine. Although strategic bombing did not win wars on its own (despite the claims of its early champions), it struck crippling blows against the Third Reich.

It devastated vital war industries and undermined the economy for eventual collapse. It helped clear the skies for the land army's push to Berlin. And as for its objective of breaking the will of the German people, the *United States Bombing Survey* concluded, "The mental reaction of the German people to air attack is significant."

Present-day, translated words give testimony to the effect of strategic bombing on morale in World War II Germany:

"When I came home from the Russian front for holidays, I was totally shocked," said one German soldier. "I thought, *What are we fighting for, when we're subjected to these raids in our own country?* From that day on, I doubted our victory. Many of comrades felt the same."

"Food was okay till the end of 1944, when it became less and worse, though we [on the fire brigade] were better fed than the rest of the population because of the importance of our work during the raids," according to one German man. "It was difficult to drive vehicles after these attacks, due to the rubbish on the streets and the danger of falling facades. My greatest fear was for my wife and daughter, who had to stay in a normal cellar, while I was in the safer fire brigade's cellar. Surviving depended very

147

The oil refinery at Merseburg in the aftermath. Photo taken on May 25, 1945. USAF via Frank Halm

Bremen in the aftermath. 7th Photo Recon Group

Instead of a windswept airfield somewhere in England, a windswept Arizona desert valley became the resting place for once proud aircraft. Some remained mothballed for a time. Parts were stripped off many and were eventually broken up and sent to the smelter. Others became drones or were transferred to the air forces of countries like India, Israel and Brazil. A few survived. These P–38s and B–24s await their demise at Chino, California. Michael O'Leary

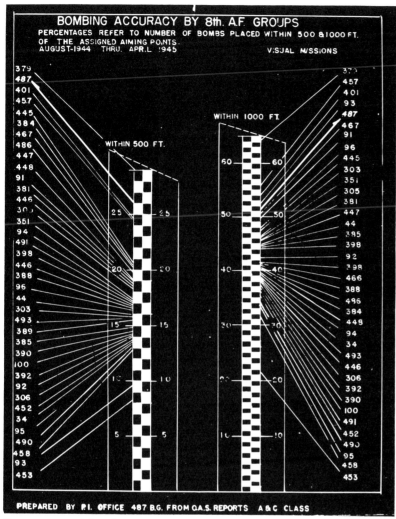

A US propaganda leaflet. The message translates to "To die in vain."

Comparison of bombing accuracy between bomb groups from August 1944 through April 1945. The 379th Bomb Group placed 29 percent of its bombs within 500 feet of the aiming point and over 64 percent within 1,000 feet. USAF via Clyde Coenen

"Two days after VE-day in London, I met a girl and asked her if she wanted to go for a drink. She said, 'There isn't anything left but water.' Celebrations had drained London dry."
—Ralph Ballinger, 904th Signal Company (at Alconbury)

much on the safety of one's cellar. . . ."

"When the British attacked, it burnt. When the Americans attacked, it crashed," remembered one German woman, twenty-six years old in 1945.

"People in the cellars were calm and serious. Some prayed. I was furious because of the Allies, but also because of our own leaders. Sometimes I feared this could be the revenge for what we have done to the Jews," said a German woman, thirty-four years old in 1945.

"A lot of our streets were nothing but long rows of ruins by 1944," according to one German man. "Sometimes we didn't recognize where we were. Nobody could imagine then how it would be after the

war. We felt depressed, but not able to react against the Nazi leaders."

"I remember best the first raids in 1942 and 1943, when an air raid shelter was the sensation in Munich," said one German woman. "When a street or a house was badly damaged, all the people were running to look at it. This changed very much when we had attacks nearly every day in 1944—American raids during the day and English during the night. Then people became more and more depressed. From autumn 1944 till the end, it became worse and worse. Nearly half of the population—mostly mothers and their children—was already evacuated. I had no children and had to stay in my work, but things became more and more disorganized. It was harder every day to get to work, because there was so much rubbish everywhere. Trains and trams couldn't come through again. When my flat was bombed out in November 1944, I felt very hopeless. When war ended and the Americans came into our town, I was glad. I thought to myself, *Whatever happens will happen. But there will be no more air raids—that's the most important thing.*"

"I looked out over Germany and wondered how the Germans lasted so long through the hammering we gave them."
—C. L. Anderson, 390th Bomb Group (H)

"After we returned from Stuttgart, Radio Berlin broadcast that the Eighth Air Force had been out in full force that day and that 5,000 were dead and 50,000 were homeless. I asked [another airman] how he felt about that. He said he felt OK—that we had done our job. I felt the same. That's what happened to us—that's what war does to a person. But it was a real sobering thought."
—Harry Crosby, 100th Bomb Group (H)

Mercy missions

In the days just before and after Germany's surrender, field operations orders in the Third Air Division continued with about the same regularity as the previous three years. But this time, instead of specifying bombloads, they specified tonnage of ten-in-one rations to be dropped to desperate civilians cut off from supply in Holland and other countries.

"We flew a mission with the bomb bays filled with K-rations and medical supplies," said Ray Patulski. "We flew over in a loose formation and came down very low—landing gear and flaps down—just over the rooftops. It seemed like everyone living there was standing on top of the buildings—waving and waving. I never saw so many assortments of American home-made flags."

There were other types of mercy missions flown, like evacuation of refugees in war-devastated areas. Patulski continued: "With a minimum crew aboard, we picked up planeloads of [Hungarian] refugees and took them to Paris. A couple who spoke English came into the nose and sat with me. They transmitted messages to the rear telling the others where we were. When we got over France, there was wailing and tears of joy throughout the whole ship."

And Eighth Air Force aircraft were assigned other non-bombing duties. "When the war in Europe was about over, our B–17s were used to transport infantry troops from England to Casablanca for deployment to the Asian Theater," explained Carl Lose. "The crew chiefs made these long flights to help ensure the return of the B–17s to England. It was a long flight, ten hours, and took every gallon of gas we could haul. We used wingtip tanks and added two tanks in the bomb bay."

Redeployment and evacuation

Redeployment to the Asian Theater was a prevalent and unwelcome thought on Eighth Air Force stations. It would be ninety-nine more days after VE-day before Japan also surrendered. For ground personnel weary after three years preparing for maximum effort missions and fliers who had not quite completed their quota of missions, thoughts of home were front and center.

On July 16, 1945, the Eighth Air Force was re-established on the island of Okinawa in the South China Sea. The Eighth's new bombardment groups were to be equipped with B–29 Superfortresses and fighter groups trained for transition to the new, long-range P–47N. However, Japan surrendered before the groups became operational.

Meanwhile, back in East Anglia, most US airfields were evacuated without delay. Some groups (92nd, 94th, 96th, 100th, 303rd, 305th, 306th, 379th and 384th Bomb Groups, and 55th, 355th and 357th Fighter Groups) remained in Europe. When the last elements of the 306th Bomb Group left Thurleigh on Dec. 15, 1945, they had spent three years and three months—longest of all American combat units in England.

While the fighter groups remained temporarily at airfields in England, the retained bomb groups became part of the occupation forces on the Continent. "When we left Chelveston to become part of the occupation forces in Belgium," said Elmer E. Anderson, former 305th Bomb Group crew chief, "we had a huge bonfire. Everything that couldn't be taken along—leather flight jackets and pants, equipment, rations, and lumber from temporary buildings and bomb boxes—was gathered into a pile measuring at least two city blocks long and thirty feet high to be set ablaze."

Going home

The rest received orders to the States without delay. Much of the ground echelon were shuttled to ports for embarkation on liberty ships and other transports—including great luxury liners, like the *Queen Mary*, pressed into service as a troop carrier.

Lloyd Hoeft was booked passage aboard the *Queen Elizabeth*: "Accommodations were nice—even though thousands of us were aboard and slept in hammocks crammed into huge ballrooms and other places all over the ship. But no one cared about overcrowding—we were caught up in the joy of going home."

Narrow East Anglian roads—once teeming with jeeps, six-by-six trucks and olive drab bicyclists—fell silent.

The Americans jubilantly loaded their aircraft and kicked aside chocks for

> I wonder, Dad, if you realize how fortunate you & your generation have really been. True, you had your war—but it seems to me that you had much more to look forward to. I may be wrong in this, as it's a momentary thought, but it seems more like we live from day to day & even more so into the past. What the future has in store for us is so out of any person's realization that no plans could possibly be laid. Furthermore those wild dreams of world satisfaction are hopeless in view of the world's dry well of leadership. Forsight is something I know I lack—but I sincerely doubt that there is a man alive today big & strong enough to cope with the problems of the day, let alone the future. That, of course, is one man's opinion.
>
> —Jack Kirschbraun,
> March 14, 1944
> letter to father

Robert Brismaster's certificate of embarkation.

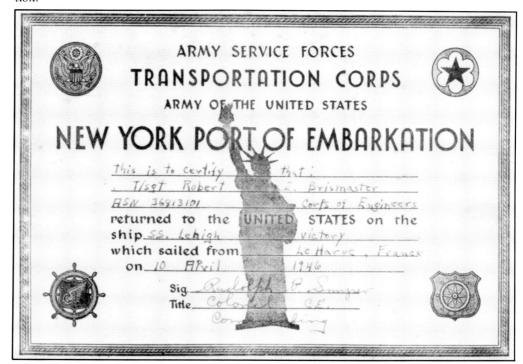

9,438 Planes Destroyed by 8thAF Fighters

8th FIGHTER COMMAND HQ, England—The 15 fighter groups of the 8th Air Force, which fought in the European air war under the command of Lt. Gen. James H. Doolittle, destroyed a total of 9,438 enemy aircraft, according to final tabulations. Of this total 5,291 were destroyed in aerial combat and 4,146 by strafing attacks against airfields. An additional 464 were listed as "probable" kills and 4,642 recorded damaged.

These figures compare with a total of exactly 3,000 fighters lost by the 8th during the war.

Many secondary targets came under the guns of the fighters. Nearly 5,000 locomotives were immobilized and 2,500 damaged. Almost 3,000 oil tank cars were shot up and more than 30,000 other types of railroad cars destroyed or damaged.

All reports by fighter pilots were checked against the film from the motion picture cameras that worked automatically in the wing of each fighter whenever the guns were fired.

This USAAF press release announced the victory tally for the Eighth Air Force's fighters.

the last time on English airfields. Then American fighters and bombers lifted off into the dawn of a new day when they no longer formed up to do battle in European skies. And all at once it seemed, the hyperactivity in the East Anglian skies ceased.

"I saw the last plane fly away," said Percy Kindred, about the departure of the 390th Bombardment Group. "I was on the perimeter track. The plane's crew knew they were the last ones to leave and they waved to me. After that plane went, I sat down and cried. I'm not one to do that kind of thing—but the place just seemed dead."

Gerry Darnell commented: "When the war ended, I was really lost. No more watching the 'Forts' go out and return, no more hearing the screech of brakes, the firing of the guns in the butts or engines revving to full power for takeoff."

"It seemed flat after they left," was a general consensus, voiced by John Gray.

The last elements of the Eighth Air Force vacated from Honington in February 1946. Eighth Fighter Command's Brig. Gen. Emil Kiel handed the keys to the station to the RAF's Air Marshal Sir James Robb on February 26. In the best tradition of the then-popular Western movies that inevitably ended with the hero riding off in the sunset, Kiel was to board the last remaining B-17 and take the metaphoric western heading toward home. True to form, however, English weather interfered with the carefully staged ceremony. Low overcast and rain delayed the flight.

John Mills offered: "When the Eighth pulled out, there was a sense of change. In [Roger Freeman's book] *The Mighty Eighth*, a chapter is titled, 'The Skies Were Never Still.' And certainly from late 1942 until mid-1945, that was true. There was nearly always one or more aircraft in sight. When the Eighth pulled out and went away, a great stillness descended. The silence was so impressive and it felt strange—you felt deprived in a way. You found yourself wondering where all the aircraft had gone. Then it occurred to you they'd all flown home. We missed the aircraft. We missed the many good-natured young men."

Shortly after the first members of the Eighth Air Force had arrived in 1942, Gen. Ira Eaker diplomatically stated to a gathering of British military and civilian officials: "We won't do much talking until we've done more fighting. We hope that when we leave, you'll be glad we came."

They succeeded—probably beyond General Eaker's wildest dreams. Members of the Eighth Air Force left behind a feeling of good will that continues strong today.

One gesture of good will and "a gift that keeps giving" is the Second Air Division Memorial Library at Norwich. "After they sent the combat crews home and began to dismantle the Second Air Division," explained Evelyn Cohen of Second Air Division Headquarters, "everyone remaining was asked to contribute a pound toward the building of a memorial library. Of course, no one then knew what that would eventually become."

Goodbye GI; now you know the way
Come back and see us in a brighter day,
When England's free and "Scotch" is
    cheap but strong

"I was glad to get home and it sure did look good to me—as good as I remembered it."
—Norm Schleitwiler, 351st Bomb Group (H)

"We were treated like kings when we came back. At a bar you couldn't spend any money. I went back to college. In 1945-46, campuses were filled with people wearing remnants of their old uniforms—they never wore out."
—John Ziebell, 357th Fighter Group

Going Back to Civilian Life *booklet, created by the War and Navy departments, was distributed to all military personnel being separated from active duty. It briefly explained veterans benefits, like mustering-out payment ("... if you have served 60 or more days overseas or in Alaska, you will receive a total of $300, payable $100 with your final pay, $100 mailed to you 1 month after your release or discharge, and $100 mailed to you 2 months after your release or discharge.") and the GI Bill ("The Veterans' Administration will pay to the educational or training institution the customary cost of tuition and such laboratory, library, infirmary, and similar payments as customarily charged. . . . The Veterans' Administration will, in most cases provide a subsistence allowance during the education or training period, of $50 a month if you have no dependents, $75 if you have.") and guaranteed loans for homes.* John T. Bradley

And you can bring your pretty wives along.
Goodbye GI; don't leave us quite alone;
Somewhere in England we must write, in stone,
How Britain was invaded by the "Yanks"
And under that, a big and hearty *Thanks.*
A. P. Herbert, British playwright
(written in a 1945 brochure for the Stage Door Canteen)

But the Eighth Air Force won much more than the lasting Anglo-American kinship. They won generations of peace in Europe. No more impossible missions that decimated young airmen and devastated people on the ground.

Ghost stations

When the Americans vacated, they left over a hundred ghost towns. The Brit-

ish government faced a glut of airfields, some of which reverted back to original (civilian) tenants. Others were inexplicably retained.

Percy Kindred explained:

"We didn't get the land back for a long time. The air ministry bought the airfield after the war. They had only requisitioned it during the war, paying me 15 shillings an acre each year. I didn't mind that a bit, but they said they'd return it to me after the hostilities ceased in its *original* condition.

"The government changed after the war. They had a look at it and said, 'Oh, my God. We could never do that—it'd cost more to put it right than it cost to build the thing.' So they put an act of Parliament through right quick making compulsory purchases and they paid the value of the land, not when they bought it, but when they first requisitioned it in the early part of the war—thirty-five pounds per acre. It was worth much more when they did buy it, even as it was. But this was take-it-or-leave it. No choice."

Ten generations of the Orlebar family occupied an expansive estate in North Bedfordshire, where 800 acres were requisitioned for Podington's airfield. Mike Orlebar commented: "The land wasn't derequisitioned until 1958. All acreage had been covered by woods. It was handed back mostly devoid of woods and with an airfield on it."

Half-chuckling, Kindred added: "They had stripped everything they could from the area—everything they could raise up, every bit of cable—to sell. Even the railings off the tower. The pole with the wind sock was cut with a torch. Then they said, 'We don't need this land anymore. And you being the original owner, we'll let you have the first offer.'" Kindred did buy the land and made possible the restoration of the 390th Bomb Group's control tower at Framlingham.

And what the British government began, many land owners finished. At Horham, home of the "Red Feather" Bomb Group, and at many other fields, land owners ground up the thick concrete runways to sell as valuable hardcore for British roads. Buildings set on precious farm acreage were brought down.

Planes to pots

Meanwhile, the aircraft that had served the Eighth Air Force well were in their final formations—wingtip to wing-

Bungay club stands in good condition. Andrew
Morland

*Billet for the Seething-based 448th Bomb
Group.* Andrew Moreland

tip, row after row at storage depots. In place of a windswept East Anglian airfield, a windswept Arizona desert valley became the last stop for many of them. At Kingman, Arizona, the largest of the storage depots, 7,000 "retired" Army Air Force aircraft stretched for six miles along Route 66 in 1947.

Fiery winds whistled down from the Hualapai Mountains in Arizona and smoothly through the multitude of aerodynamic shapes. Here and there a dust devil meandered under the high wing of a Liberator. A ghostly rudder pulsed side to side like the tail of a sleeping dog dreaming of past glories.

Colorful markings on their noses told the story—rows of stenciled bombs and swastikas, and prized artwork of for-gotten artists. Innumerable patches and mismatched parts—olive drab engine cowlings, wing panels and fuselage sections on otherwise natural aluminum-finish ships—were additional indications of the action their aircrews had faced. Who knows how many wing panel replacements, flak-hole patchings and engine changes their ground crews had performed—doing whatever it took to meet the call for a maximum performance mission.

There's something special about a plane to the crews who flew them or serviced them. There's also something special about the places they were based. For anyone who has to ask what makes them special, the response won't help.

Chapter 12

Odysseys of lost airmen

They shall grow not old, as we that are left grow old:
Age shall not weary them, nor the years condemn
At the going down of the sun and in the morning—
We will remember them.

—Laurence Binyon, "For the Fallen"

Reflecting on oft-pondered sentiments about friends killed in the war, Ralph Price murmured: "All I can do is sit back and wonder, 'Why them and not me?' After all these years, I'm still asking that question."

For survivors, there is the pride of contributing toward victory commingled with something akin to guilt for having survived when random, violent death snatched so many comrades.

A 306th Bomb Group navigator stood plaintively alongside the runway at Thurleigh. He looked almost expectantly toward the east. His eyes glistened. And after an aborted attempt to stifle them, tears began to stream down his cheeks. "I stood here forty years ago and watched my crew take off. I wasn't with them because I had a cold and couldn't fly. I watched them get off the end of the runway and crash in the field. None of them survived."

Over 26,000 men of the Eighth Air Force died on active service. Over 6,000 of the Eighth's bombers and fighters were officially listed as missing in action between August 1942 to May 1945. Hidden in the broad sweeps of those statistics are countless small brush strokes of ex-

traordinary heroism. Stories of bravery— stranger and more incredible than the most fantastic fiction—are now vanished

Grave at Cambridge American Cemetery.

"We didn't grieve too long at the time, since things were hectic. However, one never forgets—I remember vividly each and every one lost."
—Carl Lose, 94th Bomb Group (H)

from all but human memory, or never have been told when no one survived to tell them. We'll never know what sacrifices were made, what acts of gallantry and valor went unrewarded in the thousands of aircraft that never returned.

Every Eighth Air Force fighter and bomb group is represented at Cambridge American Cemetery, located near Madingly. The grounds are an immaculate iteration of Arlington National Cemetery—equal in quality but of a smaller scale. It is a worthy tribute to those whose names are inscribed there.

Buried under the white caps of a great sea of graves are 3,811 Americans, many of whom died on active service with the Eighth Air Force.

On Cambridge's great Wall of the Missing are the names of 5,126 who gave the full measure for their country, but whose remains were never recovered or identified.

The cemetery grounds, thirty and a half acres, were donated by Cambridge University during the war to be forever American soil. The only World War II American cemetery in the British Isles, it is not likely to grow larger, according to the cemetery's superintendent: "The only way someone else can be buried here now is if the person died on active service during World War II and happens to be currently buried in Europe."

Yet the number of visitors is dramatically increasing. He surmises that many with a close connection to people buried here "are now into retirement age and have the time to reminisce and to travel. Fifty percent of the Americans who come have never seen the grave of the loved one before."

Behind each of Cambridge's inscribed names lies a story. Behind each was an individual willing to put his life on the line for his friends, his country. Behind each were family members—mothers, fathers, brothers, sisters, wives and sometimes children never seen—waiting anxiously at home.

On most any day at these grounds, one can see among the white markers a remorseful gathering or an individual standing by a grave, openly sobbing or quietly fighting back tears. Some are children grown to adulthood while the dead slept. The superintendent added, "People often break down and are unable to speak when they finally see and touch a tangible link to someone lost so long ago."

People run their fingers slowly across carved names on the Wall of the Missing as if it is Braille, searching for a reassuring message from the silent dead and from the simpler time in which they had lived.

As devastatingly high as Eighth Air Force losses were, the air war's very nature veiled death, making it abstract and detached from reality. There wasn't the constant firsthand exposure to death experienced by infantry troops, who smelled, touched and saw death—making it appallingly real.

As evidenced by the Wall of the Missing, death often snatched airborne comrades without leaving a trace. Frank Halm's best friend was lost on a Nov. 4, 1944 raid:

"He was flying off my right wing. None of us realized he was in trouble because he didn't Mayday at all. He just dropped out of formation over the North Sea without complaint. The assumption was he would follow the formation in. It wasn't until two or three days later that we realized he hadn't landed *anywhere*.

"For the first few days he was just missing and we figured that he'd found an emergency field on the coast or somewhere else. But they never found him. His name, and the names of his crew, are on the Wall of the Missing."

James Goodson commented: "When pilots did not return from a mission, there was usually a chance that they were still alive. Even if we guessed a friend had been killed, there was no body and no funeral. He just wasn't around anymore."

There was no funeral to give focus to the grief. No rite according the death ritual of our culture. No "goodbyes." It was a more subtle and perhaps more acceptable loss, at least initially. But it's the kind that crouches in the subconscious and creeps to the forefront later—and finally in a quiet moment the hot slash of realization grazes the mind that "he'd never be back. Never speak or chum with us again," as one veteran at Cambridge Cemetery said.

After the passage of decades full of the joys and sorrows, triumphs and defeats of life, the raising of families and pursuit of careers, thoughts persist of *what could have been for them* in a rich world they helped save from despotism. That's why tears now come freely as a bugler's haunting melody of taps pierces the heart.

Gazing from Cambridge Cemetery's gentle slope, a natural amphitheater to the sky framed by woodlands on the west and the south, it's hard not to think of great armadas of aircraft that shook this very sky and earth during the war. "They lay below us now," murmured a British visitor.

They didn't go home, except in the hearts of survivors. Lloyd Nelson said: "It was a terrible thing to see all the young men killed. . . . They were some of the finest fellows I will ever know. And I will always remember them." What follows are the odysseys of Eighth airmen who lost their lives. Their stories are as much about the survivors left to carry the memory.

Harold "Freddie" Henslin's story

Apr. 28, 1944. It was 1st Lt. Harold "Freddie" Henslin's twenty-first mission—four to go. The Henslin crew was assigned to lead the 381st Bomb Group.

Everyone exited the briefing room feeling relieved. It was a relatively minor mission, the proverbial "milk run," to an aerodrome at St. Avord, France. The crew had been on far deeper and more dangerous penetrations.

Intelligence officers had briefed the crews that flak would be relatively light. "Flak wasn't heavy at all," affirmed Henslin's right waist gunner, William Blackmon, Jr. "But I saw one burst, then another one closer. I thought, 'The next one's going to be close.'"

Flak batteries were tracking the lead ship. Suddenly, with violent unreality, a direct flak burst tore into number two engine, the one closest to the pilot's seat. The stricken B–17 instantly plummeted from its lead position in the formation.

Inside the spiraling aircraft, crewmen tumbled. Initial spinning and spasms gave way to a steep dive that shackled everyone in the invisible chains of G-forces. Blackmon was thrown against the left waist gunner, Clarence Williams, who had been a "ground gripper" only recently assigned to the combat crew. "I could hear him screaming in my ear," said Blackmon. "And I could feel his head just crushing under my weight from that dive."

No one could escape the grim reaper's grip to reach the salvation of a hatch. Then, equally unreal as the flak explosion itself, "the bomber righted itself" according to observers in the formation.

"I tore away from the oxygen and intercom system and heated suit [connections]," Blackmon said. "I managed to

get hold of the edge [of the open waist door] and pulled myself out. I had only one eye on my chest pack chute hooked. I never did get the other hooked. It was so quiet out there. It felt like I was just laying there—I had no sensation of falling. I looked down and saw two chutes way down below me. . . ."

The tail gunner was also seen bailing out, but his chute opened too soon. It caught on the huge Fortress tail—pulling him along in the aircraft's screaming descent toward earth.

Blackmon, the copilot, and the radio operator parachuted to the airfield they had just bombed, where they were promptly captured.

The bomber righting itself was no fortuitous happening. Lt. Henslin had stayed alone in the cockpit and bought

"[Lt. Henslin] was the kind who would have stayed until the last man was out. He was a gentleman and a real pilot."
—William Blackmon, Jr., 381st Bomb Group (H)

"It was a strange thing. For one crew, the flight could be a milk run. And in the plane next to them it could be the most harrowing experience imaginable."
—John Wood, 381st Bomb Group (H) (Lt. Henslin's was the only plane in the formation to go down that day)

> Lt. Clore & his crew were killed in a crash near the field. They cracked up right after take-off on a mission to Kiel. It would have been Clores' 25th mission but fate intervened. The dead were Clore, Newell, Dille, Waldman (Kaufman's navigator), Trainer, Bozzette, Howard, Robinson, Streicher and Ingmire. Fate sure does play mean. They were killed in "278"—our new plane. If our crew had flown today—we would have been the ill-fated crew. We were very lucky. I get sick when I think of what happened.
>
> —Ken Stone, January 4, 1944 diary entry

Jan. 6th - Thursday

Woke up at 12:00 noon. ate dinner. Got dressed in my O.D.'s & went down to the Chapel. Rode on a truck to an american cemetery outside of Cambridge. Most of the old combat crews were there. The services for Lt. Clare's crew was held in a military fashion. We marched out in front of the ten caskets draped with american flags. The Chaplains said prayers. We saluted the crew and as three volleys were fired and taps played. We then marched away from the graves.

—Ken Stone,
January 6, 1944
diary entry

This letter should be sort of a "so long letter", Marnie - at least, so long for awhile - there are many things I want to write you, that seem so hard to write - will you read between the lines -

My thoughts are, mostly, of our family, and of your little family. There was never anything but happiness in ours, and there can never be anything but happiness in yours - and this is my inspiration -

—Harold Henslin,
October 13, 1943
letter to sister

1st Lt. Harold F. Henslin, Dec. 6, 1944. USAF via Karen Laws

precious heartbeats of seconds for his crew to bail out.

When the blazing number two engine sheared away from the wing, the plane went into its death throes, again spiraling wildly through the cloudless sky. Seconds later, the plane disintegrated. Still at the controls, Lieutenant Henslin perished.

Who can speak more eloquently of the freedom we enjoy now—of valor, of the willingness of a man to die for his crew—than Freddie Henslin, silenced forever on Apr. 28, 1944 at the age of twenty-one?

A niece remembers

Karen Laws, niece and godchild of Lt. Henslin, met Blackmon for the first time in 1984, forty years after the episode. She had researched the wartime life of her uncle extensively.

From contacts with others in the formation that day, she knew that a fourth crewmember, tail gunner Ed Sell, was able to exit the plane but was killed because his parachute became entangled on the tail. Blackmon, who remained a prisoner the rest of the war, knew nothing about the individual fates of the crew left on board. "Bill Blackmon never knew

"I thought if anyone would get out of that aircraft, it would be [the ball turret gunner, Little Mac]. But Little Mac didn't make it."
—Thomas O'Brien, 381st Bomb Group (H) (witness to Henslin's aircraft spinning out of control)

159

that Sell had gotten out and his chute had caught," said Laws. "He broke down when he heard it."

Not yet a year old when her uncle died, she has no firsthand recollection of "Uncle Harold," except when his body was brought back from a French graveyard in 1948. "I remember seeing a guard standing by the casket," said Laws. "I wondered why.

"As I grew up, he was 'the uncle who died in World War II.' Nothing more. Then, as I researched [years later], a real person began to take form. Piecing together the letters, telegrams, and photos jumbled together in a box in the attic, a personality emerged.

"In the letters, I sense great optimism. The little phrases really got to me. He would refer to Mother, Dad and me— there were a lot of references to me because I was his new niece."

A small chunk of mortar and a short length of ornate wrought iron from Ridgewell's airfield now occupy a prominent place on Laws' sitting room shelf. Laws had traveled to England and to Ridgewell, where her uncle took off for the last time. She said, "Standing on the remnants of runway, I didn't feel a sense of loss. It was just the opposite, in fact. Something missing was filled in."

William A. Rautenbush's story

Forty-five years after a vicious dogfight over Dalsch, Germany, 1st Lt. William A. Rautenbush's family learned for the first time the details of his fate. Previously, there had been only vague reports that the twenty-four-year-old fighter pilot had been lost over Germany, no precise information known.

A close friend in the squadron, Stan Rames, who had become a POW, visited the family after the war and told what he knew about Rautenbush. In the savage dogfight in which the men grappled for their lives, he could not recount with certainty the details of the loss. No one saw him go down.

Then, suddenly, word came from the Rotary Club of Verden, West Germany, that in 1989 a memorial had been erected on the site of a World War II crash. Then the details started to unfold.

Piloting a new Mustang fighter, Lt. Rautenbush lifted smoothly from Bottisham's steel mat runway on May 8, 1944. Since the 361st Fighter Group was converting from P-47 Thunderbolts to P-51 Mustangs at the time, six P-51s and eight

1st Lt. William Rautenbush. Don Ritchie

"There might be just a few bursts of flak off your wing, but down would go another airplane. It just happened to hit right. I once saw a single burst of flak hit a P-51 flying by and that was the end of it."
—Joe Curley, 486th Bomb Group (H)

P-47s formed up to escort bombers on a deep penetration. The Eighth Air Force sent 729 fighters to escort 807 bombers to six targets in Germany.

The 361st Fighter Group was to accompany a B-17 formation from the First Air Division until relieved by the 4th Fighter Group. Fifteen miles southeast of Bremen, the formation of bombers were attacked head-on by twenty Fw 190s. Rautenbush's squadron immediately split up and pursued the bandits.

He and his wingman, Murray C. Bell, spotted an Fw and immediately dove in pursuit. When the enemy sought invisibility in the undercast, Rautenbush and Bell plunged downward at high speed, not knowing what peril awaited them in the low-hanging clouds.

The speed attained in the dive was too great. The leading edge of the wings split the air, creating a vacuum behind that prevented effective function of the elevator of the tail. Bell was able to pull out of the dive just above the ground— literally stripping paint from his plane from the severity of the swoop. But when he climbed back upstairs, he found himself alone.

In the heat of pursuit, Lt. Rautenbush had sent his shrieking aircraft into an irrecoverable dive toward earth and plunged into a marsh with such tremendous force that it literally buried itself. The body of the young American

WESTERN UNION

A. N. WILLIAMS
PRESIDENT

1201

The filing time shown in the date line on telegrams and day letters is STANDARD TIME at point of origin. Time of receipt is STANDARD TIME at point of destination.

GUB6   44 GOVT=WMU WASHINGTON DC MAY 23 420A

ARTHUR W RITCHIE=

GREENWOOD FARM

:THE SECRETARY OF WAR DESIRES ME TO EXPRESS HIS DEEP
REGRET THAT YOUR WARD FIRST LIEUTENANT WILLIAM A
RAUTENBUSH HAS BEEN REPORTED MISSING IN ACTION SINCE EIGHT
MAY OVER GERMANY PERIOD IF FURTHER DETAILS OR OTHER
INFORMATION ARE RECEIVED YOU WILL BE PROMPTLY NOTIFIED=

DUNLOP ACTING THE ADJUTANT GENERAL.

817A.

"They were flying ahead of us when flak scored a direct hit on their ball turret. We flew through the pieces, debris hitting our plane. I saw the blood on our aircraft's nose. They buried one crewman's arm at Cambridge."
—John Houk, 92nd Bomb Group (H)

pilot was left in the ruins of his Mustang.

A German who led efforts to erect the memorial, Dr. Peter Clasen, explained: "When it was clear that a pilot could not be alive, they left him in the ground where he died . . . because of the danger of exploding ammunition. This [cautious handling of crash sites applied to] German and Allied air force soldiers in the same way."

Years later they buried his body at the American World War II Cemetery at Ardennes, Belgium. (The Ardennes cemetery is a ninety-acre site commonly associated with the Battle of the Bulge, for the large number of infantrymen who died in that battle.)

On a cold Saturday in March 1989, members of the Verden Rotary Club, several US Air Force officers from Bremerhaven and Osterholz-Scharmbeck, Germany, representatives from the German corps and from the Association of British officers from Verden gathered at the site. They came to dedicate the memorial, intended to "remind us that our own dead of World War II, as well as those of other nations, must be an obligation for lasting peace," in the translated words of Gerhard Beier, Rotary Club president. "This obligation should not be words only, but should be permanently taken to heart. . . . This memorial hour at the crash site of the American Air Force officer should serve that purpose."

Behind the white cross of plot D, row 5, grave 53, among the 5,327 markers at Ardennes, is the story of an individual who knew laughter, sorrow, hopes and

dreams. Bill Rautenbush was an orphan who had weathered the Depression in a Chicago orphanage. As a young boy, growing tall and straight, he learned the self-reliance which later would serve him as a fighter pilot.

Behind bright, clear eyes was a mind full of promise—but painfully lacking opportunity. One day, a farm family by the name of Ritchie took him in. And after his sophomore year of high school Rautenbush found—for the first time in memory—a place he called home. His first report card was mediocre and his foster mother, who was an elementary school teacher, remarked, "Surely you can do better than this, Bill." He shrugged and responded, "I've never known anybody who cared how I did." From then on, Rautenbush was at the top of his class, which graduated in 1939.

He enlisted in October 1941, just before America entered the fight. During a short stint in the tanks corps that left him wanting more excitement, his ambition became clear: he wanted to be a fighter pilot.

He earned his wings and was assigned to the 361st Fighter Group at Bottisham. He flew approximately forty missions in P-47 Thunderbolts, before the group changed over to the P-51 Mustangs.

The same week he was reported missing in action, local newspapers reported the following:

"Putting on . . . an aerial blitz of their own, four P-47 Thunderbolt pilots in ten minutes of action turned a total of thirty-two .50 caliber guns on two enemy airfields in France and returned home with the following score: two Messerschmitt 109s destroyed; one Me-110 destroyed; one FW-190 destroyed, and several hangars, a power line and other ground installations shot full of holes.

"Lt. Rautenbush blasted a silver-colored Ju-88 and as he passed over it a tremendous explosion occurred and his plane was splattered with debris. In [flight leader] Captain Dayton Casto's words, 'Lt. Rautenbush reduced the Ju-88 to atoms or slightly larger pieces.'"

An addendum to the article otherwise proclaiming his victories read somberly that he was missing in action at press time. William Rautenbush was posthumously awarded the Distinguished Flying Cross.

Now a small, solitary, white sign with black letters shows the way "to the pilot's grave" in a marshy, wooded area

From the gun camera of Lt. William Rautenbush on a strafing mission in late April 1944: "If the Luftwaffe wouldn't come up to fight, we'll go down to them." Lt. Rautenbush scores a strafing bull's-eye on an Me 110. USAF via Dayton Casto

near Dalsch. Eighty paces from the highway is a large, water-filled crater where, on May 8, 1944, the aircraft plunged into the soft earth.

Less than 2,000 meters away from Rautenbush's aircraft is another crash site. Ensign-Master Sgt. Heinz Schrader, a German fighter pilot, also remained buried in the cockpit of his Me 109.

Jack Kirschbraun's story

An April 1944 Western Union telegram bore familiar words dreaded by every family with a service flag hanging in the window: "THE SECRETARY OF WAR ASKS THAT I ASSURE YOU OF HIS DEEP SYMPATHY IN THE LOSS OF YOUR SON SERGEANT JACK KIRSCHBRAUN . . . AS RESULT OF WOUNDS RECEIVED IN ACTION OVER GERMANY. . . ."

Mortally wounded over Germany, Sgt. Jack Kirschbraun had survived the flight back to England, but died hours after landing.

The wife of an army anesthesiologist in England wrote a letter to the Kirschbraun family a short time later:

"On March 23, my husband was called to surgery, and being somewhat in a nostalgic mood, recalling that this day was our son's birthday (who was also KIA), he took one look at [Jack] and realized how awful the ravages of war are in that one's children are subjected to such risks and uncertainties. The surgery lasted several hours. . . .

Sgt. Jack Kirschbraun. Frank Kirschbraun

2/28/44

DEAR FOLKS,

Still no mail. My new address is:

16129578

92nd BOMB GROUP

327th BOMB SQDN. A.P.O.#634

NEW YORK CITY, N.Y.

—Jack Kirschbraun,
February 28, 1944
letter to parents

"The thought that he was someone's son was omnipresent. . . . In my husband's own words, 'I shall never forget this boy. . . . [He] stayed by him until the end came.

"Your brother's passing will not have been in vain. . . . I am most certain in years to come your cherished memories . . . are something no one can take away."

Jack Kirschbraun's family took his death especially hard. His brother, Frank, one and a half years senior, described their relationship as one of extraordinary closeness: "We participated jointly in nearly every activity during our lives."

Frank Kirschbraun was also in uniform and on his way back home for a furlough at the time word reached home:

"We disembarked in Seattle and things are a blur except that I vividly recall that I was at the rail station before boarding the Great Northern for Chicago when a GI who was a stranger to me came up to me for a brief conversation. When he heard my name, he asked if I had a brother in the Air Force. I replied that I did and when I asked why, he said, 'Oh, never mind. . . .' I recall that I probed about how he knew, but he evaded my question.

"At first I was agitated and then forced any concern out of my mind—yet it must have subconsciously bothered me, because I had been perfectly healthy for the previous two and a half years, but I felt ill by the time the train reached Chicago.

"I carried my barracks bag to the station doorway and found my father there with a business associate at his side. I knew something was wrong because my mother was not there. . . . I asked, 'Is it Jack?' My father broke down. I remember walking with him and hugging him tightly because I couldn't talk."

Frank Kirschbraun described the reaction as "a huge rush of adrenaline" and "for a few seconds the thought processes implode." He pointed out that the alarming loss rate of aircraft in 1943 and 1944 was not commonly known by the general public. However, he harbors no bitterness about that: "If the press of the present era had been of the same bent at the time of World War II, Hitler would be in charge of the world right now. Those were the times when the nation was united and we didn't question the mission America had embarked upon."

Leon Vance, Jr.'s story

On June 5, 1944, the day before D-day, Lt. Col. Leon Vance, Jr., of the 489th Bomb Group, led a mission to destroy coastal defenses to help pave the way for invasion forces. Serving as command pilot (not piloting a bomber, but controlling the formation in the lead ship), he directed a strike on the target. Other B-24s in the formation dropped their bombs, but his B-24's bombs failed to release and he ordered a second pass.

In an interview with radio show host Bebe Daniels, Lt. Col. Vance and others in the crew described the mission:

Vance: "We didn't meet any fighters on the way in, but we met a lot of flak—enough to knock out three of our engines ten seconds before arriving over our target. But we went on in and delivered our bombs and the group hit the target right on the nose. That's when my foot was shot off and our first pilot, Capt. Lewis Mazure, was killed."

Daniels: "Was he killed instantly?"

Vance: "Yes, but not before he heard the bombardier say I hit it right on the nose. Capt. Mazure was just strong enough to reply, 'Good boy.' Those were his last words. Then the copilot took over while Lt. Bernard Bail put a tourniquet around my leg. Just then the ship stalled and I took over."

Lt. Col. Leon R. Vance, Jr. Sharon Vance
Kiernan

Daniels: "With your leg in that condition?"

Vance: "You don't think about what's wrong with you in an emergency like that, Bebe."

Daniels: "I see. Then what happened?"

Vance: "It was then that I heard that our radio operator, Staff Sgt. Quentin Skufca, had been hit."

Daniels: "What happened to him?"

Vance: "He and Tech Sgt. Hoppie, my engineer, are here with me at this hospital. Lt. Kilgore was here with us until yesterday, but he's gone back to the States with a well-mended broken leg."

Daniels: "I'm glad to hear that."

Vance: "This is Tech Sgt. Earl Hoppie from Chicago. He's our engineer I was telling you about, Bebe."

Hoppie: "I was in the top turret when I heard the Colonel say over the intercom the number one engine was smoking. So I got out of the turret to shut off the gas. Just then, there was another burst of flak under the ship and it cut off all the gas lines. I tried stopping the leak by wrapping my jacket around the pipe, but it didn't work. The fumes were terrific and my eyes were full of gas. I kept the bomb doors open to let the gas out, but it was

hopeless. So I went up to the flight deck and told Col. Vance, who ordered us to bail out and we did."

Daniels: "You couldn't land though, could you Colonel?"

Vance: "Not very well. The plane would have exploded with all that gas in it and besides, all four motors were dead by then. I had feathered three of the props, but the fourth wouldn't feather. It was still wind-milling. By that time we were over England at about 12,000 feet and still gliding."

Daniels: "Did you bail out Colonel?"

Vance: "No, I was told that Sgt. Skufca was still in the waist, so badly injured he couldn't bail out, so naturally I couldn't leave him. All the rest did bail out and I flew the ship down to crash-land in the Channel. The windshield was cloudy with vapor and frozen so that you could hardly see forward. I was lying on my stomach between the pilot and copilot seats with my hands on the wheel. I tried to get up, but my foot was lodged in the armor plating. I couldn't take my hands off the controls to get my legs loose because the ship would have stalled. It was hard to hold the ship level, because the right elevator was shot away. Somehow or other I got down close to the water where I put my parachute pack on my head so that I wouldn't break my neck from the shock of impact.

"When the ship hit the water, the top turret came off, pinning me down. It was lying across my back and I was under about six feet of water. I figured that was the end of the line for me. Then I did something rather odd. I knew pilot Mazure was dead, but I reached over with my left hand and released his safety belt and held him up over my head to the escape hatch. And then just as I thought my lungs were going to burst, something inside the ship exploded and I was blown to the surface.

"After I got out, I tried to climb back over to the top of the ship to get to Sgt. Skufca, the injured radio operator. But I just didn't have the strength. It was just as well, because unbeknownst to me, the two waist gunners had bailed him out. I just had sufficient strength left to inflate my Mae West and the last thing I remember was the British Air-Sea Rescue ship. Later I woke up in a hospital.

"By the way, Bebe, I forgot to tell you the name of my ship."

Daniels: "What is it Col. Vance?"

Vance: I call her the *Sharon D.*"

Lt. Col. Leon Vance holding daughter, Sharon D., in front of the B-24 named for her. The Sharon D. was not the B-24 that Lt. Col. Vance ditched in the English Channel. The Sharon D. *went on to fly many subsequent missions with the 489th Bomb Group (H) and later the 445th Bomb Group (H).* Sharon Vance Kiernan

Daniels: "Is it named after someone in particular?"

Vance: "Somebody very particular. My little daughter Sharon Drury, not yet two years old."

Daniels: "I'm sure Sharon Drury and her mommy are very proud of you Col. Vance. As a matter of fact, all of America is proud of you."

In the difficult period that followed his foot amputation, Vance went through bouts of depression—his combat pilot days likely over. While he ambled on crutches down a London Street, an eight-year-old boy yelled to him, "You'll never miss it, Yank." Promptly apologizing to Vance for the outburst, the boy's mother explained that her son lost his foot in the blitz and was getting along fine with an artificial one. But an apology for the remark was the last thing Vance needed to hear. He said, "That was the biggest boost I got. Felt a devil of a lot better after that."

In his good humor, he wrote to his wife: "You'll have five toes to tickle instead of ten."

In July 1944, the C-54 carrying Vance home for convalescent leave went down between Iceland and Newfoundland. No trace was ever found.

The Congressional Medal of Honor was presented posthumously, live on TV, to Vance's daughter, Sharon.

A daughter pays tribute

In May 1987, Sharon D. (Vance) Kiernan traveled from California to Cambridge for the first time. There was no grave for her to see. What awaited her was a name on the Wall of the Missing—a name inscribed in the letters of gold reserved exclusively for those who received America's highest military award, the Congressional Medal of Honor. "It was truly moving," she said.

Even more moving, she felt, was seeing the 489th Bomb Group's airfield at Halesworth, where the runway still lies intact. "It was like going back in time," she said. "The environmental system at the farm [now occupying the site] produces a steady hum—like the drone of many aircraft. When you listen to that sound and look toward the English sky, you almost feel like you can see bombers approaching the field. I walked on the runway alone—and I cried."

Someone once asked Lt. Col. Vance what it was like when it seemed sure he would die. He had replied that there was

Maj. Gen. J. P. Hodges presents the Congressional Medal of Honor to Sharon D. Vance at Enid Air Force Base in Oklahoma. Five years after this ceremony, on July 9, 1949, Enid Air Force Base was renamed Vance Air Force *Base to honor the memory of Lt. Col. Leon Vance, who had spent most his life in Enid, Oklahoma, including graduation from Enid High School. Sharon Vance Kiernan*

incredible sadness—not specifically that his life was over, but that he'd "never see Shari smile again. Or hear Georgette [his wife] laugh again."

"As I was growing up, I went through a period of wishful thinking," Kiernan said. "I wished I had my father. I have the 78 r.p.m. record of his interview with Bebe Daniels from shortly after the mission. I wore that record's grooves deeper from listening to it so much as a child. Even at this late date, I've cried. I do feel like I got shorted a bit. Through frustration or reverting back to being a little girl again, I find myself asking, *Why couldn't it have been? Why?* I've never really stopped asking that."

Sharon Kiernan found herself a ce-lebrity during the trip to England. She was pictured in the *East Anglian Times* and the BBC sought an interview with her. People asked for her autograph. And the English bid her to visit the Triple Plea Pub (near Halesworth's airfield), where conspicuously displayed is a large photo of Colonel Vance holding his two-year-old daughter in front of the B–24 named for her—the *Sharon D.*

"I hadn't realized what a tribute the English pay," she commented. "The English don't forget—they're still saying thank you forty-plus years later. I was asked to autograph the photo in the pub, which I did. They needed something human to connect to my father, to the *Sharon D.* and to the mission."

Royal Netherlands Air Force recovery specialist with "find," A B-17 prop. Royal Netherlands Air Force

Recovering wreckage forty-five years later

Aerial traffic over Holland in World War II was among the heaviest in the world. The location made it a direct route for England-based aircraft traveling to and from the Ruhr Valley and other German targets. A day of "heavy traffic" like that of Feb. 19, 1945, saw more than 941 bombers and 700 fighters from the Eighth Air Force flying over. Much of the traffic passed above an inland body of water once called the Zuider Zee (now diked, it is now called the IJsselmeer). Flying over water was naturally preferred to flying over land, since the route over water was not defended as well.

Still, approximately 1,200 USAAF aircraft fell there—mostly Eighth Air Force Flying Fortresses, Liberators, Lightnings, Thunderbolts and Mustangs—from flak, air-to-air combat and collisions. Dutch experts estimate that more than 7,000 total German and Allied aircraft crashed in Holland during World War II.

For hundreds of years, the Dutch have been draining the land to "create" livable and farmable land from the inland sea. And since World War II, as dikes have been constructed and water has been pumped into the North Sea, aircraft wreckage is discovered. Men and machines listed on the books for decades as "missing in action" are found.

So many wrecks have surfaced that the Royal Netherlands Air Force formed a team of recovery specialists to handle the dangerous wrecks, many still bearing live bombs and ammunition. The team's medical specialists work to determine identities of remains. US and Dutch authorities work together, using official combat reports, to determine what type of ordnance and what airmen were aboard. Sometimes the process is easy, like in the discovery of virtually intact aircraft that bellied in and sank gently to the sandy bottom. Their group markings and tail numbers are plainly visible. Other times, a shattered wing is all that's available to begin the research. But relying on eyewitness accounts and other debris, many of the mysteries are eventually solved.

Identification of remains presents a challenge. But forensic experts can often make positive identification from partial remains: Even a few remaining bones can be used to determine body build, approximate weight and height; teeth can be matched against dental records; and a few shreds of clothing can give clues about whether the airman was a pilot or gunner.

Once identified, airmen who died in the hostile skies of Europe long ago finally come home. And a family learns for certain the fate of a missing son, father, brother or husband.

Receding waters exposed a B-17G, nicknamed Dinah Might, *from the 452nd Bomb Group (H), based at Deopham Green. The Fortress, serial number 237950, was shot down Feb. 10, 1944, on what was believed to be her first mission, a raid on Brunswick, Germany. Three crewmen were captured and seven evaded capture with the help of the Dutch Underground.* Royal Netherlands Air Force

Epilogue

War is hell, but the freedom we enjoy is worth fighting for and if necessary I would do it again.

—Ralph Price

Veterans who travel back to England find the airfields now standing like specters in the English fog. But in them is reassurance—a link to a time when people laid down their lives for clear values. At last sight, in the mid 1940s, the fields were a place of unbearable hours, constant cold, fear and sadness for friends lost. In short, it was a place one was happy to leave.

But in retrospect, all is changed. In their desolation, those fields stand as silent testimony to a unique and remarkable time. A time when the youth of America answered the call and became part of the greatest air armada ever assembled—sent to vanquish an evil foe in a black-and-white world. The days are gone. And the world is a more treacherous place.

Who they were

"I was adventurous and a true believer in the war and terribly naive," said Robert Bieck. "I had absolutely no difficulty equating my obvious role with what was expected of me—none whatsoever. I adopted a fatalistic attitude about it all. If something happens, it will happen.

"I'd describe myself as serious, enthusiastic, committed, with no doubts about the justice of our cause. Today I would possibly be called naive," according to James Goodson."

"There was an unusual physical and mental strength and a love for adventure shared by most men in bomber crews," said Willard Klockow, M.D.

"We were young and learning fast," recalled John Ziebell.

A brick and stucco Bungay building with asbestos roof long ago disappeared. Andrew Moreland

A complex of buildings at Bungay. Andrew Moreland

"I was a young kid at that time, full of curiosity as to what it was all about and at the same time wondering if I had what it took to complete my tour," recalled Ralph Price.

"I didn't feel very young at the time," said Charles Cummins (a twenty-four-year-old major when he returned to the States after seventy-five fighter missions).

Lessons learned

"Being deprived of freedom for 748 days," said G. W. Pederson, "I've always appreciated doing ordinary things that people do in life. And having been so close to death, I live on a higher plane than I would have otherwise. Nearly half the people I flew with died, so each day I appreciate being here."

"Friends are important," said Carl Lose.

"We were shot at by fighters and flak [batteries], and watched helplessly as our friends were shot out of the sky. I felt that in the future no person or situation could be as unnerving or threatening to me as what I went through on those nine bombing missions," recalls Gilbert Falck.

"At the time it was happening, you had so much adrenaline flowing through that you don't have any reaction when you place bullets in an enemy's canopy.

Your life is on the line. In later reflection on such an incident, it occurred to me that he might have been married, might have had kids. I thought about him as an individual like me, not about Hitler and the six million Jews killed," said Howard Moebius.

"It was interesting how pilots outdid themselves trying to look after someone with a problem—even if they had to break away from the safety of group to bring them home," recalled Charles Cummins. "We were all working toward the same thing and we were trying to protect each other. Genuine camaraderie."

"From any angle, war is *bad*," said Willard Klockow.

"The experience changed my life. I came out with an education and occupation I've loved my entire life," said Howard Dicken, expressing gratitude for his lifelong career in civilian air control.

"Our quarters had thirty-two men in double bunks. I learned how to get along with thirty-one roommates," said Roger Lyons.

"It taught me how short life can be, how you need to live life to the fullest and not just plan for the day you retire. And I came away with lifelong friends—members of the crew were tighter knit than even a family," said C. L. Anderson.

"War is hell—and a poor way to settle differences. It's the vicious epitome of man's inhumanity to man," according to Andrew Low.

"I learned about the falling of mankind. It led me to become interested in international relations—I wanted an increased understanding about the forces that lead to cataclysms like this," said John Houk.

"I learned initiative, independence, and appreciation of being alive," said James Goodson.

"I saw people work harder, more devotedly, more courageously than I had seen before or have seen since," according to Harry Crosby. "We believed in the war, in our country, in ourselves and in each other. And things *worked*."

"It's long ago. And for thirty years I had pretty much forgotten about it," said Jack Ilfrey. "When we got older, and many of us started retiring, we got together again. We talk about the days. And we miss the people who were lost, but we stay on the humorous side, because there were some very humorous things that happened—though we didn't think of them that way at the time. But we want to keep the memory of the time alive—to pass along the message to the younger generations about the bad side of war, in hopes that they'll learn and that it won't happen to them or future generations."

"War is hell, but the freedom we enjoy is worth fighting for and if necessary I would do it again," said Ralph Price.

I have been through a lot of hardships, seen a lot of the world. It's been a wonderful experience. I wouldn't trade it for anything in the world but hope I never will have to go through all this again

—Leroy Kuest
September 19, 1945
diary entry

D. Lande 89

Bibliography

Books

Ackerman, Robert W. *The Maintenance of Army Aircraft in the United States. 1939–1945.* A.A.F. Historical Study No. 88, 1954.

Bailey, Ronald H. *The Air War in Europe.* Time-Life Books, 1981.

Bekker, Cajus. *The Luftwaffe War Diaries.* Doubleday and Co., Inc., 1964.

Birdsall, Steve. *B-24 Liberator in Action.* Squadron/Signal, 1975.

Bowman, Martin W. *Fields of Little America.* Wensum Books, 1977.

———. *Castles in the Air: The Story of the B-17 Flying Fortress Crews of the U.S. Eighth Air Force.* Sterling, 1985.

Bowyer, Chaz. *Tales of the Bombers.* William Kimber & Co., Ltd., 1985.

Brooks, Elston. *I've Heard those Songs Before: The Weekly Top Ten Tunes for the Last Fifty Years.* Morrow Quill Paperbacks, 1981.

Caidin, Martin. *Flying Forts.* Meredith Press, 1968.

Callahan, John F. and Farbstein, Harold, eds. *Contrails: My War Record.* Contrails Publication, Inc., 1947.

Carter, Kit C., and Robert Mueller. *The Army Air Forces in World War II: Combat Chronology 1941–1945.* Office of Air Force History, 1973.

Cole, J. A. *Lord Haw-Haw & William Joyce.* Farrar, Straus, Giroux, 1964.

Craven, Wesley Frank, and Cate, James Lea, eds. *The Army Air Forces in World War II.* Vol. I, *Plans and Early Operations, January 1939 to August 1942.* The University of Chicago Press, 1948.

———. Vol. II, *Europe: Torch to Pointblank, August 1942 to December 1943.* The University of Chicago Press, 1949.

———. Vol. III, *Europe, Argument to V-E Day, January 1944 to May 1945.* The University of Chicago Press, 1951.

De Seversky, Alexander P. *Victory Through Air Power.* Simon and Schuster, 1942.

Frankland, Noble. *Bomber Offensive: The Devastation of Europe.* Ballantine Books, Inc., 1970.

Freeman, Roger A. *Airfields of the Eighth Then and Now.* Battle of Britain Prints International Limited, 1978.

———. *The Mighty Eighth.* Doubleday and Co., Inc., 1970.

———. *The Mighty Eighth War Diary.* Motorbooks International, 1991.

———. *The Mighty Eighth War Manual.* Motorbooks International, 1991.

Goodson, James A. *Tumult in the Clouds.* St. Martin's Press, 1983.

Hess, William N. *Fighting Mustang.* Doubleday and Co., Inc., 1970.

Hurley, Alfred F. *Billy Mitchell: Crusader for Air Power.* Indiana University, 1975.

Jablonski, Edward. *Flying Fortress.* Doubleday and Company, 1965.

Korson, George. *At His Side: The Story of the American Red Cross Overseas in World War II.* Coward-McCann, Inc., 1945.

Lay, Bierne, Jr., and Bartlett, Sy. *Twelve O'Clock High!* Ballantine Books, 1948.

Lepley, William H., ed. *Psychological Research in the Theater of War.* Government Printing Office, 1947.

Longmate, Norman. *The G.I.'s: The Americans in Britain 1942–1945.* Hutchinson of London, 1975.

Marrin, Albert. *The Airmen's War.* Atheneum, 1982.

Maurer, Maurer, ed. *Air Force Combat Units of World War II.* USAF Historical Division, 1960.

Sims, Edward H. *American Aces.* Harper and Bros., 1968.

Toliver, Raymond F., and Constable, Trevor J. *Fighter Aces of the USA.* Aero Publishers, Inc., 1979.

Turner, Lt. Col. Richard E., USAF (Ret.), *Big Friend, Little Friend.* Doubleday and Co., Inc., 1969.

Verrier, Anthony. *The Bomber Offensive.* Macmillan, 1968.

Vining, Donald. *American Diaries of World War II.* Pepys Press, 1982.

Woolnough, John H. *The 8th Air Force Album.* Eighth Air Force News, 1978.

———. *The 8th Air Force Yearbook.* Eighth Air Force News, 1981.

Periodicals

Air Classics magazine, April 1974.

Life magazine, 1942–1945.

National Geographic magazine, 1942–1945.

Nostalgic Notes. The 94th Bomb Group newsletter, through 1990.

Saturday Evening Post magazine, April 24, 1943.

Second Air Division Newsletter. Through 1989.

Smithsonian magazine, April 1986.

Splasher Six. The 100th Bomb Group newsletter, through 1989.

8th AF News. The Eighth Air Force Historical Society, Inc., through 1989.

Index